# Photographer's Guide to the
# Panasonic ZS100/TZ100

# Photographer's Guide to the Panasonic ZS100/TZ100

Getting the Most from Panasonic's Advanced Compact Camera

**Alexander S. White**

WHITE KNIGHT PRESS
HENRICO, VIRGINIA

The publisher does not assume responsibility for any damage or injury to property or person that results from the use of any of the advice, information, or suggestions contained in this book. Although the information in this book has been checked carefully for errors, the information is not guaranteed. Corrections and updates will be posted as needed at whiteknightpress.com.

Product names, brand names, and company names mentioned in this book are protected by trademarks, which are acknowledged.

Published by
White Knight Press
9704 Old Club Trace
Henrico, Virginia 23238
www.whiteknightpress.com
contact@whiteknightpress.com

ISBN: 978-1-937986-52-0 (paperback)
        978-1-937986-53-7 (ebook)


Printed in the United States of America

To my wife, Clenise.

# Contents

# CHAPTER 6: PLAYBACK 114

## Chapter 7: The Custom Menu and the Setup Menu 131

Zoom Lever . . . . . . . . . . . . . . . . . . . . . . . . . . . . . . . . . . . 145
Zoom Resume . . . . . . . . . . . . . . . . . . . . . . . . . . . . . . . . . 145
Quick Menu (Q.Menu) . . . . . . . . . . . . . . . . . . . . . . . . . . . 145
Ring/Dial Set . . . . . . . . . . . . . . . . . . . . . . . . . . . . . . . . . . 146
Eye Sensor . . . . . . . . . . . . . . . . . . . . . . . . . . . . . . . . . . . . 147
Touch Settings . . . . . . . . . . . . . . . . . . . . . . . . . . . . . . . . . 147
    Touch Screen . . . . . . . . . . . . . . . . . . . . . . . . . . . . . . . 147
    Touch Tab . . . . . . . . . . . . . . . . . . . . . . . . . . . . . . . . . 147
    Touch AF . . . . . . . . . . . . . . . . . . . . . . . . . . . . . . . . . . 148
    Touch Pad AF . . . . . . . . . . . . . . . . . . . . . . . . . . . . . . . 148
Touch Scroll . . . . . . . . . . . . . . . . . . . . . . . . . . . . . . . . . . 148
Menu Guide . . . . . . . . . . . . . . . . . . . . . . . . . . . . . . . . . . 148
The Setup Menu . . . . . . . . . . . . . . . . . . . . . . . . . . . . . . . . . 149
Online Manual . . . . . . . . . . . . . . . . . . . . . . . . . . . . . . . . . 149
Clock Set . . . . . . . . . . . . . . . . . . . . . . . . . . . . . . . . . . . . 149
World Time . . . . . . . . . . . . . . . . . . . . . . . . . . . . . . . . . . . 150
Travel Date . . . . . . . . . . . . . . . . . . . . . . . . . . . . . . . . . . . 150
Wi-Fi . . . . . . . . . . . . . . . . . . . . . . . . . . . . . . . . . . . . . . . 151
Beep . . . . . . . . . . . . . . . . . . . . . . . . . . . . . . . . . . . . . . . 151
Live View Mode . . . . . . . . . . . . . . . . . . . . . . . . . . . . . . . . 151
Monitor Display/Viewfinder . . . . . . . . . . . . . . . . . . . . . . . . 151
Monitor Luminance . . . . . . . . . . . . . . . . . . . . . . . . . . . . . . 152
Economy . . . . . . . . . . . . . . . . . . . . . . . . . . . . . . . . . . . . 152
    Sleep Mode . . . . . . . . . . . . . . . . . . . . . . . . . . . . . . . . 152
    Auto LVF/Monitor Off . . . . . . . . . . . . . . . . . . . . . . . . . . 152
USB Mode . . . . . . . . . . . . . . . . . . . . . . . . . . . . . . . . . . . 153
TV Connection . . . . . . . . . . . . . . . . . . . . . . . . . . . . . . . . . 153
m/ft . . . . . . . . . . . . . . . . . . . . . . . . . . . . . . . . . . . . . . . 153
Menu Resume . . . . . . . . . . . . . . . . . . . . . . . . . . . . . . . . . 154
Menu Background . . . . . . . . . . . . . . . . . . . . . . . . . . . . . . 154
Menu Information . . . . . . . . . . . . . . . . . . . . . . . . . . . . . . . 154
Language . . . . . . . . . . . . . . . . . . . . . . . . . . . . . . . . . . . . 154
Version Display . . . . . . . . . . . . . . . . . . . . . . . . . . . . . . . . 155
Exposure Compensation Reset . . . . . . . . . . . . . . . . . . . . . . 155
Self Timer Auto Off . . . . . . . . . . . . . . . . . . . . . . . . . . . . . . 155
Number Reset . . . . . . . . . . . . . . . . . . . . . . . . . . . . . . . . . 155
Reset . . . . . . . . . . . . . . . . . . . . . . . . . . . . . . . . . . . . . . . 156
Reset Wi-Fi Settings . . . . . . . . . . . . . . . . . . . . . . . . . . . . . 156
Demo Mode . . . . . . . . . . . . . . . . . . . . . . . . . . . . . . . . . . 156
Format . . . . . . . . . . . . . . . . . . . . . . . . . . . . . . . . . . . . . . 156

## CHAPTER 8: MOTION PICTURES  157

# Chapter 9: Wi-Fi and Other Topics 173

# Appendix A: Accessories 184

# Appendix B: Quick Tips 189

# Appendix C: Resources for Further Information 191

# INTRODUCTION

This book is a guide to the operation, features, and capabilities of the Panasonic Lumix DMC-ZS100, one of the most capable and versatile "point-and-shoot" digital compact cameras available today. (The camera is known as the ZS110, TZ100, TZ101, or TZ110 outside of North America, but I am located in the United States and my camera is labeled ZS100, so I will use that designation in this book.)

I chose this camera to write about partly because of my experience with other Panasonic compact models, including the DMC-LX3, LX5, LX7, and LX100, but also because this camera stands out from other compact cameras for several reasons.

To begin with, the ZS100 uses a "one-inch-type" image sensor, the same size sensor used in several other advanced compact models, such as the Sony DSC-RX100 and its three (as of this writing) successor models. This sensor is larger than those of many compact cameras, and lets the ZS100 provide great image quality and blurred backgrounds.

The camera also has an excellent optical zoom range of 25mm to 250mm and advanced features such as Raw image quality, manual control of exposure and focus, and excellent burst capability for continuous shooting. The ZS100 also provides very good video features, centered around its capability to capture 4K (ultra-HD) video. In addition, the camera has a large, 3-inch (7.5 cm) diagonal and very sharp (1,000,000 pixels) LCD monitor with touch-screen features; a high-quality Leica-branded lens with a wide 25mm equivalent focal length, and a built-in electronic viewfinder with more than one million pixels of resolution. It has a strong set of Wi-Fi features, enabling remote control from a smartphone and transfer of images from the camera to other devices over a wireless network.

Many photographers will welcome the inclusion of physical switches and dials on the ZS100 to control many functions, so they don't have to navigate through menus to adjust exposure compensation, white balance, Drive Mode, and other settings. Several of these controls are programmable to operate any one of numerous functions, and the camera also has five "virtual" function buttons included with its touch screen capabilities.

Also, the ZS100 includes a self-timer, macro (closeup shooting) mode, a wide range of shutter speeds (1/16000 second to 60 seconds as well as longer time exposures), many different "filter effects" settings (such as miniature effect, soft focus, sepia, and monochrome, among others), and several features for capturing images with broad dynamic range, including a built-in HDR (high dynamic range) option. The camera is equipped with Panasonic's "Depth from Defocus" system, which provides faster autofocus performance than that of many comparable cameras.

Is anything lacking in the ZS100? Some people would like the camera to be smaller, so it could fit more easily into a pocket. It also would be nice if the LCD screen could swivel and tilt. The camera could use better audio recording features, such as a jack for an external microphone, to support its excellent video capability. It also lacks the ability to connect to a smartphone or tablet using the NFC (near field communication) protocol, though it can connect using standard procedures through menus and apps, and it has no accessory shoe for a larger flash or other accessories.

But given that no camera can meet every possible need, the ZS100 is an outstanding example of an advanced compact camera. My goal is to provide a useful introduction to the ZS100's controls and operation along with tips and advice as to when and how to use various features. This book does not provide advanced technical information. If you already understand how to use every feature of the camera and when to use it and are looking for new insights, I have included some references in the Appendices that can provide further information. This book is geared to the beginning to intermediate user who is not satisfied with the documentation provided with the camera, and who is looking for a reference guide that offers additional help in mastering the camera's features.

One final note: Panasonic sells another model, known as the ZS60 in North America and the TZ80 elsewhere, which is very similar to the ZS100 but is equipped with a smaller sensor and different lens. That model is so similar to the ZS100 that it is covered by the same Panasonic users guide. Although I do not discuss the details of that model in this book, much of the information in the book is applicable to the operation of the ZS60/TZ80 model.

# CHAPTER 1: PRELIMINARY SETUP

When you first receive your ZS100, the box should contain the camera itself, battery, battery charger, USB cable, hand strap, shoulder strap adapter, and brief instruction pamphlet. There is no software disc in the box, but Panasonic provides links for downloading software for processing your photographs and videos. For PHOTOfunSTUDIO software, which can be used for editing both stills and movies on Windows-based computers, go to http://panasonic.jp/support/global/cs/soft/download/d_pfs98pe.html. To download SilkyPix software, which lets you process Raw files on Windows-based or Macintosh computers, go to http://www.isl.co.jp/SILKYPIX/english/p/. To download a 30-day free trial of LoiLoScope software for editing videos on Windows-based computers, go to http://loilo.tv/product/20.

## Charging and Inserting the Battery

The ZS100 ships with a single rechargeable lithium-ion battery, model number DMW-BLG10PP. This battery is designed to be charged inside the camera, but it also can be charged in an external charger. I will discuss various options for powering the camera and recharging batteries in Appendix A.

To charge the battery in the camera, slide the latch on the camera's bottom and open the battery compartment door. You can only insert the battery into the camera one way; look for the set of four goldish-colored metal contact strips on the battery, then look for the corresponding set of contacts inside the camera, and insert the battery so the two sets of contacts will meet, as shown in Figures 1-1 and 1-2.

Slide the battery all the way in so it is firmly seated in the camera with the latch clicked into place above the battery, as shown in Figure 1-3, and close and latch the battery compartment door.

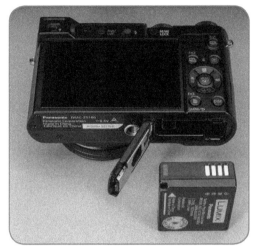

**Figure 1-1.** Battery Ready to Go Into Camera

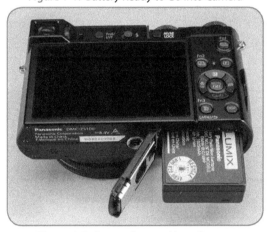

**Figure 1-2.** Battery Inserted Into Camera

**Figure 1-3.** Battery Secured by Latch

With the battery inserted, plug the small end of the camera's USB cable into the USB charging port, which is the lower port located inside a small flap on the right side of the camera, as shown in Figure 1-4.

Figure 1-4. **Battery Charger Connected to Camera**

Plug the larger end of the cable into the AC adapter, and plug the adapter into an electrical outlet. A red light on the back of the camera, to the left of the Playback button, will glow steadily while charging is in progress, and will turn off when charging is complete. It should take about 190 minutes to charge the battery fully.

## Inserting the Memory Card

The ZS100 does not ship with a memory card. If you turn the camera on with no card inserted, you will see the message "No memory card" in the center of the screen. If you ignore this message and press the shutter button to take a picture, don't be fooled into thinking that the camera is somehow storing it in internal memory. Some camera models have a small amount of built-in memory so you can take and store a few pictures even without a card, but the ZS100 does not have that safety net.

To avoid the frustration of having a great camera that can't save images, you need to use a memory card. The ZS100 uses 3 varieties of card: Secure Digital (SD), Secure Digital High-Capacity (SDHC), and Secure Digital Extended Capacity (SDXC), representative samples of which are shown in Figure 1-5. All 3 types of SD card are the same size, about the size of a postage stamp. The standard card, SD, comes in capacities from 8 MB (megabytes) to 2 GB (gigabytes). The higher-capacity card, SDHC, comes in sizes from 4 GB to 32 GB.

Figure 1-5. **Examples of Memory Cards**

The newest type, SDXC, at this writing is available in a 48 GB, 64 GB, 128 GB, 256 GB, or 512 GB size, though its maximum capacity theoretically is 2 terabytes, or about 2,000 GB. Currently 512 GB cards are selling for between $200.00 and $360.00, so they may be impractical for most photographers.

A 128 GB card, though, can be a good option, which I have used successfully in the ZS100. I also have used a 256 GB card with no problems, and I have used a SanDisk Extreme Pro 512 GB SDXC card in the ZS100 with excellent results.

When choosing a memory card, there is one important point to bear in mind: If you want to use the excellent 4K motion picture recording capability of the ZS100, you have to use a card rated in UHS Speed Class 3, for ultra-high speed class 3. Examples of such cards are shown in Figure 1-6. The numeral 3 inside the U shape on the label indicates this speed class.

Figure 1-6. **High-Speed Memory Cards**

I recommend you purchase a card of that speed class, because it will help with burst shooting as well as with 4K video.

If you're not planning to use the camera's 4K video features, you still should get a large-sized, high-speed card if possible. If you're planning to record a good deal of high-definition (HD) video or many Raw photos, you need a card with a fairly large capacity. There are several variables to take into account in computing how many images or videos you can store on a particular size of card, such as the aspect ratio you're using (1:1, 3:2, 4:3, or 16:9), picture size, and quality.

I installed a 64 GB SDXC card and formatted it in the camera to see how many images could be stored using various settings. I set the aspect ratio to 3:2 for all options. Table 1-1 shows the results.

Table 1-1. **Number of Still Images That Can be Stored on 64 GB Card at Large Size**

| | |
|---|---|
| Raw + Fine | 1815 |
| Raw | 2659 |
| Fine | 5726 |
| Standard | 9999+ |

For video, using the same 64 GB card, you can store just one hour and 20 minutes of the highest quality 4K video; with the highest quality of AVCHD video, you can store 5 hours. Note, though, that there is an important caveat for video recording lengths with the ZS100, as with most compact cameras designed primarily for still photography. There are built-in limitations on the length of any continuous video recording. In most cases, you can record only about 30 minutes of video in any one scene; you then have to stop and re-start your recording. With 4K video, the limit for continuous recording is 15 minutes. Also, as you may expect, some video formats consume memory very rapidly, so some smaller SD cards cannot record for the full amount of time that the camera would permit. There are some other considerations to be discussed with regard to recording limits; I will discuss video recording in more detail in Chapter 8.

One other consideration is the speed of the card. I often use a 64 GB SanDisk Extreme Pro card, rated at a transfer level of 95 MB/second. That speed is more than enough to get good results for recording still images and AVCHD video with this camera. You should try to find a card whose speed is rated in Class 10 or higher if you're going to record HD video. The fastest cards are rated with the UHS designation, for ultra high speed. As noted above, if you are planning to record 4K video, the highest quality format available, you need to use a card with a speed designation of UHS Speed Class 3. (If the card has a UHS-I or UHS-II designation, that label has to do with a certain type of transport system the card uses, not the speed. You need to make sure the Speed Class is UHS-3.)

Whatever type of SD card you get, once you have the card, open the same door on the bottom of the camera that covers the battery compartment and slide the card

in until it catches. The card goes in with its label facing the front of the camera, as shown in Figure 1-7.

Figure 1-7. SD Card Going Into Camera

Once the card has been pushed down until it catches, close the compartment door and push the latch back to the locking position. To remove the card, push down on it until it releases and springs up so you can grab it.

When the ZS100 is recording images or videos to an SD card, a red icon appears on the left side of the screen showing an arrow pointing to the right inside a little box representing the SD card, as shown in Figure 1-8, which gives an enlarged view of the upper left corner of the display screen.

Figure 1-8. Red Icon Indicating Writing to Memory Card

When that indicator is visible on the display, it's important not to turn off the camera or otherwise interrupt its functioning, such as by taking out the battery or disconnecting an AC power adapter. You need to let the card complete its recording process.

## Introduction to Main Controls

Before I discuss options for setting up the camera using the menu system and controls, I will introduce the main controls so you'll have a better idea of which button or dial is which. I won't discuss all of the controls here; they will be covered in some detail in Chapter 5. For now, I'm including a series of images that show the major items. You may want to refer back to these images for a reminder about each control.

### TOP OF CAMERA

On top of the camera are some of the more important controls, as shown in Figure 1-9.

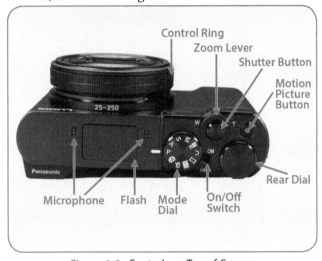

Figure 1-9. Controls on Top of Camera

You press the shutter button all the way down to take a picture; press it halfway to cause the camera to evaluate focus and exposure. The Mode dial sets the camera to a shooting mode for still images or movies. The zoom lever, surrounding the shutter button, zooms the lens from the wide-angle (W) setting to the telephoto (T) setting. The on/off switch turns the camera on and off. The flash is stored inside the top of the camera; you pop it up with the flash release button on the camera's back. The two microphone openings receive sounds to be recorded with videos. The control ring is used for focus and other operations, depending on current settings. The red motion picture button starts and stops the recording of a movie sequence. The ridged rear dial acts as a rotary wheel for changing settings, moving through menu items and options on various screens of settings, as well as for other purposes, such as moving through recorded images and videos. You can program it to handle one particular function, if you want.

### BACK OF CAMERA

Figure 1-10 shows the major controls on the camera's back.

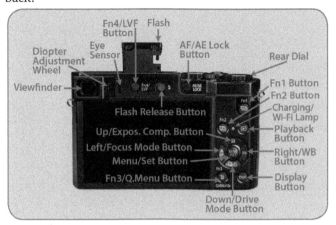

Figure 1-10. Controls on Back of Camera

The viewfinder window is where you look to see the view through the camera's electronic viewfinder, or live viewfinder (LVF). The slit to its right is the eye sensor, which senses the presence of your head and switches between the LVF and the LCD screen display. The diopter adjustment wheel lets you adjust the view in the LVF for your vision. The flash release button is used to release the camera's built-in flash unit so it will pop up, ready for use.

The AF/AE Lock button is used to lock exposure and/or focus, depending on settings you make through the menu system. The Playback button puts the camera into playback mode so you can review your recorded images and videos. The four cursor buttons (called the Up, Down, Left, and Right buttons in this book) control the settings of exposure compensation, Drive Mode, focus mode, and white balance. The Menu/Set button, in the center of the dial, is used to get access to the menu system and to select or confirm various menu options.

The four function buttons are initially assigned to particular operations, but they all can be assigned to other purposes through the menu system. The Fn1 button is initially assigned as the 4K button, to give you access to the camera's 4K photo shooting ability. The Fn2 button is initially set as the Post Focus button, which lets you shoot images whose focus point can be set after shooting. The Fn3 button is initially assigned as the Q.Menu button, which activates the Quick Menu system that gives instant access to various menu settings. The Fn4 button is initially set as the LVF button, which lets you set the live viewfinder so it is automatically switched by the eye sensor, or so either the LVF or the LCD screen is active.

The Display button is used to switch among the various displays of information in the LVF and on the LCD screen in both shooting and playback modes, and to move through the menus a full screen at a time. The LCD monitor displays the live view, control settings, and other information when you are not using the viewfinder. It displays recorded images and videos when the camera is in playback mode.

The LCD screen also has extensive touch capabilities, letting you control many of the camera's features by touching icons or other areas on the screen. The charging/Wi-Fi lamp, located between the Fn2 and Playback buttons, lights up red when the battery is being charged inside the camera or when the camera's Wi-Fi capability is active.

## FRONT OF CAMERA

There are only a few items to point out on the camera's front, shown in Figure 1-11. The AF Assist/Self-timer lamp lights up to indicate the operation of the self-timer and also turns on in dim light to assist the camera's autofocus system, unless you disable it for that purpose through the menu system. The lens is a high-quality zoom lens with a maximum aperture of f/2.8 at the wide-angle setting, changing to a maximum of f/5.9 at the telephoto end of its range.

Figure 1-11. Items on Front of Camera

The focal length of the lens varies from 9.1mm at the wide-angle range to 91mm at the telephoto setting. Ordinarily, these focal lengths are stated using "35mm-equivalent" figures, meaning the values that these

figures would correspond to for a camera using a full-frame, 35mm image sensor. Therefore, the focal length range of the lens is ordinarily stated as from 25mm to 250mm.

## RIGHT SIDE OF CAMERA

Inside the door on the right side of the camera are the HDMI port and the USB port, as seen in Figure 1-12.

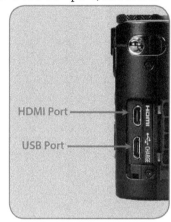

Figure 1-12. Ports on Right Side of Camera

The HDMI port is where you plug in an HDMI cable to display images and videos from the camera on an HDTV set. The USB port is where you plug in the camera's USB cable to charge the battery or to transfer images and videos to a computer. And, you can use this port to connect to a PictBridge-compliant printer to print images directly from the camera.

## BOTTOM OF CAMERA

Finally, as shown in Figure 1-13, on the bottom of the camera are the speaker, the tripod socket, the door for the battery and memory card compartment, and the small flap that is used to accommodate the cord for the AC adapter when it is connected to the camera, as discussed in Appendix A.

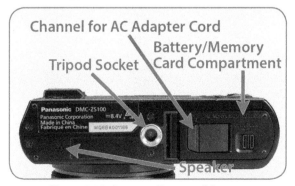

Figure 1-13. Items on Bottom of Camera

## Setting the Date, Time, and Language

It's important to set the date and time correctly before you start taking pictures, because the camera records that information invisibly with each image, and displays it later if you want. Someday you may be very glad to have the date (and even the time of day) correctly recorded with your archives of digital images.

To get these basic items set, move the camera's power switch, on the top of the camera, to the On position. Then press the Menu/Set button (in the center of the cursor buttons on the camera's back). Push the Left button to move the selection into the column for choosing the menu type (Intelligent Auto, Recording, Creative Video, Custom, Setup, or Playback). The line at the left side of the display will turn yellow to indicate that the column of menu icons is now active, as shown in Figure 1-14.

Press the Down button to highlight the wrench icon that represents the Setup menu, then press the Right button to place the yellow selection rectangle in the list of Setup menu items.

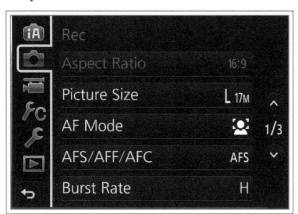

Figure 1-14. Yellow Line Showing Menu Icons Are Active

By turning the rear dial or pressing the Up and Down buttons, move the yellow rectangle until Clock Set is highlighted on the first Setup menu screen. Then press the Right button to get access to the time and date settings, as shown in Figure 1-15.

Figure 1-15. Time and Date Settings Screen

Navigate by pressing the Left and Right buttons or by turning the rear dial, and select values with the Up and Down buttons. When you're done, press the Right button enough times to highlight the Set icon in the lower right corner of the screen, and press the Menu/Set button to save the settings. Then, using a similar procedure, navigate to the Language option on the fourth screen of the Setup menu, if necessary, and change the language the camera uses for menus and messages.

If you prefer to use the camera's touch-screen capabilities, you can navigate through the menu system and make selections by touching the menu selections and icons on the camera's LCD display. I will discuss the use of the touch screen in Chapter 5.

# CHAPTER 2: BASIC OPERATIONS

## Taking Pictures

Once the camera has the correct time and date set and has a fully charged battery inserted along with a memory card, it is ready for picture-taking. For now, I won't get into discussions of the various options and why you might choose one over another. I'll just describe a set of actions for recording a good image on your memory card.

### FULLY AUTOMATIC: INTELLIGENT AUTO MODE

Here's a set of steps to follow to set the camera to its most automatic mode and let it make most of the decisions for you. This is a good setup if you need to grab a quick shot without fiddling with settings, or if you want to get good results without having to provide much input by making numerous decisions.

1. Move the power switch on the camera's top to the On position. The camera makes a whirring sound, the lens extends outward to its open position, and the LCD screen lights up.

2. Turn the Mode dial on top of the camera to the iA position, which selects the Intelligent Auto mode of shooting. You should see a red icon with iA and possibly a plus sign in white letters in the upper left corner of the display, as shown in Figure 2-1. (If you don't see this icon, press the Display button at the lower right of the camera's back one or more times until the icon appears.)

3. Press the Left button (marked with a flower and MF). The camera will display the focus mode menu, as shown in Figure 2-2.

Figure 2-1. Icon for Intelligent Auto in Upper Left of Screen

4. Use the cursor buttons (or the touch screen) to select AF, the left-most option, if it is not already selected. That sets the camera to use autofocus instead of manual focus.

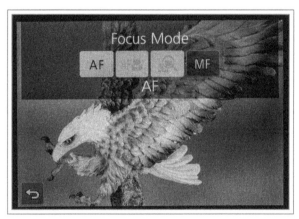

Figure 2-2. Focus Mode Menu in iA Mode

5. Press the Menu/Set button in the center of the cursor buttons on the back of the camera to call up the menu system. Press the Left button if necessary to highlight the line of icons at the far left of the screen; when they are highlighted, you will see a yellow line, as in Figure 2-3.

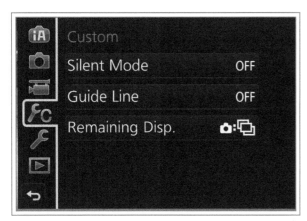

Figure 2-3. Yellow Line Highlighting Menu Icons

6. Use the Up and Down buttons as necessary to highlight the iA icon at the top of the line of icons, as shown in Figure 2-4. Then press the Right button to move to the two icons on the menu, iA and iA+. Use the buttons as necessary to make sure the iA icon is highlighted in yellow, as shown in Figure 2-5. (You can press menu items and icons on the touch screen to make selections if you prefer.)

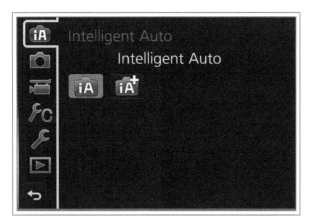

Figure 2-4. iA Icon Highlighted in List of Menu Icons

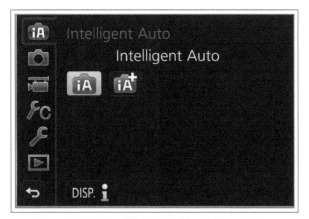

Figure 2-5. iA Icon Highlighted for iA Menu Option

7. Navigate to the red camera icon for the Recording menu, then press the Right button to move

the highlight into the menu screen. Using the procedure discussed above, make the settings in Table 2-1 for the other items on the Recording menu. (If you prefer to use the touch screen to make these settings, just touch the appropriate menu options and icons to select them.)

Table 2-1. **Recommended Settings for General Shooting in Intelligent Auto Mode**

| Menu Option | Setting |
| --- | --- |
| Aspect Ratio | 3:2 |
| Picture Size | L |
| AF Mode | Face/Eye Detection |
| AFS/AFF/AFC | AFS |
| Burst Rate | H |
| 4K Photo | 4K |
| Self Timer | Any setting |
| Post Focus | Off |
| iHandheld Night Shot | Off |
| iHDR | Off |
| Time Lapse Shot | No setting needed |
| Stop Motion Animation | No setting needed |
| Face Recognition | Off |

8. If you're taking a picture indoors, or it's dark enough that you think you might need the camera's flash, find the flash release button at the top center of the camera's back and slide it to the left to pop up the built-in flash. If the camera determines that flash is needed, the flash will fire automatically; you cannot change the flash mode setting in this shooting mode. (When you're done with the flash, press it gently back down into the top of the camera.)

9. Aim the camera at the subject and look at the screen (or into the viewfinder window) to compose the picture as you want it. Locate the zoom lever on the ring that surrounds the shutter button on the top right of the camera. Push that lever to the left, toward the W, to get a wider-angle shot (including more of the scene in the picture), or to the right, toward the T, to get a telephoto, zoomed-in shot.

10. Once the picture looks good on the display, press the shutter button halfway down. You should hear a beep and see a steady (not blinking) green dot in the upper right corner of the screen, indicating that the picture will be in focus, as shown in Figure 2-6.

Figure 2-6. Steady Green Dot for Good Focus

11. You also may see some green focus frames. (If you hear a series of 4 quick beeps and see a blinking green dot, that means the picture is not in focus. Try moving to a slightly different angle and then test the focus again by pressing the shutter button halfway down.) Then press the shutter button all the way down to take the picture.

## VARIATIONS FROM FULLY AUTOMATIC

Although the ZS100 takes care of several settings for you when it's set to Intelligent Auto mode, the camera still lets you make a few adjustments to fine-tune the shooting process. I will discuss some of these options next. For this discussion I am assuming the default settings are in effect. If some options, such as MF Assist and peaking, do not work as described below, go to the Setup menu and select the Reset option on screen 5 to reset the settings to their factory configuration.

### Focus

In Intelligent Auto mode, the ZS100 has limited options for focus settings. If you want to use some of the more sophisticated autofocus settings, you have to switch to an advanced shooting mode, such as Program or Aperture Priority. In Intelligent Auto mode, though, you can adjust some aspects of how the camera uses autofocus and you can choose manual focus.

First, when the camera is set to autofocus mode, you can choose between Face/Eye Detection and Tracking Focus. As discussed earlier, enter the menu system by pressing the Menu/Set button, then press the Left button to move to the list of menu icons; make sure the red camera icon, for the Recording menu, is highlighted. Then press the Right button to put the yellow selection rectangle

into the list of menu items. Highlight the AF Mode item on the first screen of the menu, as shown in Figure 2-7.

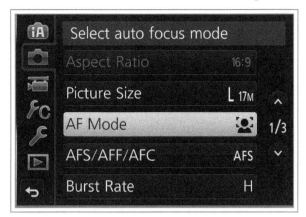

Figure 2-7. AF Mode Highlighted on Menu

In Table 2-1, I recommended that you choose the first option on the left for this menu item—Face/Eye Detection. With that setting, the camera uses its face detection focusing system. It will display a yellow focus frame if it detects a human face. This system works well for portraits and other shots including people, especially if they are not moving. If you are photographing moving subjects, whether people or objects, you may prefer to use tracking focus.

To change to tracking focus, select the second option for AF Mode, whose icon looks like a series of small frames, as shown in Figure 2-8.

Figure 2-8. Focus Tracking Icon Highlighted

With this setting, when you first aim at the subject you should see on the shooting screen a white focus frame with small lines protruding in horizontal and vertical directions, as shown in Figure 2-9.

Figure 2-9. Focus Tracking Frame

Aim the white focus-tracking frame at your subject and press the shutter button halfway. If the camera can lock on the subject, the frame will turn yellow and then green as focus is locked. Release the shutter button, and the yellow frame will follow a moving subject to maintain focus as the distance changes.

When you are ready, press the shutter button halfway down to lock focus, and all the way down to take the picture. To release the frame so you can start focusing again, press the Menu/Set button.

When the camera is in Intelligent Auto mode, there is also another way to change from Face/Eye Detection focus to Tracking Focus. Just aim the camera at a subject and touch the subject on the touch screen with your finger, and the camera will switch to tracking focus and begin tracking that subject.

Another autofocus option you can control in this shooting mode is the AFS/AFF/AFC setting. To make this choice, navigate to that setting on the first screen of the Recording menu, and press the Right button or Menu/Set to move to the list of three options for this setting, as shown in Figure 2-10.

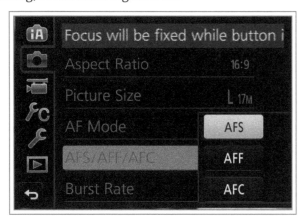

Figure 2-10. AFS/AFF/AFC Menu Options Screen

The three available choices control how the camera uses its autofocus process. If you select AFS, for autofocus single, the camera will focus on the subject when you press the shutter button halfway and it will keep the focus locked while you hold it in that position.

If you choose AFF, for autofocus flexible, the camera will focus on the subject as with AFS, but, if the subject then moves, the camera will adjust its focus as needed. With the final option, AFC, for autofocus continuous, the camera will continuously adjust the focus, even if the subject is not moving. This option uses more battery power than the other two.

If you are taking photographs of subjects in motion, such as pets or children at play, using the AFC setting will keep the focus approximately correct as the subjects move, and it should result in more accurate focusing when you press the shutter button to take the picture. If you are photographing stationary subjects, stick with the AFS setting to save battery power. I rarely use AFF, though you may find situations in which it is useful.

### Manual Focus

The other major option for focusing is manual focus, which requires you to adjust focus yourself. Many photographers like the control that comes from setting the focus exactly how they want it. In some situations, such as shooting in dark areas or areas behind glass, where there are objects at various distances from the camera, or when you're shooting a small object at a very close distance, and only a narrow range of the subject can be in sharp focus, it may be useful to control exactly where the point of sharpest focus lies.

To use manual focus, press the Left cursor button to display the focus mode menu, as shown earlier in Figure 2-2. In the Intelligent Auto shooting mode, the only choices that can be selected are AF and MF, for autofocus or manual focus. Using the cursor buttons or the touch screen, select MF, and the letters MF will appear in the upper right corner of the screen. Now, instead of relying on the camera to focus automatically, you now need to use the control ring (the large, ridged ring around the lens) to adjust focus manually.

When you start turning the ring, the camera will enlarge the display to assist you in deciding when focus is sharp, as shown in Figure 2-11.

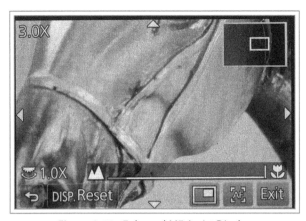

Figure 2-11. Enlarged MF Assist Display

(In recording modes other than Intelligent Auto, including Intelligent Auto Plus, you need to use the MF Assist option on screen 3 of the Custom menu to activate this enlargement feature. See Chapter 7 for details about the MF Assist menu option.)

You can use the four direction buttons or scroll the touch screen with your finger to select the area that is enlarged, and you can turn the rear dial (on the right side of the camera's top), or pinch and pull the screen with your fingers, to change the enlargement factor. To reset the enlarged area to the center of the scene, press the Display button. To return to the normal-sized display, press the Menu/Set button. Continue turning the control ring until the part of the scene that needs to be in focus looks sharp and clear.

The camera also will add colored pixels to the display to outline areas that are in sharp focus, using a feature known as peaking. When an area of colored pixels appears at its strongest, the image should be in focus at that point. (The peaking feature is automatically activated by default when the camera is in Intelligent Auto mode. In other recording modes, you need to turn it on or off through screen 4 of the Custom menu.)

## Defocus Control Option

Another feature that is available in Intelligent Auto mode is defocus control. That option lets you set a wider aperture, which may result in a pleasantly blurred background. As I will discuss in Chapter 3, in Aperture Priority mode you can control the aperture setting more directly. The wider the aperture (the lower the aperture number, such as f/2.8), the more likely it is that the background will be blurred, while the foreground remains sharp.

In Intelligent Auto mode, the camera selects the aperture initially, based on its automatic exposure reading. However, you can activate the defocus control option by pressing the Up button, which is labeled with a plus and minus sign. (In other shooting modes, this button controls exposure compensation, which is designated by the plus and minus icon).

When you press the Up button, the camera displays two simulated dials, as shown in Figure 2-12. The top dial shows the shutter speed, and the bottom one shows the aperture. If you turn the rear dial, these settings will change. The lower the aperture number you can set, the better the chance there will be of having a blurred background.

Figure 2-12. Graphic Dials for Defocus Control Option

Figure 2-13 shows an image that was taken using this option, with the aperture set to f/2.8, the widest possible, resulting in a nicely blurred background.

Figure 2-13. Image Taken Using Defocus Control Option

When the defocus control option is in effect, the camera sets the autofocus mode to 1-Area, which I will discuss in Chapter 4. The camera uses a single autofocus frame, which you can move around the screen with your finger.

## Drive Mode

In Intelligent Auto mode, you can control several options for burst shooting and the self-timer using the Drive Mode menu. I will discuss the basics of these features here; further details are in Chapter 5, where I discuss the physical controls.

The self-timer causes the camera to delay for a few seconds after you press the shutter button, before it actually takes a picture. To use this feature, press the Down button, which is labeled with icons for a stack of frames and a timer dial. The camera will display the Drive Mode menu, as shown in Figure 2-14.

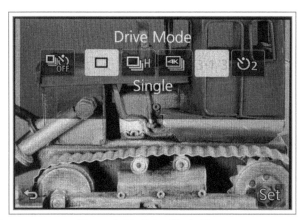

Figure 2-14. **Drive Mode Menu**

Using the cursor buttons, the rear dial, or the touch screen, navigate to the dial icon at the far right. When it is highlighted, press the Up button or the More Settings icon on the screen to move to the self-timer settings screen, as shown in Figure 2-15.

Figure 2-15. **Self-timer Settings Screen**

From the left, the choices are ten-second delay; ten-second delay with multiple shots; and two-second delay. With the middle option, the camera will take three shots after the delay instead of just one. Highlight your

choice and press the Menu/Set button to confirm it and return to the shooting screen.

Choose the ten-second delay when you need to leave the camera on a tripod and join a group picture. The two-second setting is useful when the camera is on a tripod and you want to make sure the camera is not moved when you press the shutter button to take a picture. This setting is especially important when you are taking a closeup shot or a shot using a long telephoto setting, when any motion of the camera is likely to blur the image. The setting with three shots is good when taking a group photo, to make it more likely that the camera will capture at least one image with everybody having their eyes open and smiling.

You also can use the Drive Mode menu to select either standard burst shooting or 4K burst shooting. With these settings, the camera will capture a rapid burst of shots while you hold down the shutter button. I will discuss these features in more detail in Chapter 5. For now, if you encounter a situation where burst shooting would be useful, such as a sporting event, select one of these settings and hold down the shutter button to capture a group of images.

To turn off all Drive Mode settings and return to normal shooting, select either of the two left-most icons on the Drive Mode menu.

## Intelligent Auto Plus Mode

There is another important setting available when the camera's Mode dial is set to the Intelligent Auto position. That setting lets you choose between two different varieties of Intelligent Auto mode: basic Intelligent Auto and Intelligent Auto Plus. In this chapter, I have been discussing the use of basic Intelligent Auto mode, in which the camera controls most settings and leaves few menu options that you can change. If you choose Intelligent Auto Plus instead, the camera opens up numerous other options for adjustment.

To make this setting, with the Mode dial at Intelligent Auto, press the Menu/Set button, then press the Left button to highlight the list of menu icons at the far left. Using the rear dial, cursor buttons, or touch screen, navigate to and highlight the iA icon at the top of the list of icons. Then, using the Right button or the touch screen, highlight the iA+ icon on the right, and press the Menu/Set button to select it and return to the shooting screen. You should now see the iA+ icon in the top left corner of the screen. (You may instead see an icon showing what kind of scene the camera has detected, such as macro or portrait.)

For a quicker way to switch between Intelligent Auto and Intelligent Auto Plus modes, if the touch screen is turned on, just touch the iA or iA+ icon in the upper left corner of the display, and the camera will display a screen for selecting one of those two modes. On that screen, touch the icon for the mode you want and then touch the Set icon in the lower right corner of the display to confirm the setting.

When Intelligent Auto Plus mode is in effect, probably the most important difference from the standard mode is that you can adjust exposure compensation. To do that, press the Up button and then make a brightness adjustment on the camera's display, to compensate for a subject that is excessively bright or dark. I will discuss that process in Chapter 5, where I discuss the physical controls.

In addition, with Intelligent Auto Plus selected, the camera lets you choose many more options from the Recording, Creative Video, and Custom menus than in Intelligent Auto mode. For example, you can select Photo Style, Quality, Shutter Type, Color Space, Stabilizer, and Profile Setup from the Recording menu, as well as Half Press Release, Focus/Release Priority, MF Assist, and others from the Custom menu.

There still are some important settings you cannot make in Intelligent Auto Plus mode, such as ISO sensitivity, HDR, and Multiple Exposure. For those settings, you need to select an advanced shooting mode such as Program, Aperture Priority, Shutter Priority, or Manual. However, you may sometimes want to select Intelligent Auto Plus mode so you can make some settings that are unavailable in Intelligent Auto mode.

## Motion Picture Recording

Next, I'll discuss the basic steps for recording a motion picture sequence with the ZS100. Later, I'll discuss other options for movie recording, but for now I'll stick to the basics.

1.  With the camera set to Intelligent Auto mode, press the Menu/Set button to enter the menu system,

and then press the Left button followed by the Up or Down button, to highlight the Creative Video menu, symbolized by the icon of a movie camera, as shown in Figure 2-16.

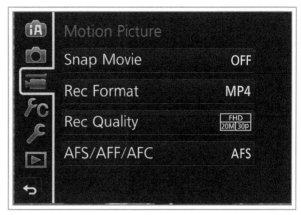
Figure 2-16. Creative Video Menu Icon Highlighted

2.  Press the Right button to go to the list of menu options. Highlight Rec Format, the second option, and press the Right button, giving the choices of AVCHD and MP4, as shown in Figure 2-17. (AVCHD stands for Advanced Video Coding High Definition; it and MP4 are video encoding formats.)

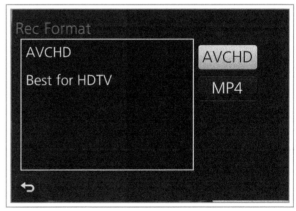
Figure 2-17. Record Format Menu Options Screen

3.  Highlight MP4 and press the Menu/Set button to select it and return to the menu screen. Then highlight the next option down, Rec Quality, and select FHD/20M/30p, for High Definition, the fourth option down, and press Menu/Set to select it. Then press the Fn3/Q.Menu button to return to the shooting screen.

4.  Be sure the focus mode is set to AF. If it is not, press the Left button to select the focus mode menu and select AF.

5.  Compose the shot the way you want it, and when you're ready, press the red motion picture button

on top of the camera, to the right of the shutter button. Don't hold the button down; just press and release it. The LCD screen will show a blinking red dot as a recording indicator along with a countdown of recording time remaining and a counter of elapsed time, as seen in Figure 2-18. The camera will keep recording until it runs out of storage space or reaches a recording limit, or until you press the motion picture button again to stop the recording.

Figure 2-18. Video Recording Screen with Red Dot

6. The ZS100 will adjust focus and exposure automatically as necessary, and you are free to zoom in and out as the movie is recording. (The sound of the zooming mechanism may be audible on the sound track, though, so you may want to keep zooming to a minimum.)

There are many other options and considerations for motion picture recording, which I will discuss in Chapter 8.

## Basic Playback

Playback of images or videos is activated by pressing the Playback button, the button near the top right on the back of the camera with a triangle icon. When you press that button, if there are pictures or videos on the memory card, you will see one of them displayed. It will be whatever image or video was last displayed; the camera remembers which item was most recently on display even after being turned off and back on.

To move to the next picture or video, press the Right button; to move back one item, press the Left button. You can hold either of those buttons down to move quickly through the images and videos. If you prefer, you can move through the items with left or right turns

of the rear dial or by scrolling the touch screen with your finger. The display on the screen will tell you the number of the picture being displayed. (If it doesn't, press the Display button until it does.) This number will have a three-digit prefix, followed by a dash and then a sequence number. For example, the card in my camera right now is showing picture number 100-0111; the next one is 100-0112.

If you would rather see an index view of multiple pictures, use the zoom lever on the top of the camera. Move it to the left, toward the W, one time, and the display changes to show 12 images in three rows of four, as shown in Figure 2-19.

Figure 2-19. Index Screen with 12 Images

Move it to the left one more time, and it shows 30 pictures at a time, as shown in Figure 2-20.

Figure 2-20. Index Screen with 30 Images

Give it one final leftward push and the screen shows a calendar from which you can select a date to view all images taken on that date, as shown in Figure 2-21.

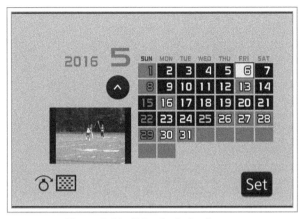

Figure 2-21. Calendar index Screen

You can also move the zoom lever to the right to retrace your steps through the options for multi-image viewing and back to viewing single images.

For now, move the zoom lever once to the left to see the 12-picture screen. Note that the Right and Left buttons now move you through the pictures on this screen one at a time, while the Up and Down buttons move you up and down through the rows. If you move to the last row or the last image, the proper button will move you to the next screen of images. Once you've moved the selector to the image you want to view, press the Menu/Set button, and that image is chosen for individual viewing.

Once you have the single image you want displayed on the screen, you have more options. Press the zoom lever once to the right, toward the T, to zoom the image to twice its normal size, as shown in Figure 2-22.

Figure 2-22. Playback Screen Enlarged to 2.0x

Press the lever repeatedly to zoom up to 16 times normal size. Press the zoom lever back to the left to shrink the image down in the same increments. Or, you can press the Menu/Set button to return the image immediately to normal size. You can pinch and pull

on the touch screen with your fingers to change the enlargement of the image, also.

While the zoomed picture is displayed, you can scroll it in any direction with the direction buttons or by scrolling the touch screen with your finger. Also, you can review other images at the same zoom level by turning the rear dial to navigate to the next or prior image, while the image is still zoomed.

## PLAYING MOVIES

To play back movies, navigate through the images by the methods described above until you find an image that has a movie-camera icon with a yellow upward-pointing triangle at the upper left and a playback triangle icon in the center, as shown in Figure 2-23. (If you don't see the movie-camera icon for a movie file, press the Display button until the screen that shows the icon appears.)

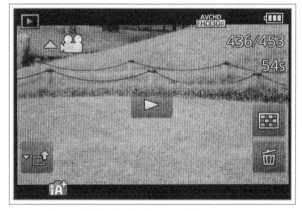

Figure 2-23. Movie Ready to Play in Camera

The yellow icon indicates that you press the Up button to start the movie playing. With the first frame of the motion picture displayed on the screen, press the Up button to start playback.

Figure 2-24. Movie Playback Control Icons

After the movie starts to play, you can use the four direction buttons as a set of DVR controls; the camera will briefly display icons that show the arrangement of those controls, as seen in Figure 2-24. The Up button is Play/Pause; the Right button is Fast Forward (or frame advance when paused); the Down button is Stop; the Left button is Rewind (or frame reverse when paused).

You can raise or lower the volume of the audio by turning the rear dial to the right or left. You will see a volume display when you activate this control, as shown in Figure 2-24. (This volume control will not appear when the camera is connected to a TV set, because the volume is adjusted by the TV's controls in that situation.)

If you want to play your MP4 movies on a computer or edit them with video-editing software, they will import nicely into software such as iMovie for the Macintosh, or into any other Mac or Windows program that can deal with video files with the extension .mp4. This is a file extension used by Apple Computer's QuickTime video software; QuickTime itself can be downloaded from Apple's website. You can edit these files on a Windows-based computer using Windows Movie Maker, Adobe Premiere Elements, or any one of a number of other programs. You also can edit AVCHD videos with most current video editing programs.

To save a frame from a movie as a single image, play the movie to the approximate location of the image you want, then press the Up button, which acts as the Play/Pause button in this context. Then press the Left and Right buttons to maneuver to the exact frame you want to save. While you are viewing this frame, press the Menu/Set button to select it, then, when prompted, on the screen shown in Figure 2-25, highlight Yes and press Menu/Set to confirm, and you will have a new still image at the end of the current group of recorded images.

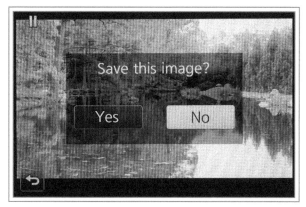

Figure 2-25. Message to Save Still Image from Movie

Press the Down button (Stop) to exit the motion picture Playback mode. Any still images saved from Full HD or HD video will not be of the highest quality; each one will be of Standard quality and no larger than 2 MP in size. If you need to save higher-quality still images from movie files, save them from 4K videos or use the 4K Photo option, discussed in Chapter 5.

# Chapter 3: The Recording Modes

Until now I have discussed basic settings for quick shots, relying heavily on Intelligent Auto mode, in which settings are controlled mostly by the camera's automation. Like other sophisticated cameras, though, the ZS100 has many options for setting up the camera to take pictures. One of the goals of this book is to explain those options clearly. To do this, I need to cover several areas, including recording modes, menu items, and physical controls. In this chapter, I will discuss the camera's recording modes and how the selection of one of these modes affects your images.

## Choosing a Recording Mode

Whenever you set out to capture still images or videos, an important first step is to select a recording mode, sometimes called a shooting mode. This "mode" controls the camera's behavior for adjusting exposure and other options. As with most advanced cameras, the ZS100 provides a standard set of modes: Intelligent Auto, Program AE (also known as Program), Aperture Priority, Shutter Priority, and Manual exposure. These last four are often known as the PASM modes, for the first letter of each mode. This camera also offers some more specialized modes: Creative Video, Custom, Panorama, Scene, and Creative Control.

Figure 3-1. Mode Dial - Creative Control

Each of the ZS100's ten shooting modes is assigned a slot on the Mode dial; you select the mode by turning the dial so the mode's icon is next to the white selector mark. For example, Figure 3-1 shows the dial when Creative Control mode is selected.

With that introduction to the recording modes, I will provide more detailed explanations of the modes in this chapter.

## Intelligent Auto Mode

This is the mode to choose if you need to have the camera ready for a quick shot in an environment with fast-paced events when you won't have time to fuss with settings. It's also handy if you need to hand the camera to a stranger to take a picture of your group.

To make this setting, turn the Mode dial on top of the camera so the iA icon is next to the white indicator mark, as shown in Figure 3-2.

Figure 3-2. Mode Dial - Intelligent Auto

You then should see a red camera icon with white characters for iA in the upper left corner of the screen, as shown in Figure 3-3.

Figure 3-3. iA Icon on Shooting Screen

If the icon has a white plus sign at the right, as shown in Figure 3-4, the camera is set to Intelligent Auto Plus mode. To change it back to the standard Intelligent Auto mode, press the Menu/Set button to enter the menu system, navigate to the iA icon on the far left of the screen, and then, on the right side of the menu screen, select the icon for iA instead of iA Plus. (I will discuss the differences between the two iA modes later in this section; for now, it will be simpler to leave the camera in iA mode.) Or, you can just touch the iA+ icon to bring up a screen for changing to iA mode.

Figure 3-4. iA+ Icon on Shooting Screen

In iA mode, the camera limits the settings you can make, in order to simplify things. For example, you cannot adjust items such as exposure compensation, white balance, ISO, Photo Style, Metering Mode, Filter Settings, most settings for Autofocus Mode (setting the area for autofocus) and several others. You can select manual focus, though.

The camera turns on several settings, including Auto White Balance, scene detection, image stabilization, and backlight compensation, all of which are useful settings that will not unduly limit your options in most cases. I'll discuss all of those items in Chapter 4 in connection with Recording menu settings, except scene detection and backlight compensation, which I will discuss here, because they are not menu options; the camera uses them automatically in Intelligent Auto mode.

With scene detection, the camera attempts to figure out if a particular scene type should be used for the current situation. The camera uses its programming to detect certain subjects or environments. For example, it looks for people; babies (if you have registered them using the Face Recognition menu option); night scenes; close-ups; sunsets; food; and portraits. It will identify scenes calling for the iHandheld Night Shot setting if that option is turned on through the menu system. That

feature is discussed in Chapter 4. If the camera detects one of these factors, it displays an icon for that type of scene and adjusts its settings accordingly. Otherwise, it displays the standard iA icon.

For example, in Figure 3-5, the camera detected the mannequin's face and displayed the icon for portrait scene detection.

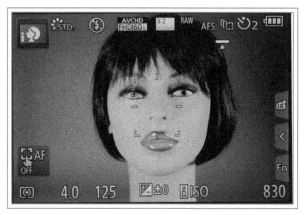

Figure 3-5. Portrait Scene Detection Icon

In Figure 3-6, the camera detected a closeup situation when I took a picture of an eraser, and it displayed the flower icon that indicates a macro shot.

Figure 3-6. Macro Scene Detection Icon

When shooting motion pictures or using the 4K Photo or Post Focus features, the camera detects fewer scene types: only portraits, scenery, low light, and macro shots.

With backlight compensation, the camera will try to detect situations in which the subject of the photograph is lighted from behind. This sort of lighting can "fool" the camera's metering system into making the exposure too dark, because of the light shining toward the lens. The result would be a subject that is too dark, without backlight compensation. With this setting, the camera automatically adjusts its exposure to be brighter, to overcome the effects of the backlighting.

Even though the ZS100 makes several automatic settings in Intelligent Auto mode, there are still some options you can adjust using the menu system and, to some extent, the physical control buttons.

First, you can use the Recording menu to select certain settings, although the choices are sharply limited compared to the many options that are available in other still-shooting modes. In those other modes (including Intelligent Auto Plus), there are eight screens of options available on the Recording menu; in basic Intelligent Auto mode, there are only three screens of options. I will discuss those options in Chapter 4. I included a table of recommended settings for general picture-taking in this mode in Chapter 2.

Second, you can press the Up button (marked with the plus and minus icon) to activate the defocus control option. As I discussed in Chapter 2, when you press that button in this mode, the camera displays two dials showing shutter speed on top and aperture on the bottom. Turn the rear dial to select a wider aperture (lower number on bottom dial) to get the camera to blur the background of the scene.

Third, you can press the Left button to bring up the focus mode menu and select either AF for autofocus or MF for manual focus. I discussed the general use of those settings in Chapter 2 and I will provide more details in Chapter 5.

Fourth, you can press the Down button to call up the Drive Mode menu, which I mentioned briefly in Chapter 2. In Intelligent Auto mode, you can select burst shooting or the self-timer (but not exposure bracketing) from the Drive Mode menu. I will provide further information in Chapter 5.

You also can use other controls for their intended purposes in this mode, such as the 4K button to get access to the 4K settings and the Q.Menu button to get access to the Quick Menu. You can pop up the flash with the flash release button, but the camera will decide whether to use it. I will discuss those options, among others, in Chapter 5.

In summary, although the Intelligent Auto shooting mode lets the camera make most of the technical

decisions, you still can have a fair amount of involvement in making settings for photographs (and movies). Especially when you're just starting out to use the ZS100, the basic Intelligent Auto mode provides a good start for exploring the camera's features. The automation in this mode is sophisticated and will often produce excellent results; the drawback is that you don't have as much creative control as you might like. But for ordinary picture-taking opportunities, vacation photos, and quick shots when you don't have much time to decide on particular settings, Intelligent Auto is a wonderful tool to have at your fingertips.

## INTELLIGENT AUTO PLUS MODE

If you want the camera to make its own decisions for several options but you want to be able to make more settings from the menus and physical controls, you can select Intelligent Auto Plus mode. As I discussed earlier, to set this mode, navigate to the iA icon at the top of the line of menu icons at the far left of the menu system, then move back to the right side and select the iA icon with a plus sign, as shown in Figure 3-7.

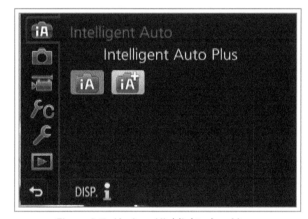

Figure 3-7. iA+ Icon Highlighted on Menu

In this mode, the camera displays seven screens of the Recording menu, instead of only three screens, as in the basic Intelligent Auto mode. (The camera skips over screen 6.) However, some of the menu items, such as Filter Settings, Sensitivity, Metering Mode, Highlight Shadow, and others, are dimmed and unavailable for selection because the camera chooses those settings automatically in this mode. The ZS100 also gives you access to many more options on the Custom menu than are available in basic Intelligent Auto mode, including items such as Half Press Release, Focus/Release Priority, MF Assist, and others. Those features are discussed in Chapter 7.

## Using the Up Button: Defocus Control and Exposure Compensation

In addition, with Intelligent Auto Plus mode in effect, you can press the Up button to get access to the exposure compensation function, as well as to the defocus control option, which I discussed earlier. The camera will select those two features in sequence when you press the Up button. A third press will return the camera to normal operation.

To use exposure compensation, press the Up button one or more times until the adjustment scale shown in Figure 3-8 appears.

Figure 3-8. Exposure Compensation Adjustment Screen

With that scale on the display, use the rear dial, the Left and Right buttons, or the touch screen to select a value for positive or negative exposure compensation, up to 5 EV (exposure value) units in either direction. The screen will grow brighter or darker to indicate the effect of the setting.

Figure 3-9. Exposure Compensation Adjusted +1.0 EV

Press the Up button one or more times, or press the Q.Menu button or the Menu/Set button, to return to the normal shooting screen. A scale at the bottom

center of the screen will show the degree of exposure compensation that is in effect, as seen in Figure 3-9, which shows +1.0 EV (exposure value). I will provide an example of the use of exposure compensation in Chapter 5.

## Using the Right Button: Color Control

When the camera is in Intelligent Auto Plus mode, if you press the Right button, the camera will display a screen for adjusting color tone, as shown in Figure 3-10.

Figure 3-10. Color Tone Adjustment Screen

If you then turn the rear dial to the right, colors will be adjusted to the bluish, or "cooler" side; if you turn it to the left, they will be adjusted to the reddish, or "warmer" side. If any such adjustment is made, a small color block will appear in the lower right corner of the shooting screen, as shown in Figure 3-11.

Figure 3-11. Color Block Indicating Color Adjustment

In Intelligent Auto Plus mode, as in basic Intelligent Auto mode, you can pop up the camera's built-in flash unit, but you have no control over whether the camera will cause it to fire; that process will be handled automatically by the camera. If you don't want the flash to fire, leave it retracted inside the camera.

## Program Mode

Program mode, also known as Program AE (for autoexposure), with the Mode dial set as shown in Figure 3-12, is the most automatic of the advanced (PASM) recording modes.

Figure 3-12. **Mode Dial - Program**

In this mode, the camera displays a P icon in the upper left corner of the display, as shown in Figure 3-13.

Figure 3-13. **Program Mode Icon in Upper Left Corner of Screen**

When you aim the camera at your subject, the exposure metering system will evaluate the light and choose both the shutter speed and aperture, which will be displayed in the lower left corner of the display when you press the shutter button halfway.

If those two values flash in red, that means the camera is unable to find settings that will yield a proper exposure. In that case, you may need to adjust the ISO setting or change the lighting conditions by using flash or taking other steps. In this mode, the camera can use its full range of aperture settings, from f/2.8 to f/8.0, and shutter speeds from 1/2000 second to 60 seconds if the mechanical shutter is in use, or from 1/16000 second to one second if the electronic shutter is in use.

If you want to alter the camera's settings by selecting a different shutter speed or aperture while keeping the same overall exposure, you can do that (if conditions permit) by using a feature called Program Shift. After you press the shutter button halfway to evaluate

exposure, you can turn the rear dial (on back of the camera) or the control ring (around the lens) within the next 10 seconds, and the camera will try to select another combination of shutter speed and aperture settings that will result in a normal exposure.

For example, if the camera initially selects settings of f/4.5 and 1/125 second, when you turn the control ring or the rear dial, the camera may change the settings to f/5.0 and 1/100 second, or f/5.6 and 1/80 second. If you turn the ring or dial in the other direction, the camera may change the settings to f/4.0 and 1/160 second, or f/3.5 and 1/200 second.

However, if ISO is set to Auto ISO instead of a specific numerical value, the camera may shift the aperture value and ISO value, but not the shutter speed. If ISO is set to Intelligent ISO, Program Shift is not available. (ISO settings are discussed in Chapter 4.)

Program Shift can be useful if you want to have the camera make the initial choice of settings, but you want to tweak them to use a slightly higher shutter speed to stop action, or a wider aperture to blur the background, for example. When Program Shift is in effect, the camera displays the P icon with a double-ended arrow in the lower left corner of the screen, as shown in Figure 3-14.

Figure 3-14. **Program Shift Icon in Lower Left Corner of Screen**

In addition, if the Exposure Meter option is turned on through screen 5 of the Custom menu, the camera will show the shutter speed and aperture settings in two moving strips, as seen in Figure 3-15. Program Shift is not available when recording motion pictures or 4K photos, or when using the Post Focus feature.

Figure 3-15. Exposure Meter Dials and Program Shift Icon on Screen

With Program mode, as with Intelligent Auto mode, the camera will select both the shutter speed and the aperture. However, unlike Intelligent Auto mode, with Program mode you can control many settings besides shutter speed and aperture. You don't have to make a lot of decisions if you don't want to, however, because the camera will make reasonable choices for you as defaults.

Program mode greatly expands the choices available through the Recording menu. You will be able to make choices involving white balance, image stabilization, ISO sensitivity, filter effects, metering method, autofocus area, and others. I won't discuss all of those choices here; if you want to explore that topic, see the discussion of the Recording menu in Chapter 4.

Besides unlocking many options in the Recording menu, choosing Program mode provides you with access to settings in the Custom menu that are not available in Intelligent Auto Mode, such as various focus-related settings and options for setting how the camera's controls operate, including the AF/AE Lock button. I will discuss those options in Chapter 7.

Using Program mode does involve some tradeoffs. The most obvious issue is that you don't have complete control over the camera's settings. You can set many options, such as Photo Style, Quality, Picture Size, and ISO, but you can't directly control the aperture or shutter speed, which are set according to the camera's programming. You can exercise a good deal of control through exposure compensation and exposure bracketing (discussed in Chapter 5) and Program Shift (discussed above), but that's not the same as selecting a particular aperture or shutter speed at the outset. If

you want that degree of control, you'll need to select Aperture Priority, Shutter Priority, or Manual exposure for your recording mode.

## Aperture Priority Mode

This mode is similar to Program mode in the functions available for you to control, but, as the name implies, it gives you more control over the camera's aperture.

Figure 3-16. Mode Dial - Aperture Priority

In this mode, set by turning the Mode dial to A, as shown in Figure 3-16, you select the aperture setting and the camera will select a shutter speed that will result in normal exposure, if possible. The camera will choose a shutter speed anywhere from 60 seconds to 1/2000 second. (The range is one second to 1/16000 second when the electronic shutter is in use; that feature is discussed in Chapter 4.) If none of these values results in a normal exposure, both the shutter speed and aperture values will turn red and flash. In that case, you may need to adjust the aperture or the ISO setting, or change the lighting conditions.

The main reason to choose this mode is so you can select an aperture to achieve a broad depth of field, with objects in focus at different distances from the lens, or a shallow depth of field, with only one subject in sharp focus and other parts of the image blurred to reduce distractions. With a narrow aperture (higher f-stop number) such as f/8.0, the depth of field will be relatively broad; with a wide aperture such as f/2.8, it will be more shallow, resulting in the possibility of a blurred background.

Because the range between the widest and narrowest aperture settings available on the ZS100 is not very great, this camera does not readily produce dramatically blurred backgrounds just from changing the aperture. However, there can be a noticeable difference from this setting. For example, in Figures 3-17 and 3-18, I made the same shot with two very different aperture settings. I focused on the vase in the foreground in each case.

Figure 3-17. Aperture Set to f/2.8

Figure 3-18. Aperture Set to f/8.0

For Figure 3-17, I set the aperture of the ZS100 to f/2.8, the widest possible. With this setting, because the depth of field at this aperture was relatively shallow, the items in the background are blurry. I took Figure 3-18 with the camera's aperture set to f/8.0, the narrowest possible setting, resulting in a broader depth of field, and bringing the background into sharper focus.

These two photos show the effects of varying the aperture by setting it wide (low numbers) to blur the background or narrow (high numbers) to achieve a broad depth of field and keep subjects at varying distances in sharp focus. There are two other ways to achieve a blurred background. First, you can zoom the lens in to a telephoto setting, which reduces the depth of field and renders the background blurry, if the foreground subject is not too distant from the lens. Second, if you focus on a subject at a very close distance, the depth of field will be minimal, and the background will be blurry.

Of course, with either of those techniques, you have to accept the other effects of the setting—either a telephoto shot or a closeup shot, which may not be practical for the image you are making. For example, with a portrait, you may find that the best option

for blurring the background is to choose the widest possible aperture.

Figure 3-19 is an image I took with the lens focused very close, in macro mode, to show how that setting can produce a blurred background apart from the aperture setting.

Figure 3-19. Blurred Background with Macro Shot

To set the aperture, turn either the rear dial or the control ring, and the number of the f-stop will appear in the lower left corner of the screen, as shown in Figure 3-20, where the value is f/5.6.

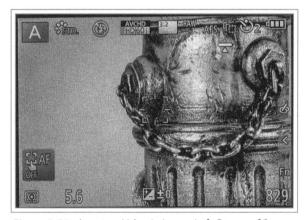

Figure 3-20. Aperture Value in Lower Left Corner of Screen

The shutter speed will be displayed also, but not until you have pressed the shutter button halfway down to let the camera evaluate the exposure.

If you turn on the Exposure Meter option on screen 5 of the Custom menu, the camera will display two dials showing the shutter speed and the aperture, as seen earlier in Figure 3-15.

It is important to note that not all apertures are available at all times. In particular, the widest-open aperture, f/2.8, is available only when the lens is zoomed out to its wide-angle setting (moved toward the W indicator). At higher zoom levels, the widest aperture available changes steadily, until, when the lens is fully zoomed in to the 250mm level, the widest aperture available is f/5.9.

To see an illustration of this point, here is a quick test. Zoom the lens out by moving the zoom lever all the way to the left, toward the W. Then select Aperture Priority mode and set the aperture to f/2.8 by turning the rear dial or the control ring all the way to the f/2.8 setting. Now zoom the lens in by moving the zoom lever to the right, toward the T. After the zoom is complete, you will see that the aperture has changed to f/5.9, because that is the widest the aperture can be at the maximum zoom level. (The aperture will change back to f/2.8 if you move the zoom back to the wide-angle setting; so you need to check your aperture after zooming out as well as after zooming in, to make sure you will not be surprised by an unexpected aperture setting.)

## Shutter Priority Mode

The next shooting mode is a complement to Aperture Priority mode. In Shutter Priority mode, with the Mode dial at the S position as shown in Figure 3-21, you choose the shutter speed and the camera will set the corresponding aperture in order to achieve a proper exposure of the image.

Figure 3-21. Mode Dial - Shutter Priority

In this mode, you can set the shutter for a variety of intervals ranging from 60 full seconds to 1/2000 of a second when using the mechanical shutter. With the electronic shutter, the range is from one second to 1/16000 second. I will discuss the Shutter Type menu option in Chapter 4. (The available shutter speed settings are different for motion pictures.) The camera will select an aperture from its full range of f/2.8 to f/8.0, unless the lens is zoomed in. In that case, as discussed in connection with Aperture Priority mode, the widest aperture available is f/5.9.

If the camera cannot set an aperture to result in a normal exposure, the shutter speed and aperture values will flash red. If you are photographing fast action, such as a baseball swing or a hurdles event at a track meet, and you want to stop the action with a minimum of blur, you should select a fast shutter speed, such as 1/500 of a second. You can use a slow shutter speed, such as 1/8 second or slower, to cause motion blur for effect, such as to smooth out the appearance of flowing water.

Figure 3-22. Shutter Speed Set to 1/2000 Second

In Figures 3-22 and 3-23 I photographed the same action using different shutter speeds to illustrate the different effects. In both cases, I took a picture as I was pouring a cup of uncooked rice into a pitcher. In Figure 3-22, using a shutter speed of 1/2000 second, the camera froze the rice in mid-air, letting you see the grains of rice individually. In Figure 3-23, using a shutter speed of 1/30 second, the rice appears to form a single stream of white, because that shutter speed was not fast enough to stop the action.

Figure 3-23. Shutter Speed Set to 1/30 Second

You select the shutter speed by turning the rear dial or the control ring. For example, to set a value of 1/500 second, turn the dial or the ring so the 500 indication appears. Values faster than 1/2000 second are available only if the Shutter Type option on screen 5 of the Recording menu is set to Auto or Electronic, shown as ESHTR on the menu.

On the shutter speed display, be sure to distinguish between the fractions of a second and the times that are one second or longer. The longer times are displayed with what looks like double quotation marks to the right, as in Figure 3-24, which shows a shutter speed setting of four seconds.

Figure 3-24. Shutter Speed Setting of 4 Seconds on Screen

One aspect of the camera's display that can be confusing is that some times are a combination of fractions and decimals, such as 1/2.5 and 1/3.2. I find these numbers hard to translate mentally into a time I can understand. Here is a table that translates these numbers into a more understandable form:

Table 3-1. **Shutter Speed Equivalents**

| | |
|---|---|
| 3.2 | 1/3.2 = 0.31 or 5/16 second |
| 2.5 | 1/2.5 = 0.4 = 2/5 second |
| 1.6 | 1/1.6 = 0.625 = 5/8 second |
| 1.3 | 1/1.3 = 0.77 = 10/13 second (0.8 sec) |

When Shutter Priority mode is in effect, you cannot use the Intelligent ISO setting. If it was set, the camera will reset it to Auto ISO.

## Manual Exposure Mode

Manual exposure mode, set by turning the Mode dial to M, as shown in Figure 3-25, helps you take full control over exposure decisions.

Figure 3-25. Mode Dial - Manual Exposure

For example, you may want to underexpose or overexpose an image to convey a feeling or to produce an effect, such as a silhouette. Or, if your subject is deeply shadowed you may prefer to use manual settings of aperture and shutter speed rather than relying on exposure compensation or settings such as i.Dynamic to expose the subject properly.

I find Manual exposure mode useful when taking shots to be combined in software to create HDR (high dynamic range) composite images. The HDR technique, which I will discuss further in Chapter 4, often is used when the scene is partly in darkness and partly in bright light. To even out the contrast, you can take a series of shots, some considerably underexposed and others overexposed. You then combine these shots in special software that blends differently exposed portions from several shots, resulting in a composite image that is well exposed through a wide range of lighting values.

Figure 3-26 is an example using Manual exposure mode for a shot I took using the LumoPro LP180 optical slave flash, which is discussed in Appendix A. When using an off-camera flash like that one, I use Manual mode because the camera's autoexposure modes cannot take into account the flash from the off-camera unit.

Figure 3-26. Image Taken Using Manual Exposure Mode

The technique for using Manual exposure mode is not far removed from that for the Aperture Priority and Shutter Priority modes. To control exposure manually, set the shutter speed by turning the rear dial and set the aperture by turning the control ring. (If you press the Up button, the roles of those controls will reverse, and the rear dial will set the aperture while the control ring will adjust the shutter speed.)

Figure 3-27. Shooting Screen in Manual Exposure Mode

The camera will display the aperture and shutter speed in the lower left corner, as shown in Figure 3-27. You also will see at the bottom center of the display either an exposure compensation icon, as shown in Figure 3-27, or a small exposure scale ranging from –3 EV to +3 EV (exposure value), as shown in Figure 3-28. As you change the exposure settings, the camera will display tick marks along the scale if the exposure as metered

is too bright or too dark. For example, in Figure 3-28, there are tick marks to the right, indicating that the exposure as metered is too bright.

Figure 3-28. Exposure Compensation Scale in Manual Mode

If no tick marks appear, the exposure compensation icon is displayed with the plus-or-minus zero symbol, meaning that the exposure is normal according to the camera's metering system. Of course, you do not have to be concerned with the indication on this on-screen scale, because you can make any settings you want; you may want a darker-than-normal image to create a silhouette, for example. But the EV scale is useful to help you decide what settings to make.

You also should note that the camera's display will not show the effects of your settings unless you set it to do so. That is, with normal menu options, even if you set the aperture and shutter speed to values that would produce a very dark image, the image on the display will appear basically normal, provided there is sufficient ambient light to produce a normal view. If you want to see the effects of your exposure settings, go to screen 5 of the Custom menu and turn on the Constant Preview option. Then the display will become darker or brighter as the settings change. (This feature works only with Manual exposure mode, not with Aperture Priority, Shutter Priority, or Program.)

An important feature of Manual exposure mode is that you can set ISO to Auto ISO. If you do that, then, even though the camera cannot change the aperture or the shutter speed you have set, it can vary the ISO setting within the range permitted by the Auto ISO option (discussed in Chapter 4). Therefore, the camera may be able to achieve a normal exposure by setting the ISO to an appropriate level. This is a powerful feature, which amounts in effect to giving you a new recording mode, which might be called "Aperture and Shutter Priority" mode.

For example, you might use Manual exposure mode with Auto ISO when you are taking pictures of a person working with tools in a dimly lighted workshop. You might need to use a narrow aperture such as f/8.0 in order to keep the work in focus, and a fairly fast shutter speed such as 1/250 second to avoid motion blur. You can make both of those settings and be assured that they will not vary. The camera will automatically adjust the ISO setting to achieve the best exposure possible, given the lighting conditions.

In other situations, such as when you purposely want to underexpose or overexpose an image, just set ISO to a specific numerical value and adjust the shutter speed and aperture to achieve the exposure you need. You cannot use Intelligent ISO in Manual exposure mode.

Another distinguishing feature of Manual exposure mode is that it provides you with an additional option for setting the shutter speed. With Shutter Priority mode, you can set the shutter speed anywhere from 60 seconds to 1/2000 second (when using the mechanical shutter). With Manual mode, you have the additional option of setting the shutter speed dial to the T setting, for Time exposure.

With the T setting, when you press the shutter button the shutter opens up and does not close again to end the exposure until you press it again, up to a limit of about 120 seconds. You can use this feature to take extra-long exposures of trails of cars' headlights, for fireworks, for star trails, or to turn night scenes into unusual daylight vistas. Of course, it is advisable to use a solid tripod and to trigger the camera remotely from a smartphone (as discussed in Chapter 9) when taking an exposure of this length. The time exposure feature is not available if you are using the electronic shutter, which is discussed in Chapter 4.

## Panorama Mode

This shooting mode is designed for a very specific purpose—the shooting of panoramic images. If you follow the fairly simple steps involved, the camera will stitch together a series of images internally and produce a high-quality final result that sets forth a

dramatic, wide (or tall) view of a scenic view or other subject that lends itself to panoramic depiction.

Figure 3-29. **Mode Dial - Panorama**

Once you turn the Mode dial to the Panorama position, as seen in Figure 3-29, you will briefly see the display shown in Figure 3-30, showing the direction that is currently set for taking the panorama and advising you to press the shutter button and move the camera in that direction.

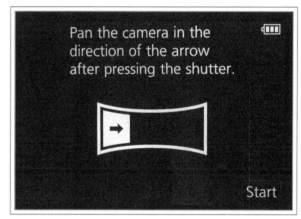

Figure 3-30. Initial Message for Panorama Shooting

When that screen disappears, you will see a display like that shown in Figure 3-31, which provides a guide line for keeping your panorama level.

Figure 3-31. Shooting Screen in Panorama Mode

When you are ready, press the shutter button all the way down and release it, while moving the camera steadily in the direction selected. You will hear a continuous clicking sound as the camera takes multiple images. You should try to keep the camera steady in a single horizontal (or vertical) plane and move it at a steady rate, so that you would complete a full circle in about eight seconds. You can keep moving the camera until the panorama ends of its own accord, or you can press the shutter button down again to stop the recording at any time.

The direction (left, right, up, or down) in which you move the camera is determined by the Panorama Settings option on screen 5 of the Recording menu. That menu option also includes a Picture Size setting, which lets you choose Standard or Wide for the size of the panorama. With the Standard setting, a horizontal panorama has a width of 8176 pixels and a height of 1920 pixels. A vertical panorama has a width of 2560 and a height of 7680. With the Wide setting, a horizontal panorama has a width of 8176 and a height of 960, but it covers a wider area than a Standard panorama. If you want the highest quality, choose Standard; choose Wide if you need to include a very wide view in the image.

Because of the different sizes of panoramas taken with the horizontal and vertical orientations, you can use the direction settings with different orientations of the camera to achieve different results than usual. For example, if you set the direction to Down and then hold the camera sideways while you sweep it to the right, you will create a horizontal panorama that has 2560 pixels in its vertical dimension rather than the standard 1920.

I tend to shoot my panoramas moving the camera from left to right, but you may have a different preference. If you move the camera either too quickly or too slowly, the panorama will not succeed; if that happens, just try again. Generally speaking, panoramas work best when the scene does not contain moving objects such as cars or pedestrians, because, when items are in motion, the multiple shots are likely to pick up the same object more than once, in different positions.

It is advisable to use a tripod if possible, so you can keep the camera steady in a single plane as it moves. Note that focus, exposure, and white balance are fixed as soon as the first image is taken for the panorama.

If for some reason you want to shoot a panorama with one of the filter effects settings in place (such as Expressive, Retro, Old Days, and the like), you can select one from the Filter Settings menu, or you can just turn the control ring or the rear dial. Those controls are both programmed by default to select that setting in this shooting mode. (If the controls do not carry out this function, check the setting of the Ring/Dial Set option on screen 8 of the Custom menu.)

When a panoramic shot is ready to be played back in the camera, the camera prompts you to press the Up cursor button (or the on-screen icon) to start it playing back; the panorama then scrolls across the screen so it can be viewed using the full area of the screen, rather than being squeezed to fit its full extent within the screen.

Figure 3-32 is a sample panorama, shot with the camera hand-held and using the Standard setting for panorama size.

Figure 3-32. **Panorama: Maymont Park, Richmond, Virginia**

## Scene Mode

Scene mode, also called Scene Guide mode, is quite different from the other shooting modes discussed so far. This mode does not have a single defining feature, such as permitting control over one or more aspects of exposure. Instead, when you select Scene mode and then choose a particular scene type within that mode, you are in effect telling the camera what sort of environment the picture is being taken in as well as what kind of image you are looking for, and you're letting the camera make a group of decisions as to what settings to use to produce that result.

Figure 3-33. Mode Dial - Scene Guide

Turning the mode dial to the SCN indicator, as shown in Figure 3-33, places the camera in Scene mode, but unless you want to settle for whatever scene setting is already in place, you now need to make another choice, and pick one from the fairly impressive list of possibilities.

To make this further choice, you can use the menu system. When you select Scene mode, the menu system itself changes. When the camera is set to Scene mode, there is a new branch of the menu system, named Scene, as shown in Figure 3-34.

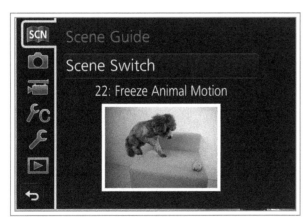

Figure 3-34. Scene Icon Highlighted in Menu System

It takes over as the first choice at the top of the menu system once you have pushed the Menu/Set button. The Scene menu also appears automatically when you select SCN on the Mode dial, if the Menu Guide option is turned on in screen 8 of the Custom menu.

To change scene types, press the Menu/Set button and navigate to the SCN icon at the top of the left side of the screen. Next, press the right button, and select the Scene Switch option, as shown in Figure 3-35.

Figure 3-35. Scene Switch Option

The camera then displays a series of images that will rotate as you touch them with your finger, as shown in Figure 3-36. You also can move through these images using the Left and Right buttons or the rear dial.

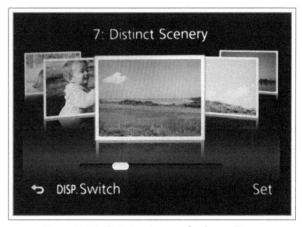

Figure 3-36. Rotating Images for Scene Types

If you press the Display button, the display changes to an arrangement that includes a text description of each setting, as shown in Figure 3-37. You can move through those screens using the Left and Right buttons and scroll through hints for each setting with the rear dial. If you press the Display button again, you will see an array of 12 images on the screen, as shown in Figure 3-38. You can scroll through those images using the touch screen, the cursor buttons, or the rear dial. Using any of the three systems of display, scroll through the 24 options and select the scene type you want.

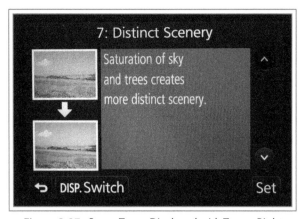

Figure 3-37. Scene Types Displayed with Text at Right

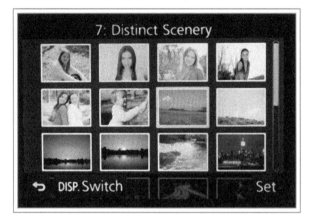

Figure 3-38. Scene Types in 12-Image Display

Another way to select one of the 24 scene types is to touch the Scene mode icon on the shooting screen, as shown in Figure 3-39.

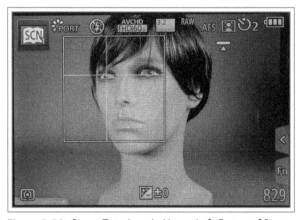

Figure 3-39. Scene Type Icon in Upper Left Corner of Screen

When you touch that icon, the camera immediately displays the Scene settings menu, so you can make a selection of a scene type. Unfortunately, each icon uses the SCN designation with a small number as the only identification of the scene type, so you either have to memorize 24 scene types or press on the icon for a reminder of what scene type is currently selected.

Each scene type carries with it a variety of settings, including things like focus mode, flash status, range of shutter speeds, sensitivity to various colors, and others.

There are limitations on settings you can make in Scene mode. No matter what scene type you select, you cannot use the Filter Settings, Sensitivity, Metering Mode, Highlight Shadow, HDR, or Multiple Exposure options. For Photo Style, you cannot select a main setting, such as Portrait, Vivid, or Natural, but you can adjust contrast, sharpness, noise reduction, and saturation (including color tone or filter effect for monochrome options). For some settings, the camera uses Auto White Balance, but you can fine-tune white balance with color axes as discussed in Chapter 5, and you can use white balance bracketing, also discussed in Chapter 5.

Except for Handheld Night Shot, with all scene settings you can set Quality to Raw. However, any special effects that are similar to the Filter Settings or Creative Control settings will not show up in the Raw images on a computer. Therefore, you should shoot using Fine, or Raw & Fine, for Quality if you use a setting of that nature. (For example, with the Glistening Water setting, the Star Filter rays will not show up in a Raw file when it is opened on a computer.)

With most of the settings you can use burst shooting, and with several you can use flash. (And with some the camera asks you to use flash.) I will provide details about each of the settings, so you can make an informed choice. I will include sample images for some of the settings. Several of the settings are self-explanatory from their names, and I will not discuss them all in detail.

Clear Portrait: This setting is designed to produce rich skin tones. You should get good results if you shoot close to the subject and set the zoom to full telephoto, so as to blur the background if possible. The camera sets itself to a wide aperture if it can and initially sets the autofocus mode to Face/Eye Detection. The flash mode is initially set to Forced On/Red-Eye Reduction, but you can change it to Forced On.

Silky Skin: This setting is similar to Portrait; it detects skin tones in faces and adds a "soft effect" to those areas, as shown in Figure 3-40. The softening increases as the image is zoomed in further. Flash mode is initially set to Forced On/Red-Eye Reduction.

Figure 3-40. **Silky Skin Portrait Example**

**Backlit Softness:** The camera uses positive exposure compensation and disables the flash.

**Clear in Backlight:** The camera sets the flash mode to Forced On and displays a message asking you to pop up the flash, if it is not popped up. However, you can still take the picture without flash if you don't pop it up. This setting is for use when the subject is lighted from behind and you need to use flash to make the subject show up clearly.

**Relaxing Tone:** The flash is disabled and the camera uses warmer, yellowish tones to add a somewhat subdued, old-time appearance to the image.

**Sweet Child's Face:** With this setting, the flash mode is initially set to Forced On/Red-eye, but you can change it to Forced On. When you touch a face on the screen, the camera takes a picture with focus and exposure set for that face, using its setting for touch shutter. As the lens is zoomed in, a softening effect is applied increasingly.

Figure 3-41. **Distinct Scenery Example**

**Distinct Scenery:** This style is intended for photographs of landscapes and subjects other than individual people. It is useful for general shots of buildings, gardens, and colorful scenery, as shown in Figure 3-41. The flash is disabled. You cannot select a white balance setting, presumably because you will be shooting your outdoor vistas in daylight conditions. However, you can tweak the white balance using the color axes and you can use white balance bracketing.

**Bright Blue Sky:** The camera uses a small amount of positive exposure compensation to allow for shadows or backlighting that might be caused by the sky's brightness. You can alter that setting as you like. The flash is disabled, and white balance can be tweaked, but the basic setting cannot be changed.

**Romantic Sunset Glow:** The camera disables the flash and adds a reddish or purplish hue to the scene to emphasize the colors of a sunrise or sunset. You can tweak white balance but not change the major setting. In Figure 3-42, I used this setting and the next one to capture the sunset from a rooftop event in the city.

Figure 3-42. **Romantic Sunset Glow Example**

Figure 3-43. **Vivid Sunset Glow Example**

**Vivid Sunset Glow:** This setting is similar to the previous one, except that the camera does not add any coloration to the scene; it uses settings that emphasize the colors that are present in the scene naturally. In Figure 3-43, I shot the sunset at the same time and place as the previous image, to show the differences between these two settings.

**Glistening Water:** The flash is disabled and the camera uses the Star Filter setting, also available with the Filter Settings option and Creative Control mode. That setting adds star-like rays to bright areas, such as the sun's reflections on water. White balance can be tweaked, but not changed to a different setting. Figure 3-44 is a shot of a lighted swimming pool. The brightest rays were formed on the reflections of lights on the white rim of the pool.

Figure 3-44. Glistening Water Example

**Clear Nightscape:** With this setting, the flash is disabled and white balance can be tweaked but not otherwise changed. The camera is likely to use a long shutter speed to capture a natural-looking scene, such as a gas station at dusk, as shown in Figure 3-45.

Figure 3-45. Clear Nightscape Example

It is advisable to use a tripod and to set the self-timer, so the camera will not be jiggled when you press the shutter button.

**Cool Night Sky:** This setting is similar to the previous one, except that the camera adds a bluish tone to the image, to make it look "cooler."

**Warm Glowing Nightscape:** This setting is similar to the previous two, but with this one the camera uses "warmer" reddish/yellowish tones.

**Artistic Nightscape:** This setting is also designed for night scenes, but in this case the camera initially sets a shutter speed of 30 seconds to capture moving trails of cars' headlights and taillights, and similar items, to create an impressionistic view of the night scene. For good results, you need to have the camera firmly anchored on a tripod and trigger it with the self-timer. You can change the shutter speed if you want to by turning the rear dial or the control ring. It may take some experimenting to find the right setting to capture an interesting mixture of lights. For Figure 3-46, which I took before the sky was totally dark, I reduced the shutter speed to 3.2 seconds to capture these trails of cars' lights without overexposing the image.

Figure 3-46. Artistic Nightscape Example

**Glittering Illuminations:** This setting is designed for capturing scenes with some bright lights. The camera uses the Star Filter effect, which adds radiant beams to the brightest areas. Here, again, it is advisable to use a tripod, though the camera is not likely to use a very long shutter speed as with the previous setting. In Figure 3-47, I used this setting to add starry rays to some bright spots on a pond.

Figure 3-47. Glittering Illuminations Example

**Handheld Night Shot:** With this setting, the ZS100 uses a special process to take high-quality images in low light. The camera takes a rapid burst of several shots and combines them internally into a composite image. Because of this processing, the camera can use a high ISO setting, and therefore can use a fast shutter speed to minimize the blur caused by camera motion during a long exposure. Although shots with high ISO settings often have unpleasant visual noise or graininess, by combining the multiple images, the camera can reduce the noise in the final result.

Figure 3-48. Handheld Night Shot

This setting is useful when you cannot use a tripod or flash, and need to take pictures in low light. Of course, because multiple images are being taken, this setting works best for subjects that are not moving, or at least are not moving rapidly. In Figure 3-48, I used this setting for a shot of a dimly lighted basement room in an historic mansion. The flash is disabled. This setting is the same as the iHandheld Night Shot option, which is available only in Intelligent Auto mode, and can be selected from the Recording menu, as discussed in Chapter 4.

**Clear Night Portrait:** With this setting, the camera expects you to use flash. If you pop up the flash, it will be set to Slow Sync with Red-eye Reduction. You cannot change that setting, but you can use the Flash Adjustment option under the Flash item on screen 6 of the Recording menu to make the flash output brighter or darker. If possible, the subject should be asked not to move for about a second while the image is being exposed. The purpose of the Slow Sync flash mode is to expose the main subject with the flash, but to keep the shutter open long enough to also expose the background with the ambient light.

**Soft Image of a Flower:** This setting is designed for a closeup (macro) shot of a subject such as a flower. The flash mode is initially set to Forced On, but you should avoid using the flash if the camera is very close to the subject, because the flash may overwhelm it or wash it out. It is advisable to use a tripod and the camera's self-timer. The ZS100 also applies a softening effect to the scene. In Figure 3-49, I used this setting for a closeup shot in a botanical garden.

Figure 3-49. Soft Image of a Flower Example

**Appetizing Food:** This scene type is for those occasions when you're in a restaurant and are so impressed by the presentation of your meal that you want to photograph it, or for people who like to document every meal they eat. Or you could use it for taking pictures for your cookbook. In any event, the idea is to take a closeup picture without flash, though the flash will be available if you want to use it. In addition, the camera allows you to control the aperture for this setting, which usually can be done only with Aperture Priority mode and Manual exposure mode. To do that, turn either the control ring or the rear dial to select a new aperture. You might want to do this if you want to select a wide aperture to blur the background, or a narrow aperture to achieve a broad depth of field and keep the entire scene in focus. For Figure 3-50, I used this setting to capture an image of artificial fruit in the dining room of an historic house.

Figure 3-50. Appetizing Food Example

Cute Dessert: This setting is very similar to the previous one, though it appears to apply somewhat more saturation and vividness to the image.

Freeze Animal Motion: This setting is intended for photos of moving pets, often taken indoors. The camera uses tracking focus and turns off the AF assist lamp to avoid startling the animal, though you can turn it back on through screen 3 of the Custom menu if you want to. The camera turns on Intelligent ISO so it can use a fast shutter speed as needed. (I'll discuss ISO, or sensitivity to light, in Chapter 4. Briefly, with a higher-numbered ISO setting, the camera is more sensitive to light, and therefore can use a faster shutter speed. The tradeoff is the possibility of added "noise" or fuzziness of the image.) You can use the flash, but only with the Forced On setting. You can turn on burst shooting through the Drive Mode settings, as discussed in Chapter 5.

Figure 3-51. Freeze Animal Motion Example

In Figure 3-51, I used this setting to catch a shot of a very active spaniel puppy as she played in the yard.

Clear Sports Shot: This style is similar to the previous one, but it is meant to stop the action of sports in bright daylight using fast shutter speeds if necessary. The AF assist lamp is not disabled by default. In Figure 3-52, I used this setting to capture some of the action at a high school lacrosse game.

Figure 3-52. Clear Sports Shot Example

Monochrome: This final setting for Scene mode sets the camera to take black-and-white images. You can use any flash setting you want.

## Creative Control Mode

Creative Control mode occupies its own place on the Mode dial, so I will discuss it here in the context of the other shooting modes, even though it is a bit of a hybrid creature. It has some attributes of the Photo Style setting on the Recording menu, and some attributes of the Scene mode settings.

For example, one of the Creative Control settings, Monochrome, is similar to the Monochrome setting of the Photo Style menu option and to the Monochrome setting of Scene mode. The Expressive setting of Creative Control mode is similar to the Vivid setting of the Photo Style option. However, there are significant differences among these various options, and the Creative Control settings offer a range of adjustments that makes these options useful for dramatic alteration of the colors and other attributes of your images.

Figure 3-53. Mode Dial - Creative Control

When you turn the Mode dial to the artist's palette position, as shown in Figure 3-53, if the Menu Guide option on screen 8 of the Custom menu is turned on, you will immediately see a screen that lets you browse through the icons for the 22 effects. You can choose from three possible arrangements of the icons by pressing the Display button repeatedly.

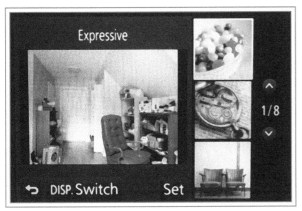

Figure 3-54. Normal Display for Creative Control Mode

With the Normal display, as shown in Figure 3-54, the camera displays a vertical line of icons at the right. As you scroll up and down through that line using the Up and Down buttons or the rear dial (or the touch screen), the camera highlights the selected icon and displays a large view at the left of the screen that applies that effect to the live view of the current scene that the camera is aimed at.

With the Guide display, as shown in Figure 3-55, the setup is the same, except that, at the left of the screen, instead of displaying the appearance of the effect, the camera displays a brief description of the effect.

With the List display, as shown in Figure 3-56, the camera displays more icons on each screen, in rows and columns. As you scroll through them, the camera displays the name of the effect at the top of the display.

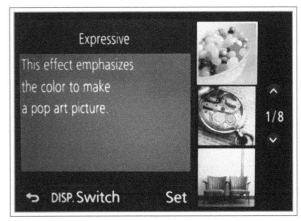

Figure 3-55. Guide Display for Creative Control Mode

Figure 3-56. List Display for Creative Control Mode

When you have scrolled through the Creative Control effect icons and highlighted the one you want to use, press the Menu/Set button (or touch the Set icon on the screen) to select it and return to the recording screen. The camera's display will show the name of the effect briefly at the left, and the appearance of the scene on the display will reflect the chosen effect, as shown in Figure 3-57, where the Sepia effect is selected.

You also can select a Creative Control effect quickly by just turning the control ring or the rear dial when the shooting screen is displayed. When you do that, the camera displays a scrolling list of effects at the bottom of the screen as shown in Figure 3-58; press the Menu/Set button to select one when it is highlighted in yellow. You also can change the current effect by touching the effect icon in the upper left corner of the screen, which calls up the standard menu screen for selecting an effect.

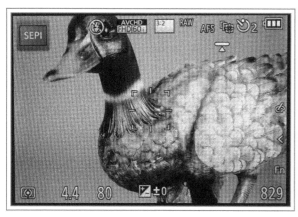

Figure 3-57. Shooting Screen with Sepia Setting in Effect

Figure 3-58. Scrolling List of Settings at Bottom of Display

The Creative Control choices provide different "looks" for your images, in some cases producing striking alterations of the normal color, texture, and brightness. It's important to note that, because the Creative Control setting occupies its own slot on the mode dial, whatever setting you make for Creative Control is only in effect when the mode dial is set to that position. So, for example, if you switch the Mode dial to Program or Aperture Priority mode, the Creative Control setting will no longer be in effect. If you later switch the dial back to Creative Control, though, whatever setting you previously made in that mode will once more take effect.

You also should note that, when you record a motion picture with the ZS100, you don't need to move the mode dial; you only need to press the red motion picture button on top of the camera. So, when you record a movie, you need to be sure the Mode dial is set where you want it. For example, if you have just taken some still photos using an exotic setting from the Creative Control selections, that setting will still be in effect if you press the red button to record a movie. If you want a more ordinary look for your movie, be sure to set the

Mode dial back to Intelligent Auto, Program, Creative Video, or some other standard mode, to avoid having the movie recorded using the Creative Control setting. On the other hand, being able to use Creative Control settings when shooting a movie can be an advantage when you want to add an atmospheric look to your motion pictures. I'll discuss movie settings in Chapter 8.

Once you have selected a Creative Control setting, you can still make some additional settings from the Recording menu and with the camera's physical controls. For example, you can use options such as Picture Size, AF Mode, and Metering Mode. However, several other settings are unavailable with the Creative Control shooting mode, including white balance, ISO, Intelligent Dynamic, and Photo Style. With some of the Creative Control options you can use burst shooting or flash; I will indicate those cases as I discuss the settings individually below.

You also can use Raw for the Quality setting with the Creative Control settings. However, as with the Filter Settings menu option, discussed in Chapter 4, there is a pitfall with that capability. If you set Quality to Raw, the Creative Control effect will not show up in the image that opens in your Raw-processing software— at least not in any software I have tried, such as Adobe Photoshop and Silkypix. The effect may appear when you view the image in the camera or view a thumbnail in your software, but it will not be included in the image when it is opened on a computer. Therefore, there is no point in using Raw for Quality with the Creative Control mode. Instead, you should use Raw & Fine or Raw & Standard. In that way, you will have an image that includes the special effect you selected, as well as a Raw image for flexibility in processing.

In addition to the settings from the Recording menu and physical controls discussed above, with the Creative Control mode you can make several other adjustments, depending on which Creative Control setting is in effect. These adjustments can be made in two ways. First, you can press the Right button, which will take you to the adjustment screen for the effect that is currently selected. For example, when the Expressive effect is active, pressing the Right button takes you to the screen shown in Figure 3-59, with a sliding scale at the bottom. Using the rear dial, the Left and Right buttons, or the touch screen, you can adjust the slider along that scale to make the vividness of the effect greater or smaller. With other effects you can adjust other values, such as coloring, contrast, or graininess.

Figure 3-59. Adjustment Screen for Expressive Effect

In this recording mode, you can also adjust background defocus and image brightness, in the same way as with Intelligent Auto Plus mode. To do that, press the Up button, and then use the on-screen scale or dial to make the adjustment using the rear dial, the Left and Right buttons, or the touch screen.

You also can adjust all of the Creative Control mode settings using the touch screen icons. To do that, touch the small icon that looks like a painter's palette at the right edge of the screen. You will then see a vertical line of three icons at the right edge of the screen, as shown in Figure 3-60.

Figure 3-60. Touch Screen Icons for Creative Control

Press the top icon to bring up the adjustment scale for the Creative Control effect. Press the middle icon to bring up the defocus control. Press the bottom icon to call up the brightness adjustment scale. Press the arrow icon to dismiss the adjustment icons.

As I discuss each Creative Control setting, I will mention what items can be controlled, if those

adjustments are different from the standard ones (brightness, background defocus, and intensity of the selected effect).

Following are details about each of the 22 Creative Control choices. Along with descriptions I will include a sample photograph taken using the setting being discussed, to give an idea of how the Creative Control settings affect images.

Expressive. I would call this mode something like "super-vivid"; some people call it "pop art." If you like your colors with strong saturation, this style is useful. However, the Vivid setting of the Photo Style menu option can produce a similar result. The Photo Style setting is available in the more advanced shooting modes such as Program, Aperture Priority, and the like; therefore, you can use more menu and other settings in conjunction with that setting than you can with the more limiting Creative Control Expressive setting. Figure 3-61 provides an illustration, with a shot of an impressive tree in an arboretum.

Figure 3-61. Expressive Example

Retro. This style appears to me to be the opposite of Expressive; it paints the scene with subdued, somewhat yellowish tones, de-emphasizing the glaring qualities of Expressive. It evokes a gentle feeling of past times. For this effect, adjusting the setting to the left on the scale increases yellowish tones, and adjusting it to the right increases reddish tones. In Figure 3-62, I used the Retro setting for a shot of a room in an historic mansion from the late 19th Century, to emphasize the antique aura of the surroundings.

Figure 3-62. **Retro Example**

**Old Days.** This effect is intended to give a "nostalgic" look by lowering the saturation of colors and reducing contrast for an old-fashioned look. With the adjustment slider, you can vary the contrast. In Figure 3-63, I used this setting to give an aged appearance to another room in the historic mansion shown in the previous image.

Figure 3-63. **Old Days Example**

**High Key.** "High key" is a technique in which a studio photographer uses high-intensity lighting throughout the scene, striving for a bright look with light colors and few shadows. This technique often is used in advertising photography. With the ZS100, this single setting cannot necessarily remake your image to look like a traditional high key shot, but the camera does boost the exposure to produce a brighter-than-normal image. Moving the slider for the effect to the left produces more pinkish tones, while setting it to the right yields bluer hues. Figure 3-64 provides an

example, showing another room from the historic mansion shown in the previous two images. I used this setting because the lighting was dim, and I felt that the High Key setting brightened up the scene. I used a small amount of negative exposure compensation to avoid making the image too bright.

Figure 3-64. **High Key Example**

**Low Key.** "Low key" lighting, of course, is the opposite of "high key." With this approach, the photographer welcomes shadows and dark areas in the photograph. Here again, the ZS100 cannot produce a true "low key" image all by itself; what it can do is reduce the exposure and otherwise process the photograph to look more dark and shadowy than normal. Here again, as with the High Key setting, the effect's adjustment slider can be moved to the left for a redder look, or to the right for a bluer appearance. In Figure 3-65, I used this setting in the arboretum to emphasize the bright colors used for the artistic wrap on a massive tree.

Figure 3-65. **Low Key Example**

**Sepia.** With the Sepia setting, as shown in Figure 3-66, the ZS100 produces a monochrome image with a sepia (brownish) tone and softens the contrast somewhat to give the look of an antique photograph. In this case, adjusting the setting of the adjustment slider decreases the overall contrast of the image, while moving it to the right increases the contrast, producing a somewhat harsher, darker appearance. For Figure 3-66, I used this setting for a scene inside the historic mansion shown earlier, to show how this setting compares to others.

Figure 3-66. Sepia Example

**Monochrome.** This setting gives you another way, other than the Photo Style menu option and the Scene mode option, to capture an image in traditional black and white. The adjustment slider lets you add a color tone, ranging from yellowish to bluish. For Figure 3-67, I used this setting for a shot of an historic inn in a city park.

Figure 3-67. Monochrome Example

**Dynamic Monochrome.** This setting, illustrated in Figure 3-68, converts the image to black and white, but with heightened contrast to produce a more dramatic effect. As with Sepia, you can use the left or right adjustments to decrease or increase contrast. For Figure 3-68, I used this setting to add dramatic impact to a shot of an impressive old tree against the sky.

Figure 3-68. Dynamic Monochrome Example

**Rough Monochrome.** With this setting, the camera also records a monochrome image, but this time with the appearance altered to add grain by inducing visual noise, like the noise that results from using a high ISO setting. This option can be good for street photography or for other situations in which you want the somewhat primitive look of a grainy image. The adjustment slider lets you reduce or increase the amount of graininess. For Figure 3-69, I used this setting for a shot of a tree with unusually shaped branches as a way to emphasize its structure.

Figure 3-69. Rough Monochrome Example

**Silky Monochrome.** This option gives you another way to take a monochrome image. In this case, the camera puts the image slightly out of focus to add a soft or dreamlike look. With the adjustment slider, you can alter the amount of defocusing that is used. The left side of the scale provides a sharper, less defocused image. For Figure 3-70, I used this setting for a photo of objects on the ground near a bench on the grounds of a school, to add a slight air of fantasy to the scene.

Figure 3-70. Silky Monochrome Example

**Impressive Art.** This setting has some similarities to the Expressive, Dynamic Monochrome, and High Dynamic settings. It produces images with high contrast and dramatic variations in color intensity. Using the adjustment slider, you can alter the intensity all the way to the left to produce a monochrome image, or all the way to the right to produce an oversaturated image with exploding, vibrant colors. You can achieve some fairly dramatic effects with this setting, as seen in Figure 3-71, which shows a view of a cobblestoned street on a rainy day, enhancing the colors with stark contrast.

Figure 3-71. Impressive Art Example

**High Dynamic.** This setting is oriented less to altering the colors of the image than to leveling out the shadows and highlights. As you can see from the name, it is akin to the "high dynamic range" or HDR processing that is often done with software, and sometimes, as here, through in-camera processing. For Figure 3-72, I used

this setting for a shot of a walkway in the botanical garden on a sunny day, to even out the shadows and bright areas.

Figure 3-72. High Dynamic Example

The High Dynamic setting is useful when you're taking a picture that includes areas of both bright light and shadows. Ordinarily, a camera cannot process that sort of image and preserve the details in both areas. This setting alters the processing so more details are visible in the dark areas, and the bright areas are not so washed out and overexposed. As with the Impressive Art setting, above, the adjustment slider lets you adjust the image from monochrome at the left to oversaturated color at the right.

**Cross Process.** This setting gives you the ability to add a distinctive color tint to your images, in either green, blue, yellow, or red. In this case, you use the adjustment made available through the bottom icon at the right of the screen to select one of those colors, as shown in Figure 3-73.

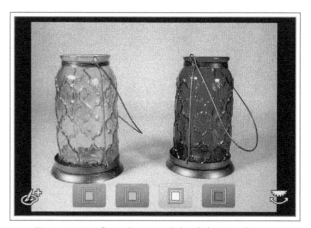

Figure 3-73. Cross Process Color Selection Screen

Once that selection has been made, your images will be tinted with the selected color. Figure 3-74 is an example of using this setting for a blue sculpture in the arboretum. This composite image shows all four settings. Clockwise from upper left, the settings are green, blue, red, and yellow.

Figure 3-74. Cross Process Composite Example

**Toy Effect.** As with some of the other Creative Control selections, this one is not strictly an example of color processing. Rather, this setting tries to reproduce the effects that are achieved with a primitive "toy" camera. There has been a popular movement for this sort of photography in recent years, using cameras like the Holga and Diana, which are purposely constructed to lack sharpness and to suffer from vignetting at the corners. The photographs from such cameras can be quite appealing in their own way, and the Toy Effect setting lets you experiment with a good simulation of this sort of image.

Figure 3-75. Toy Effect Example

It can be a pleasing way to highlight a single subject in the middle of the frame, as shown in Figure 3-75, which

shows a decorative bell hanging in a garden. With this setting, the bottom icon's adjustment produces more reddish or orange tones to the left, and more bluish ones to the right.

**Toy Pop.** With this setting, the camera combines the vivid, bright appearance of the Expressive setting with the vignetting of Toy Effect, discussed above. In this case, the adjustment slider controls the amount of vignetting. At the left of the scale, the vignetting is reduced so more of the image is bright; at the right, the vignetting increases to darken more of the corners. For Figure 3-76, I found that this setting was a good one to place a vignette around a picturesque house in the arboretum.

Figure 3-76. Toy Pop Example

**Bleach Bypass.** This option causes images to have increased contrast and lowered color saturation, to produce a bleached, washed-out appearance. You can reduce the contrast by moving the adjustment slider to the left or increase it by moving the slider to the right. For Figure 3-77, I took a view of the same city street shown earlier in Figure 3-71, for comparison.

Figure 3-77. Bleach Bypass Example

**Miniature.** The next Creative Control setting is called the Miniature effect. When you apply this option to an image, the camera adds blurring at one or more sides of an image or at the image's top or bottom, to simulate the appearance of a photograph of a tabletop model or miniature. Such images often appear blurred in one area, either because of the narrow depth of field of these close-up photos, or because of the use of a tilt-and-shift lens, which causes blurring at the edges.

For this feature to work well, you need to choose an appropriate subject. I have found that the effect looks interesting when applied to something like a street scene or a house, which might actually be reproduced in a tabletop model. For example, if you are able to get a high vantage point above a road intersection or a parking area on a street, as in Figure 3-78, you may be able to use this effect to make it look as if you had photographed a high-quality mock-up of an area with model cars.

Figure 3-78. Miniature Effect Example

With this setting, three icons appear at the right side of the screen when you touch the artist's-palette icon at the right side of the screen. The bottom icon adjusts brightness and the middle one adjusts the intensity of the colors. In order to adjust the settings for the miniature effect itself, you use the top icon, which looks like a rectangle with arrows pointing up and down.

When the Miniature setting has been selected, touch the artist's palette icon then touch the top (rectangle) icon, and a long yellow frame will appear on the screen, as shown in Figure 3-79.

Figure 3-79. Miniature Setting Adjustment Frame

This frame represents the area of the image that will remain in sharp focus. The areas outside of that frame will be defocused and fuzzy, contributing to the overall effect. So, for example, if you are shooting from an overpass down toward a highway intersection, you may want to line up the yellow frame over the road that you want to remain in focus, leaving the areas outside the frame to be out of focus.

To move the yellow frame, use the four cursor buttons. When you see triangles on the frame, press the buttons corresponding to those triangles to move the frame in the direction of the triangle. Use the other two cursor buttons to flip the frame to a different orientation (horizontal or vertical). Then, turn the rear dial to change the size of the frame. When you have the frame oriented and sized as you want it, press the Menu/Set button to return to the shooting screen and take your picture. You also can use your fingers on the touch screen to move the rectangle, to pinch it to make it larger or smaller, or to change its orientation between horizontal and vertical.

You can press the Right button to get to the adjustment slider, which adjusts color saturation. With this setting, you cannot use burst shooting or the flash, although you can use Raw image quality. Also, note that you can use the Miniature setting when shooting movies. If you do so, no audio is recorded, and the action is speeded up to about ten times normal speed, which helps reinforce the illusion that you are filming a model scene rather than a life-sized one.

**Soft Focus.** With this setting, the camera defocuses the overall image to achieve a soft, hazy look, as seen in Figure 3-80. You can still use the icons at the right of the screen to control brightness, background defocus, and the overall intensity of the general defocusing effect. You cannot use burst shooting or record movies with this setting in effect.

Figure 3-80. Soft Focus Example

**Fantasy.** With this option, the camera alters the intensity of colors and adds a bluish color cast to the scene, with the idea of producing a hazy, fantasy-like appearance. With the adjustment slider, you can vary the intensity of the colors. For Figure 3-81, I felt that this setting was appropriate for a swan-themed bedroom in a 19th-Century mansion.

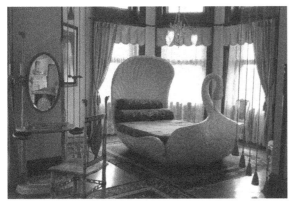

Figure 3-81. Fantasy Example

**Star Filter.** This setting lets you add cross-shaped "stars" of light to your images at bright points in the scene, giving a sparkling effect. This effect can be pleasing with a subject that lends itself to this look, like the baseball stadium and neighboring buildings with their bright lights in Figure 3-82. The effect's adjustment slider controls the size of the rays of light; adjust to the left for shorter rays, and to the right for longer ones. You cannot use this effect with burst shooting or when recording movies.

Figure 3-82. Star Filter Example

**One Point Color.** This is a setting that I enjoy quite a bit. It lets you select any one color in a scene for the camera to retain, while turning the rest of the image black and white. You can achieve a dramatic effect with this setting, by placing a clear emphasis on a small part of the scene that is in color.

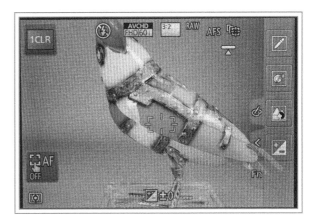

Figure 3-83. One Point Color Touch Icons

To select the color that is retained, press the icon for the artist's palette at the right edge of the screen to bring up a line of four icons, as shown in Figure 3-83. Touch the top icon, which looks like a pencil, and a movable set of yellow arrows will appear in the center of the screen, as shown in Figure 3-84. Using the four direction buttons or your finger on the touch screen, place that square over the object whose color you want to retain, and press the Menu/Set button (or touch the Set icon) to confirm the selection.

The setting's adjustment icon (which looks like a palette with a plus sign) is used to determine how closely an item must match the selected color in order to show up in color. Move the slider to the left to restrict the color selection to the minimum, and to the right to include a broader range of similar colors.

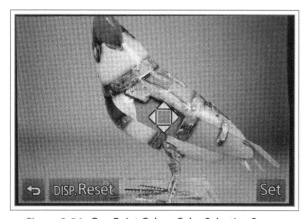

Figure 3-84. One Point Color - Color Selection Screen

Then, as shown in Figure 3-85, only objects matching that color will appear in color on the shooting screen and in the final image after you take the picture. You can use burst shooting with this setting and you also can shoot movies with it.

Figure 3-85. One Point Color Example

Sunshine. Finally, the Sunshine option lets you add a solar flare effect to your image. After you select this option, press the artist's palette icon at the right edge of the screen, then touch the top adjustment icon, which looks like the sun, and you will see a yellow circle on the display. You can move that circle around the screen using the four direction buttons or your finger on the touch screen and resize it using the rear dial or by pinching and pulling with your fingers on the screen.

When you have the solar flare sized and located as you want, press Menu/Set (or the Set icon) to lock it in. Then, press the Right button or touch the second adjustment icon (under the sun icon) and you can select yellow, red, blue, or white for the color of the flare. Press Menu/Set, and the effect will be locked in with your selections. You can move the flare outside the edges of the image to avoid having the large, bright ball in the scene.

For Figure 3-86, I used this option to add a solar flare to an image of a King Tut figurine, to add some regal atmosphere.

Figure 3-86. Sunshine Example

## Custom Mode: C Position on Mode Dial

Finally, I will briefly discuss the C position on the Mode dial, seen in Figure 3-87.

Figure 3-87. Mode Dial - Custom

(I will discuss the Creative Video mode in Chapter 8.) The C position does not represent an independent shooting mode. Instead, it is used in conjunction with the powerful Custom Set Memory menu item, which I will discuss in Chapter 7. Essentially, you can use this slot on the Mode dial to recall three sets of custom values for your important menu settings and some other settings. Once you have stored the settings, just turn the Mode dial to the C position to recall one of your three saved groups of settings—C1, C2, or C3. See Chapter 7 for further details.

# CHAPTER 4: THE RECORDING MENU AND THE QUICK MENU

Much of the power of the ZS100 lies in the options provided in the Recording menu, which gives you control over the appearance of images and how they are captured. This menu is not the only source of creative tools for this camera; there are several important settings that can be controlled with physical buttons and dials, as I will discuss in Chapter 5, and there also is the convenient Quick Menu, which gives you ready access to several often-used options. I will discuss both the Recording menu and the Quick Menu in this chapter.

## The Recording Menu

As I have discussed earlier, the main menu system of the ZS100 incudes five separate menus: Recording, Creative Video, Custom, Setup, and Playback. I'll discuss the Playback menu in Chapter 6, the Custom and Setup menus in Chapter 7, and the Creative Video menu in Chapter 8.

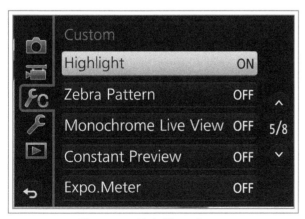

Figure 4-1. Main Menu Screen

When you press the Menu/Set button, you will initially see the main menu screen, as shown in Figure 4-1. The actual screen that is displayed depends on the setting of the Menu Resume item on screen 3 of the Setup menu.

If that option is set to On, then the menu screen you last used will appear first; if it is set to Off, the camera will display the first screen of the Recording menu. In Figure 4-1, screen 5 of the Custom menu is active, with the camera set to Program mode.

If, as in this example, the Recording menu screen is not displayed, press the Left button. That action will move the highlight into the left column of the menu screen, as shown in Figure 4-2, where you can navigate up and down with the direction buttons or the rear dial (or the touch screen) to highlight the icons for the various menu systems.

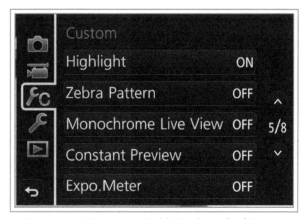

Figure 4-2. Menu Icons Highlighted at Left of Screen

For now, use the buttons to highlight the red camera icon at the top of the line of icons, indicating the Recording menu, as shown in Figure 4-3.

Then press the Right button to move back over to the main part of the screen, with the Recording menu items. The yellow selection rectangle will highlight a menu item, as shown in Figure 4-4. You can then navigate through the Recording menu to find the item you want to adjust.

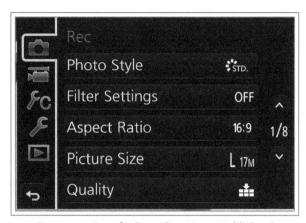

Figure 4-3. Icon for Recording Menu Highlighted

Figure 4-4. Screen 1 of Recording Menu

As I discussed earlier, the menu options will change depending on the recording mode in effect. If you're using the basic Intelligent Auto mode, the Recording menu is limited to three screens, because that mode is for a user who wants the camera to make most of the decisions without input. For the following discussion, I'm assuming you have the camera set to one of the advanced (PASM) modes, because in those modes all eight screens of the menu are available.

On the menu screen you will see a fairly long list of options, each occupying one line, with its name on the left and its current setting on the right. (In some cases, the current setting is not shown because it involves multiple options.) You have to scroll through eight screens to see all of the items.

You can scroll through the items on any screen using the Up and Down buttons or the rear dial. If you find it tedious to scroll using those methods, here's a tip for navigating the main menu system on the ZS100: You can use the zoom lever on top of the camera to speed through the menus one full screen at a time, in either direction. You also can press the Display button

to move through the menu screens, but only in the forward direction. And, you can use the touch screen capability, by touching a desired menu option, or by touching the up and down arrows at the far right of the menu screen. You can tell which numbered screen you are on by checking the numbers at the right of the screen, which show the screen numbers as 1/8, 2/8, through 8/8.

Depending on the location of a particular menu option, you may be able to reach that option more quickly by reversing direction with the direction buttons and wrapping around to reach the option you want. For example, if you're on the top line of screen 1 of the menu, at Photo Style, you can scroll up to reach the bottom option on screen 8 of the menu, Profile Setup.

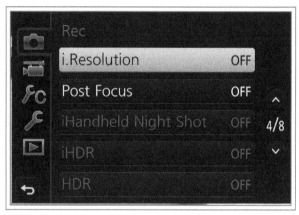

Figure 4-5. Menu Screen with Some Items Dimmed

Some menu lines may have a dimmed, "grayed-out" appearance at times, meaning they cannot be selected under the present settings. For example, in Figure 4-5, several items are dimmed on screen 4 of the Recording menu. In this case, Quality is set to Raw and the recording mode is Program. With Quality set to Raw, you cannot select HDR, which is incompatible with that setting, and both iHandheld Night Shot and iHDR are available for selection only in Intelligent Auto mode.

Also, if you have set Quality to Raw, you cannot make several other settings, including Intelligent Zoom and Digital Zoom. If you want to follow along with the discussion of the options on the Recording menu, set Quality to Fine, which is the setting represented by the icon of an arrow pointing down onto 2 rows of bricks, as shown in Figure 4-6.

Figure 4-6. Quality Setting of Fine Highlighted

To do so, scroll down using the Down button until the Quality line is highlighted, then press the Right button to pop up the sub-menu. Scroll up or down as needed to highlight the top icon with the 6 bricks, and then press the Menu/Set button to select that option.

With that setting, you will have access to most of the options on the Recording menu. I'll start at the top, and discuss each option on the list.

## PHOTO STYLE

This first item on the Recording menu gives you several options for choosing a setting that determines the overall appearance of your images. These settings yield differing results in terms of warmth, color cast, and other attributes.

Figure 4-7. Photo Style Selection Screen

To select a Photo Style setting, highlight the Photo Style line on the Recording menu and press the Right button or Menu/Set to move to the screen that displays the current setting in the upper right corner, as shown in Figure 4-7. (For all menu settings, you also can use the touch screen to make selections. I will mention

that possibility from time to time, but I won't keep repeating it for every menu option.)

Then use the Left and Right buttons or the rear dial to scroll through the available settings: Standard, Vivid, Natural, Monochrome, Scenery, Portrait, and Custom. When your chosen setting is highlighted at the top right of the screen, as shown in Figure 4-7, where the Vivid setting has been highlighted, press the Menu/Set button to select it, then press the Q.Menu button to exit to the shooting screen. Or, if you prefer, after highlighting the new setting, just press the shutter button halfway to select the setting and return to the shooting screen.

If you want to go further and fine-tune the setting, the ZS100's menu system lets you adjust four parameters that are associated with the Photo Style settings: contrast, sharpness, noise reduction, and saturation. To make adjustments to those parameters, press the Down button when the main setting (such as Vivid or Natural) is highlighted in yellow, as in Figure 4-7. A new highlight will then appear in the block that contains the value for one of the four adjustable parameters, as shown in Figure 4-8.

Figure 4-8. Adjustment Block for Photo Style Highlighted

In this case, the second line is highlighted, which means you can adjust the sharpness setting; the word Sharpness appears for a few seconds at the top left of the screen, indicating that that value can now be adjusted.

Once you have placed the highlight block on one of the four parameters, press the Left and Right buttons or turn the rear dial to change the value of that parameter up to five levels, either positive or negative. A yellow scale in the center of the screen will reflect those changes, as shown in Figure 4-9. Press Menu/Set or press the shutter button halfway to save the changes. The camera will remember those settings even when it is turned off.

Figure 4-9. Sharpness Adjustment Mode for Photo Style

There is one additional point to make about the Monochrome setting for Photo Style. Monochrome means there is no color in the image, only shades of black, white, and gray. Therefore, the saturation adjustment does not work to increase or decrease the saturation of colors for the Monochrome setting. Instead of the saturation adjustment, the camera provides two additional parameters at the bottom of the list: color tone and filter effect, as shown in Figure 4-10.

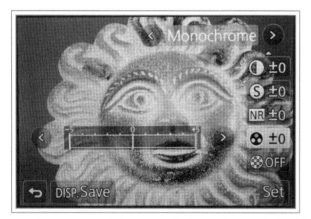

Figure 4-10. Additional Parameters for Monochrome Photo Style

With color tone, a positive adjustment makes the monochrome effect increasingly bluish or "cooler," while a negative adjustment makes it increasingly yellowish or "warmer."

The filter effect adjustment lets you add a virtual filter, simulating the effect of a glass filter, which can be used on a camera's lens for black-and-white photography to enhance contrast and for other purposes. You can

choose from a yellow, orange, red, or green filter, or choose the last setting, which turns the filter effect off.

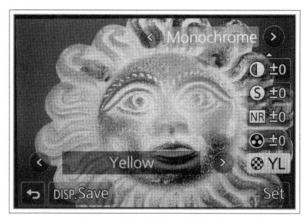

Figure 4-11. Yellow Selected for Filter Effect

For example, Figure 4-11 shows the screen when the yellow filter effect is selected. The yellow, orange, and red effects provide increasing amounts of contrast for blue subjects, and can be used to enhance the appearance of a blue sky. The green effect can be used to reduce the brightness of human skin and lips or to brighten the appearance of green foliage.

When you set Photo Style to Monochrome with Quality set to Raw, the picture you take will show up as black-and-white on the camera's LCD screen, but, when you import the image file into software that reads Raw files, the image may show up in color, depending on how the software interprets the Raw data from the sensor. With the Silkypix software provided with the camera, Raw images taken with Photo Style settings retain the Photo Style appearance, but you can convert them to other settings in the software.

The Photo Style settings are not available in the basic Intelligent Auto mode, but they are available in all other shooting modes, with the exception of Creative Control mode. In Intelligent Auto Plus mode, you can select only Standard or Monochrome for Photo Style, and you cannot adjust either setting's contrast and other parameters.

In Scene mode, the camera selects a Photo Style setting according to the scene type you select, but also lets you adjust the parameters for that type. For example, if you select Clear Portrait for the scene setting, the camera selects Portrait for the Photo Style setting, but lets you adjust the contrast and other values.

The Photo Style settings also are available for recording a movie with one of the advanced shooting modes.

Before I provide descriptions of how the Photo Style settings affect your images, I am providing a chart in Figure 4-12 that shows the same scene photographed with each of the various settings.

# Photo Style Chart for ZS100

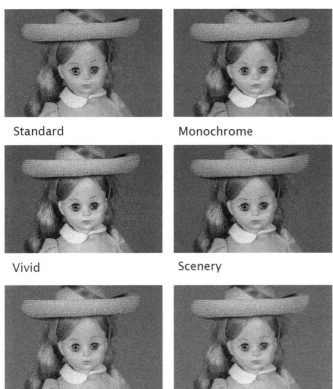

Standard

Monochrome

Vivid

Scenery

Natural

Portrait

Figure 4-12. **Photo Styles Comparison Chart**

Here are summaries of each of the Photo Style settings:

Standard: No change from the normal setting; good for general photography. The camera uses moderate sharpening and contrast to provide a clear image for everyday purposes.

Vivid: Increased saturation (intensity or vividness) and contrast of the colors in the image to make the colors "pop" out in dramatic fashion.

Natural: Reduced contrast to produce a softer, more subdued appearance.

Monochrome: Standard settings, but monochrome image, with all color removed (that is, saturation

reduced to zero), unless you use the color tone adjustment to add a yellow or blue tone. You also can use the filter effect setting to add a yellow, orange, red, or green filter effect.

Scenery: Increased emphasis on the blues and greens of outdoor scenes, with increased saturation of those hues.

Portrait: Emphasis on flesh tones.

Custom: The Custom slot is available to store a setting that you have customized using your own settings for the parameters that can be adjusted (contrast, sharpness, saturation, and noise reduction, as well as color tone and filter effect for the monochrome setting). To use this option, select any one of the basic Photo Style settings (Standard, Vivid, Natural, Monochrome, Scenery, or Portrait), then press the Down button and proceed to adjust any or all of the parameters for that setting as you want them. Next, press the Display button, as prompted by the DISP. Save message on the display, as shown in Figure 4-9.

The camera will display the message shown in Figure 4-13, asking you to confirm that you want to overwrite the current Custom setting with the settings you just made. If you highlight Yes and press Menu/Set, the settings you have made will be stored in the Custom slot of the Photo Style setting.

Figure 4-13. **Message to Save Custom Photo Style**

After you have stored the Custom setting, you can recall it at any time by selecting Custom for your setting. You can alter the Custom setting in the future by choosing a different set of settings and storing it to the Custom slot, overwriting the previous entry.

## FILTER SETTINGS

This second option on the Recording menu lets you apply special picture effects to your images. As I discussed in Chapter 3, the Creative Control shooting mode provides a set of 22 effects, including Expressive, Retro, Old Days, and 19 others. Each of these settings includes adjustments to things such as brightness, sharpness, focus, colors, and other factors, to achieve a special appearance for a given shot. I discussed the details of those settings in Chapter 3.

The Filter Settings menu option lets you apply any of these same effects without using that shooting mode. So, for example, while shooting in Program or Aperture Priority mode, you can select one of the 22 Filter Settings options to alter the look of an image or video. Using this option, you can have the benefit of the special setting while using one of the more advanced shooting modes. If you select one of the Filter Settings options while using Manual exposure mode, you can select the aperture and shutter speed you want, in order to have full creative control over the image. If you use the Creative Control shooting mode, you can apply the same effects, but you have to rely on the camera's automation for the exposure.

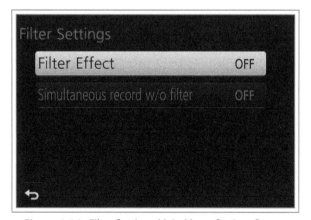

Figure 4-14. Filter Settings Main Menu Options Screen

To use this option, navigate to the Filter Settings menu option and select it. You will see a screen like that in Figure 4-14. Highlight Filter Effect and select it, and you will see a screen like that in Figure 4-15, with the choices On, Off, and Set. Select On or Off to activate or turn off the currently selected effect. Use Set to change to a different effect. When you select Set, you are taken to a screen where you can select one of the 22 available settings.

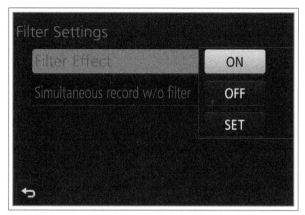

Figure 4-15. Filter Effect Settings Screen

The settings screen is the same as that discussed in Chapter 3 for Creative Control mode; see that chapter for details about selecting one of the settings.

If you want to protect against accidentally leaving one of the effects activated, you can go to the main options screen for Filter Settings and select Simultaneous Record Without Filter. That option can be selected only when Filter Effect is turned on through the menu.

If you turn this option on, then, when you take a picture using one of the special effects, such as Expressive, Retro, Miniature, or Soft Focus, the camera also takes an image at the same time that does not use that effect. This feature offers protection against accidentally taking a picture with the Filter feature turned on, resulting in an image that is not usable for ordinary purposes because of the special coloration or other effects. I usually keep this option turned on.

You have to have one of the Filter Effects turned on and Quality set to Standard or Fine in order to turn this simultaneous recording option on. If you do that, then, when all filter effects are turned off, this option will be turned off. However, if you have not purposely turned this option off, it will turn itself back on automatically as soon as you activate a filter effect. So, I recommend that you turn on a filter effect, turn on this menu option, and then turn off the filter effect. In that way, this option will be available when needed.

As is the case with the Creative Control settings, the Filter Effects settings do not affect Raw files when those files are opened on a computer. So, if you want to use one of these effects, you should shoot with Quality set to Fine or Raw & Fine.

## ASPECT RATIO

This menu option has four settings: 4:3, 3:2, 16:9, and 1:1, representing the ratio of the width of an image to its vertical height. This setting does not affect just the shape of the image; it also helps determine how many megapixels (MP or M) an image contains. When the aspect ratio is set to 3:2, the maximum resolution of 20 MP is available. When the aspect ratio is set to 4:3, the greatest possible resolution is 17.5 MP. At 16:9, the greatest possible resolution is 17 MP. At the 1:1 ratio, the largest resolution available is 13.5 MP. If you want to view the scene using the entire area of the LCD screen, choose 3:2, which is the aspect ratio of the screen. With 4:3, there will be black bars at the sides of the screen as you compose your shot; with 16:9, there will be black bars at the top and bottom of the screen; with 1:1, there also will be black bars.

Figures 4-16 through 4-19 show the shapes of images taken with the ZS100's various aspect ratio settings.

Figure 4-17. Aspect Ratio 3:2

Figure 4-18. Aspect Ratio 16:9

Figure 4-16. Aspect Ratio 4:3

Figure 4-19. Aspect Ratio 1:1

In Figure 4-16, the aspect ratio is set to 4:3. This aspect ratio crops the image slightly in the horizontal direction. Figure 4-17 is an image taken with the 3:2 setting, which uses the maximum number of available horizontal and vertical pixels. For Figure 4-18, the aspect ratio was set to the 16:9 position, which uses the maximum number of horizontal pixels, and crops the vertical pixels. Finally, the 1:1 setting was used for Figure 4-19. This setting uses the maximum number of vertical pixels, but crops the pixels in the horizontal direction.

## PICTURE SIZE

This next item on the Recording menu controls the number of megapixels in the images you record with the camera, up to and including its maximum of 20 MP. The maximum MP setting, using the L (for Large) setting for Picture Size is affected by the aspect ratio that you have set using the Aspect Ratio menu item, discussed above. If you set the aspect ratio to 3:2, the maximum Picture Size setting is the full 20 MP, as shown in Figure 4-20, using the full horizontal and vertical extent of the available pixels.

Figure 4-20. Picture Size Menu Option

As noted above in connection with the aspect ratio setting, the number of megapixels decreases with other aspect ratio settings.

The higher the Picture Size setting, the better the overall quality of the image, all other factors being equal. However, you can create a fuzzy and low-quality image with a high Picture Size setting with no trouble at all; this setting does not guarantee a great image. But if all other factors are equal, a higher megapixel count should yield noticeably higher image quality. Also, when you have a large megapixel count in your image, you have some leeway for cropping it; you can select a portion of the image to enlarge to the full size of your print, and still retain acceptable image quality.

On the other hand, images with high megapixel counts eat up storage space more quickly than those with low megapixel counts. If you are running low on space on your SD card and still have a lot of images to capture, you may need to reduce your Picture Size setting so you can fit more images on the card.

As noted earlier, the Picture Size setting is dimmed and unavailable when you have selected Raw for the Quality setting. However, if you select Raw & Fine or Raw & Standard, with which the camera records both a Raw and a JPEG image, the Picture Size option is available for setting the size of the JPEG image.

## Extended Optical Zoom

Another point to consider in setting Picture Size is how much zoom power you need to have available. You might not think that picture size is related to zoom, but with the ZS100 it is. The camera has a feature called Extended Optical Zoom, designated as EX in the user's manual illustrations. When you set the Picture Size to 5 MP (S), for example (with aspect ratio of 3:2), you will

find that you can zoom in farther than you can with Picture Size set to its maximum. You will see an EX designation appear on the menu screen to the left of the Picture Size setting of S, as shown in Figure 4-21.

Figure 4-21. EX Designation for Extended Optical Zoom

(You will not see the EX designation unless Quality is set to Fine or Standard, because Extended Optical Zoom is not available with Quality set to Raw. This feature also is incompatible with some other settings, such as 4K Photo, Handheld Night Shot, Multiple Exposure, HDR, and others.)

You will see that the zoom scale goes beyond the normal limit of 250mm as you move the zoom lever on top of the camera toward the T setting, for Telephoto, as shown in Figure 4-22.

Figure 4-22. Zoom Scale Beyond 250mm with Extended Optical Zoom

Depending on the Picture Size setting, the scale will extend to a zoom level of as much as twice normal, or about an equivalent of 500mm. (If you turn on Intelligent Zoom or Digital Zoom, discussed later in this chapter, the zoom range will extend even farther;

for now, I am assuming that both of those options are turned off.)

To summarize the situation with Extended Optical Zoom, whenever you set Picture Quality to a level below Large, you get a bit of additional zoom power because of the reduced resolution. You could achieve the same result by taking the picture at the normal zoom range with Picture Size set to the full 20M and then cropping the image in your computer to enlarge just the part you want. But with Extended Optical Zoom, you get the benefit of seeing a larger image on the display when you're composing the picture, and the benefit of having the camera perform its focus and exposure operations on the actual zoomed image that you want to capture, so the feature is not useless. You just need to decide whether it's of use to you in a particular situation.

I'll discuss Intelligent Zoom and Digital Zoom later, as other Recording Menu options.

## QUALITY

The next setting on the Recording menu is Quality. It's important to distinguish the Quality setting from the Picture Size setting. Picture Size concerns the image's resolution, or the number of megapixels in the image. Quality has to do with how the image's digital information is compressed for storage on the SD card and, later, on the computer's hard drive. There are three levels of quality available in various combinations: Raw, Fine, and Standard, as shown in Figure 4-23. From the top, the five icons stand for Fine, Standard, Raw & Fine, Raw & Standard, and Raw.

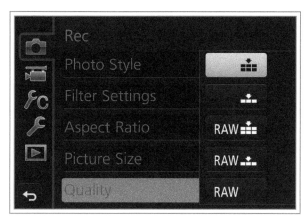

Figure 4-23. **Quality Menu Options Screen**

Raw is in a category by itself. There are both pros and cons to using Raw in this camera. First, the cons. A Raw file takes up a lot of space on your memory card,

and, if you copy it to your computer, a lot of space on your hard drive. In addition, there are various functions of the ZS100 that don't work when you're using Raw, including panorama shooting, Digital Zoom, Resize, Cropping, Title Edit, Text Stamp, Favorites, Print Set (printing directly to a photo printer), and White Balance Bracket. You also cannot get the benefit of using the Filter Settings menu option or Creative Control mode to add picture effects to your images, though you can use those effects when shooting with Raw for Quality. (The resulting image will show the effect when displayed in the camera, but not when opened on a computer.)

You cannot shoot in Raw quality with the Handheld Night Shot or HDR options. You cannot use the SH setting of burst shooting when using Raw quality, and any burst shooting will be slowed down when shooting in Raw.

Finally, you may have problems working with Raw files on your computer because of incompatibility with editing software, though those problems can be overcome by getting updates for your program.

On the other hand, using Raw files has several advantages. The main benefit is that Raw files give you an amazing amount of control and flexibility with your images. When you open up a Raw file in a compatible photo-editing program, the software gives you the opportunity to correct problems with exposure, white balance, color tints, sharpness, and other settings. If you had the aperture of the camera too narrow when you took the picture, and it looks badly underexposed, you can make exposure adjustments in the software and recover the image to a proper brightness level. Similarly, you can adjust the white balance after the fact and remove unwanted color casts. In effect, you get a second chance at making the correct settings, rather than being stuck with an unusable image because of unfortunate settings when you pressed the shutter button.

For example, Figure 4-24 is an image I took with Quality set to Raw, but with settings purposely made to result in underexposure and incorrect white balance.

Figure 4-24. Raw Image Taken with "Wrong" Settings

Figure 4-25 is the same image after I opened it using Adobe Camera Raw software and made corrections after the fact. The corrected image looks essentially as if it had been shot with proper settings to begin with.

Figure 4-25. Raw Image After Corrections with Software

The drawbacks to using Raw files are either not too severe or they are counterbalanced by the flexibility Raw gives you. The large size of the files may be an inconvenience, but the increasing size of hard drives and SD cards, with steadily dropping prices, makes file size much less of a concern than previously. I have had problems with Raw files not loading when I didn't have the latest Camera Raw plug-in for Adobe Photoshop or Photoshop Elements, but with a little effort, you can download an updated plug-in and the software will then process and display your Raw images. Panasonic provides a free download of Silkypix, a program for processing Raw files, so you don't have to buy any additional software to process Raw files.

You certainly don't have to use Raw, but you may be missing some opportunities if you avoid it.

The other two settings for Quality—Fine and Standard—are levels of compression for computer image files that use the JPEG standard. Images saved with Fine quality are subjected to less compression than those saved with Standard quality. In other words, Standard-quality images have their digital data "compressed" or "squeezed" down to a smaller size to allow more of the files to be stored on an SD card or computer drive, with a corresponding loss of image quality. The more compression an image is subjected to, the less clear detail it will contain. So unless you are running out of space on your storage medium, you probably should leave the Quality setting at Fine to ensure the best quality. (Of course, you may prefer to shoot in the Raw format for maximum quality.)

With the ZS100, besides choosing one of the individual Quality settings (Raw, Fine, or Standard), you also have the option of setting the camera to record images in Raw plus either Fine or Standard. If you choose that option, the camera will record each image in two files— one Raw, and the other a JPEG file in either Fine or Standard quality, depending on your selection. If you then play the image back in the camera, you will see only one image, but if you copy the files to your computer, you will find two image files—one with a .jpg extension and one with an .rw2 extension. The Raw file will be much larger than the JPEG one. In a few examples I just looked at on my computer, the Raw files from the ZS100 were all about 22 MB and JPEG files with Picture Size set to Large were between about 6 and 8 MB. (Note that MB stands for megabytes, a measure of file size, as distinguished from MP or M, meaning megapixels, a measure of the number of pixels in an image.)

Why would you choose the option of recording images in Raw and JPEG at the same time? If you're taking pictures of a one-time event such as a wedding or graduation, you may want to preserve them in Raw for highest quality and later processing with software, but also have them available for quick review on a computer that might not have software that reads Raw files. Or, you might want to be able to send the images to friends or post them to social media sites without translating them from Raw into a JPEG format that most people can easily view on their computers. Also, as I discussed earlier, if you are using Creative Control mode or the Filter Settings menu option to add special effects to images, those effects will not show up in Raw files when the files are opened on a computer. In order to have the benefit of the special setting as well as the benefits of a Raw file, you can use the Raw & Fine or Raw & Standard option to record images both ways.

The next menu options to discuss are on screen 2 of the Recording menu, shown in Figure 4-26.

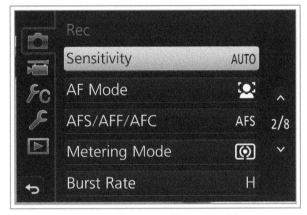

Figure 4-26. Screen 2 of Recording Menu

## SENSITIVITY (ISO)

The first setting on screen 2 of the Recording menu lets you set the camera's ISO, or sensitivity to light. On the ZS100, the available ISO settings range from 125 to 12800, though the range varies in some situations. With the lower settings, the camera produces the best image quality, but exposures require more light. With higher settings, the camera can produce good exposures in dim light, but there is likely to be an increasing amount of visual "noise" in the image as the ISO value increases.

Generally speaking, you should shoot images with the lowest ISO that will allow them to be exposed properly. (An exception is if you want the grainy look that comes with a high ISO value.) For example, if you are shooting indoors in low light, you may need to set the ISO to a high value (say, 800) so you can expose the image with a reasonably fast shutter speed. If the camera were set to a lower ISO, it would need to use a slower shutter speed to take in enough light for a proper exposure, and the resulting image would likely be blurry and possibly unusable.

The ISO setting is available only when the camera is set to one of the advanced shooting modes, including the PASM modes, Panorama, and Creative Video. To make the setting, select this menu option and a horizontal menu will appear at the bottom of the display, as shown in Figure 4-27.

Figure 4-27. Sensitivity (ISO) Menu

You can scroll through the values on this menu by pressing the Left and Right buttons, by turning the rear dial, or scrolling the menu with the touch screen. The possible numerical values are 125, 200, 400, 800, 1600, 3200, 6400, and 12800, unless you change some menu settings, discussed below, to add values below 125 and above 12800, as well as intermediate values.

When you set a numerical value for the ISO, you cannot use the ISO Limit Set option (discussed later in this chapter). When you set ISO to Auto ISO, the camera automatically adjusts ISO to a value up to the maximum value set with ISO Limit Set, if any has been set, based on the brightness of the scene. As discussed in Chapter 3, you can use Auto ISO with Manual exposure mode for still images, which lets you keep shutter speed and aperture fixed while the ISO varies.

When you use the Intelligent ISO setting, the camera adjusts the ISO based on the movement of the subject as well as the brightness, so the camera can set a higher shutter speed to stop the motion. Intelligent ISO is available with the Intelligent Auto, Program, and Aperture Priority modes, but not with the Shutter Priority or Manual exposure modes, or when using the Post Focus option.

When would you want to use a numerical value for the ISO setting, rather than setting it to Auto ISO or Intelligent ISO? One example is if you want the highest quality for your image, and you aren't worried about camera movement, either because you are using a tripod so a slow shutter speed won't result in blur, or the lighting is bright enough to use a fast shutter speed. Then you could set the ISO to its lowest possible setting of 125 (or 80 if Extended ISO is turned on) to achieve high quality. On the other hand, if you definitely want a grainy, noisy look, you can set the ISO to 3200 or even higher to introduce noise into the image. You also might want a high ISO setting so you can use a fast shutter speed to stop action or in low light. In many cases, though, you can just leave the setting at Auto or Intelligent and let the camera adjust the ISO as needed.

It is important to be aware of how much a high ISO value can affect the quality of your images. Figure 4-28 is a composite in which the left image of the doll was taken at ISO 125 and the right one was taken at ISO 25600.

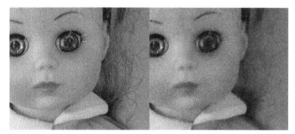

Figure 4-28. Left: ISO 125; Right: ISO 25600

As you can see, the right image shows considerable deterioration, both in the doll itself and in the plain background. You can use this high setting when absolutely necessary to get a shot, but it's advisable to avoid the highest ISO values when possible.

## AF MODE

This next menu option controls what area of the scene the camera focuses on when using its autofocus capability. (As a reminder, you select autofocus, manual focus, or macro focus by pressing the Left button to bring up the focus mode menu.)

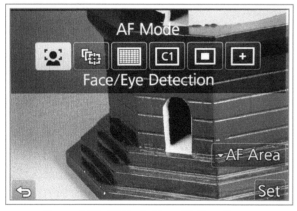

Figure 4-29. AF Mode Menu Options Screen

When you select the AF Mode menu option with the focus mode set to AF or AF Macro, the camera displays

a line of icons representing the six choices available for the AF Mode setting: Face/Eye Detection; AF Tracking; 49-Area; Custom Multi; 1-Area; and Pinpoint, as shown in Figure 4-29.

Use the rear dial or the Left and Right buttons (or the touch screen) to highlight the choice you want, then press the Menu/Set button (or touch the Set icon) or press the shutter button halfway to select that setting and return to the recording screen.

In Intelligent Auto mode, only two of these options are available: Face/Eye Detection and AF Tracking. Following are details about all six options that are available in other recording modes.

### Face/Eye Detection

When you select this setting, the camera does not display any focusing brackets or rectangles until it detects a human face. If it does, it outlines the general area of the face with a yellow rectangle. Then, after you press the shutter button halfway down, the rectangle turns green when the camera has focused on the face. If the camera detects more than one face, it displays white rectangles for secondary faces, as shown in Figure 4-30.

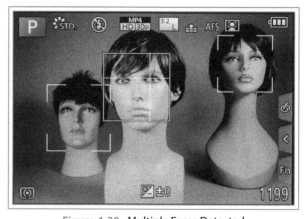

Figure 4-30. Multiple Faces Detected

Any faces that are the same distance away from the camera as the face within the yellow rectangle will also be in focus, but the focus will be controlled by the face in the yellow rectangle. If Metering Mode is set to Multi, the camera will also adjust its exposure for the main detected face.

With this setting, the camera also will look for human eyes. It will place a set of crosshairs across the closest eye it finds and fix focus there. If you want, you can change the eye that the camera focuses on. To do that, when the camera is displaying frames over detected faces, press the touch screen over the eye you want the camera to focus on, then press the shutter button halfway to focus. (Touching a different eye does not work in Intelligent Auto mode; in that mode, if you touch the screen, the AF Mode setting will change to AF Tracking.)

You also can change the face that the camera focuses on. One way to do this is to touch the screen and move the focus frame with your finger. To use that system, go to the Touch Settings item on screen 8 of the Custom menu and, under Touch Settings, set Touch AF to AF. Another way to do this is to use the Direct Focus Area option. To do that, turn on the Direct Focus Area option on screen 3 of the Custom menu. Then, when the Face/ Eye Detection frame is displayed on the screen, press any of the four cursor buttons to start moving the focus frame to the location where you want it. When the frame is being moved, you can also turn the rear dial to change the frame's size.

When the focus frame is sized and located as you want, press the Menu/Set button to lock it in place. The camera will then shift its focus to the area inside that frame. You might want to use this option if you are aiming at two faces, but you want to focus on the one that is farther away from the camera. Ordinarily, the camera will focus on the closest face, but if you move the frame over the other face, the camera will direct its focus there. To reset the frame to its original position, press the Display button while the frame is movable.

## AF Tracking

This next setting for AF Mode allows the camera to maintain focus on a moving subject. On the menu screen, highlight the second icon, which is a group of offset focus frames designed to look like a moving focus frame. Press the Menu/Set button or half-press the shutter button to select this option.

The camera will then display a special focus frame with spokes sticking out of it, in the center of the display, as shown in Figure 4-31. Move the camera to place this focus frame over your subject and press the shutter button halfway, then release the button. If the camera can identify a subject at this location, the frame will turn yellow. The camera will then do its best to keep that target in focus, even as it (or the camera) moves. The yellow bracket should stay close to the subject on the display.

Figure 4-31. **AF Tracking Frame**

When you are ready, press the shutter button to take the picture. If you want to cancel AF Tracking, press the Menu/Set button.

If the camera is not able to maintain focus on the moving subject, the focus frame will turn red and then disappear. AF Tracking will not work with certain settings, such as Time Lapse Shot and several Creative Control mode settings, including all of the Monochrome options; the camera will use 1-Area mode instead.

To use this option with the touch screen, just touch the subject on the screen to select it, and press the AF Off icon on the screen to cancel the tracking focus.

Using AF Tracking can reduce the time it takes for you to be able to take a picture of a moving subject. If you are trying to snap a picture of your restless four-year-old or a fidgety Jack Russell Terrier, AF Tracking can give you a head start, so the camera's focus is close to being correct and the focusing mechanism has less to do to achieve correct focus when you suddenly see the perfect moment to press the shutter button.

## 49-Area

This next option for AF Mode causes the camera to focus on up to 49 small focus zones within the overall autofocus area, which is the same area as that of the current aspect ratio setting. The camera then looks within the focus zones and selects however many subjects it detects that are at the same distance from the camera and can be focused on.

To make this setting, select the third icon on the AF Mode menu, which looks like a screen with multiple focus points. Then, when you push the shutter button down halfway, the camera will display green rectangles to show you which of the multiple focus areas it has selected to focus on, as shown in Figure 4-32.

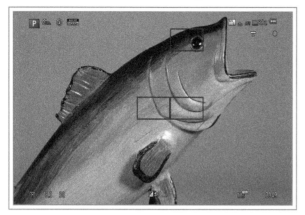

Figure 4-32. 49-Area Focus Frame in Use

The name of this setting is somewhat misleading, however, because, even though the camera has 49 focus zones, it will only use a few of those zones at any one time in this mode. By default, the camera uses the nine zones in the center of the screen. So, with the default setting, if you focus on a scene with a prominent object at the far right, the camera will choose whatever object it can find in the center of the display to focus on, and will ignore the object at the right.

If you want the camera to direct its focus somewhere other than the center of the scene, press the Down button while the 49-Area icon is highlighted on the menu screen, and then move the block of focus zones where you want them using the cursor buttons, as shown in Figure 4-33.

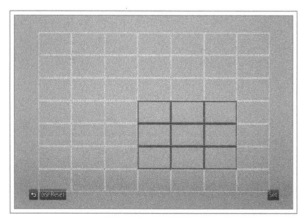

Figure 4-33. 49-Area Focus Blocks Ready to Move

If the Direct Focus Area option is enabled, you can use the cursor buttons to move the focus area around the screen when the camera is in shooting mode with the 49-Area option selected. If the Touch AF option is turned on through the Touch Settings item on screen

8 of the Custom menu, you can touch the screen in shooting mode to select the area for the focus zone.

Whenever this AF Mode setting is in use, the camera displays a small white cross on the screen to indicate the center of the block of focus zones it is currently using. The blocks near the center of the overall focus area have nine zones each, but the blocks near the edges of the display area have only six or four blocks.

The 49-Area method can be useful if your subject is likely to be located within a predictable area, and you want to have the option to adjust that area somewhat. It is a good mode to use when you are shooting landscapes or general scenes that do not require you to focus on faces or on any one particular object.

### Custom Multi

This setting lets you create a custom-tailored focus zone out of the 49 available blocks. For example, you can create a horizontal focus area that is seven blocks across, or a vertical one of the same size. You can create a zone that has 21 blocks arranged in three lines of seven, either horizontally or vertically. Or, you can create a completely free-form zone with any arrangement of blocks. Somewhat oddly, with the free-form option you can create a focus area that uses all 49 of the focus blocks, resulting in a true 49-Area focus mode, unlike the mode with that name, which can use only up to nine blocks. The process for using this option is a bit complicated, so I will lay out the steps below.

1.  Go to the AF Mode item on the Recording menu and scroll to the fourth icon from the left, with the label Custom Multi below it, as shown in Figure 4-34.

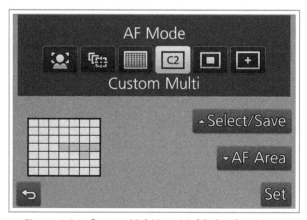

Figure 4-34. Custom Multi Icon Highlighted on Menu

2. Press the Up button to move to the line of possible patterns for the focus zone, as shown in Figure 4-35.

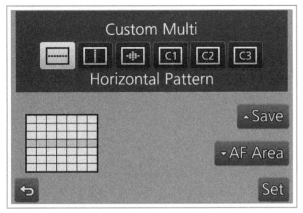

Figure 4-35. Patterns for Custom Multi Option

3. Scroll through these icons to select the one you want. The last three—C1, C2, and C3—are for free-form custom patterns you can create and save to these slots.

4. When you have selected either horizontal, vertical, central, or free-form for the shape, press the Down button to move to the AF Area option. There you will see a screen with all 49 blocks, some of which will be highlighted in yellow for the horizontal, vertical, or central choices, but all of which will be blank for the free-form options.

5. For the horizontal, vertical, or central option, turn the rear dial to the right to increase the size of the focus area, or turn it to the left to reduce it. You can move the line or lines across the display by pressing the appropriate direction buttons or by touching the screen. When you have the focus area positioned where you want it, press the Fn2 button, to the right of the LCD screen, to set the focus area in place. The blocks will display for a moment and then disappear, and this focus area will be in effect.

6. For any of the three free-form options, after pressing the Up button, scroll to the icon that says C1, C2, or C3, then press the Down button to move to the AF Area screen. You will then see a display with all 49 blocks, none of which are highlighted, with a cross in the center block. Use the direction buttons to move the cross to a block you want to add to the focus pattern, and press the Menu/Set button to highlight it. You also can touch a block with your finger to highlight it. Figure 4-36 shows

this screen after several blocks have been selected in this way.

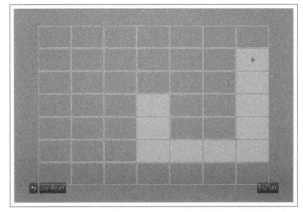

Figure 4-36. Free-form Screen with Blocks Highlighted

7. The blocks do not have to be contiguous; they can be in any pattern, up to and including selecting all 49 blocks. When you have finished selecting blocks, press the Fn2 button to lock in the pattern you have created.

8. To create and save a custom focus pattern, use the same procedure as in Steps 5 through 7. When you have finished, press the Menu/Set button and select the AF Mode menu option to bring the AF mode menu back on the screen. Then scroll to the Custom Multi option. Press the Up button to move to the line of options, and scroll to the focus pattern you just created, whether horizontal, vertical, or free-form, then press the Up button. The camera will display a screen like that in Figure 4-37, asking which Custom slot you want to save it to.

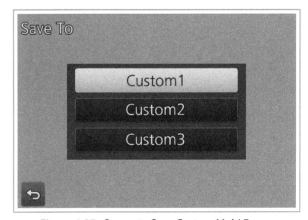

Figure 4-37. Screen to Save Custom Multi Frame

9. Highlight the one you want and press Menu/Set, then select Yes when asked if it should overwrite the existing settings. To select the saved pattern in

the future, just select C1, C2, or C3, depending on what slot the pattern was saved to.

The Custom Multi option is useful if you have a need for specially shaped focus zones. You might want to use a horizontal zone if you are focusing on a group of artifacts that are displayed in a straight line, to make sure the camera does not accidentally focus on an object outside of that line. You also might want to create a pattern that uses all 49 focus zones, so the camera will focus on the closest object, regardless of whether it is in the center of the image, or in a particular sector of the image.

## 1-Area

This AF Mode setting is selected with the next-to-last icon on the AF Mode menu, as shown in Figure 4-38. With this option, the camera uses a single focus frame, which by default is in the center of the screen. You can customize the setting by moving the single frame to any position on the display and changing its size.

Figure 4-38. 1-Area Icon Highlighted on Menu

When you have highlighted the 1-Area icon on the AF Mode menu, press the Down button to move directly to setting the location of the autofocus frame using the direction buttons or the touch screen, as shown in Figure 4-39. You can change the size of the frame by turning the rear dial or by pulling or pinching on the touch screen.

When you have finished moving and resizing the focus frame, press the Menu/Set button or press the Set icon with your finger to fix the frame in place. To move the frame back to the default location in the middle of the screen or reset its size to normal, press the Display button at the bottom right of the camera's back. If the frame has been both moved and resized, you have to

press Display once to reset the location and once more to reset the size.

Figure 4-39. 1-Area Focus Frame Ready to Move

The 1-Area method is a good setting for general shooting, because it lets you quickly position the focus area just where you want it. It is particularly helpful when you need to make sure the camera focuses on a fairly small item that is not in the center of the scene.

## Pinpoint

The last icon at the right of the line of AF Mode icons is used to select the Pinpoint option. With this setting, you can move a single focus frame around the display and resize it, and the camera will enlarge the focus area to help you get the focus frame positioned precisely where you want it.

After selecting the AF Mode option on the Recording menu, highlight the Pinpoint icon and press the Down button to move to the AF Area screen. Move the focus area around the display using the four direction buttons and resize it using the rear dial, then press the Menu/Set button to set the focus area's location and size. Then, while the focus frame is still movable, with arrows displayed, you can enlarge the display by turning the rear dial, to assist you in getting the focus area set exactly where it is needed. You also can move and resize the focus area using the touch screen.

You can control the amount of enlargement for this display using the Pinpoint AF Display item on screen 2 of the Custom menu. If you select Full for that item, the image will be enlarged from three times to ten times and the enlargement will fill the display. If you select PIP, for picture-in-picture, the enlarged area will not take up the entire display, and the enlargement will only range from three times to 6 times. When the display is enlarged, you can vary the amount of enlargement within the specified range by turning the rear dial. When the focus frame is located where you want it, press the Menu/Set button to exit to the recording screen.

When you focus on an item using this setting, place the small white cross over the subject and press the shutter button halfway. The camera will enlarge the display at that area for a short time while you keep the shutter button half-pressed, to help you determine whether focus is sharp. The length of time that the display remains enlarged with this option is determined by the Pinpoint AF Time option on screen 2 of the Custom menu; the time can range from 0.5 second to 1.5 second. The display then returns to normal size so you can evaluate the entire scene before pressing the shutter button to take the picture.

### Moving the Focus Frame or Focus Area

With all of the AF Mode options except AF Tracking, you have the ability to move the focus frame or zones. There are several ways to do this, even after you have returned the camera to the recording screen. One way to do this is to go to the AF Mode option on the Recording menu and select the current AF Mode option. Then press the Down button (or touch the AF Area icon on the screen) to go to the screen for moving the frame. Move the frame with the cursor buttons or touch screen and resize it with the rear dial or touch screen if necessary, then press Menu/ Set and you're ready to focus again with the frame in a new location.

For a faster way to move the focus frame (or broader focus area, for the 49-Area or Custom Multi setting), there are three other options. First, you can set one of the function buttons to the Focus Area Set option through the function Button Set option on screen 7 of the Custom menu, as discussed in Chapter 7. Then, if you press that Function button, the screen for moving the focus area will appear immediately. Second, you can turn on the Direct Focus Area option on screen 3 of the Custom menu. Then, from the recording screen, as soon as you press any of the four direction buttons, the focus area moving screen will appear. (A drawback of that option is that you cannot then use the direction buttons to call up options such as white balance, focus mode, and Drive Mode. You can use the Quick Menu to activate those items, though, or you can assign function buttons to those settings.) Third, you can use your finger to move the focus frame, if the Touch AF option

is turned on through the Touch Settings item on screen 8 of the Custom menu.

## AFS/AFF/AFC

This next menu option lets you choose how the autofocus system operates when the camera is using autofocus. With AFS, for autofocus single, when you press the shutter button halfway, the camera locks focus on the subject and keeps it locked while the button is held there, even if the subject moves. With AFF, for autofocus flexible, the camera locks focus but will adjust focus if the subject (or the camera) moves. With AFC, for autofocus continuous, the camera does not lock focus, but adjusts it continuously as the subject or camera moves.

If you are shooting images of a landscape or other stationary subject, AFS will work well. The camera will lock focus and keep it there, and the battery will not be drained by adjusting focus. If you are shooting handheld shots at a fairly close distance, though, you might want to use the AFF setting because the camera will adjust the focus if the camera moves slightly, and the focus could be thrown off by that movement, especially when the focus distance is small or the lens is zoomed in.

If you are shooting pictures of children or pets moving around unpredictably, you may want to use the AFC or AFF setting and let the camera continue to adjust focus as needed. With these settings, the camera's battery will be drained faster than with AFS, but it may be worth it to capture an action shot in sharp focus.

This setting is fixed at AFS in Panorama mode. With 4K Photo shooting, AFF is not available. Only AFS is available with the 4K Photo S/S setting.

## METERING MODE

The next option on the Recording menu lets you choose the method the camera uses to meter the light and determine the proper exposure. The ZS100 gives you a choice of three methods: Multiple, Center-weighted, or Spot. If you choose Multiple, the camera evaluates the brightness at multiple spots in the image shown on the display, and calculates an exposure that takes into account all of the various values. With Center-weighted, the camera gives greater emphasis to the brightness of the subject(s) in the center of the screen, while still taking into account the brightness of other areas in the image. With Spot, the camera evaluates only the brightness of the subject(s) in the small spot-metering area.

The Panasonic user's manual recommends Multiple mode for "normal usage," presumably on the theory that it produces a reasonable choice for exposure based on evaluating the overall brightness of everything in the scene. However, if you want to make sure that one particular item in the scene is properly exposed, you may want to use the Spot method, and aim the spot metering area at that object or person, then lock in the exposure. The Spot option is useful when you are photographing a performer who is lit by a spotlight on stage. For a shot with a central subject of prime importance, such as a portrait, the Center-weighted option may work best.

To make this selection, scroll to the line for Metering Mode, then press the Right button to activate the sub-menu with the three choices, as shown in Figure 4-40.

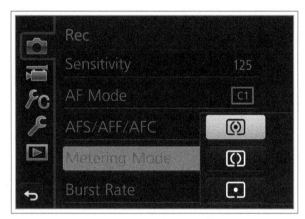

Figure 4-40. Metering Mode Menu Options Screen

The first icon, a rectangle with a circle and a dot inside, represents Multiple mode; the second, a rectangle with a circle inside, represents Center-weighted; and the third, a rectangle with just a dot inside, represents Spot.

With Multiple or Center-weighted, the metering process is simple: Point the camera at the subject(s) you want and let the camera compute the exposure. If you choose Spot as your metering technique, the process can be more involved. Presumably, you will have a fairly small area in mind as the most important area for having the correct exposure; perhaps it is a small object you are photographing for an online auction.

The LCD screen or viewfinder will display a small blue cross in the center of the focusing brackets, as shown in Figure 4-41, and you need to be sure that the cross is over the most important object.

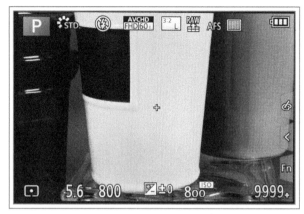

Figure 4-41. Spot Metering Cross on Shooting Screen

If your subject is not in the center of the screen, you may need to lock the exposure while the Spot-metering cross is on the subject, and then move the camera so the subject is in the proper part of the scene. To do this, press the shutter button halfway while the cross is on the subject, and hold it in that position while you move the camera back to the final position for your composition. (You also can use the AF/AE Lock button for this function, as discussed in Chapter 5.)

As another option, there is a sparsely-documented feature of the camera that lets you move the little cross around the camera's screen so you can place it right over the area of the picture that you want properly exposed. This will work only if, in addition to using the Spot metering mode, you are using one of the autofocus settings that lets you move the autofocus area, such as 1-Area or Face/Eye Detection, as discussed in Chapter 5. In that case, whenever you move the focusing target, the Spot-metering target moves along with it, so the target serves two purposes at once. For example, Figure 4-42 shows the display when both Spot metering and 1-Area autofocus are in effect.

The Metering Mode setting is not available in Intelligent Auto mode or Scene mode. When Multiple metering is selected and AF Mode is set to Face/Eye Detection, the camera will attempt to expose a person's face correctly, assuming a face has been detected. The current setting for Metering Mode is indicated by an icon in the lower left of the display, as shown in Figure 4-42.

Figure 4-42. Spot Metering Cross Moved with Focus Frame

## Burst Rate

This last item on screen 2 of the Recording menu controls the rate for burst shooting. The control for selecting burst shooting from the shooting screen is the Down button, which activates the Drive Mode settings, including burst shooting, the self-timer, and bracketing, as discussed in Chapter 5. When you press the Down button and activate burst shooting from the Drive Mode menu, you have the option to set the burst rate from that menu. However, if you want, you can set the burst rate ahead of time from this Recording menu item. In that way, you will save a step when you press the Down button to select burst shooting from the Drive Mode options.

The choices for burst rate are SH, H, M, and L, for super-high, high, medium, and low. I will discuss those options in Chapter 5, in connection with the Drive Mode options.

The third screen of the Recording menu is shown in Figure 4-43.

Figure 4-43. Screen 3 of Recording Menu

## 4K Photo

The 4K Photo menu option, like the Burst Rate option, works together with the burst-shooting features of the ZS100. 4K Photo is a special sub-option of Drive Mode. You can activate 4K Photo from the Drive Mode menu by pressing the Down button from the shooting screen, or by pressing the Fn1 button, unless you have assigned that button to another function. (That button, at the upper right of the camera's back, is labeled 4K and is assigned by default to trigger 4K Photo mode.)

As with normal burst shooting, you can choose an option for 4K burst shooting after you select 4K Photo using one of the above methods. However, you also can use the 4K Photo menu option to set the 4K shooting option ahead of time, to save time when you press a button to activate 4K shooting. I will discuss the details of the various 4K Photo settings in Chapter 5, where I discuss the physical controls.

## Auto Bracket

The Auto Bracket feature lets you set the ZS100 to take a series of images with one press of the shutter button, at different exposure settings. In this way, you will have several images to choose from, increasing your chance of having one that is exposed the way you want it. You also can use this option to shoot a group of shots with different exposure values to be combined in software to create an HDR (high dynamic range) image, as discussed later in this chapter.

The standard way to get access to this feature from the shooting screen is to press the Down button and use the Drive Mode menu to make the various settings, including the EV (exposure value) interval between exposures and the number of exposures. You can also make those settings using this menu option. In addition, you can make some settings with this menu option that are not available from the Drive Mode menu.

Those settings, shown in Figure 4-44, control whether the camera takes the multiple exposures in a single burst or requires you to press the shutter button for each one. The settings also let you select the EV interval and choose the order in which the exposures are made.

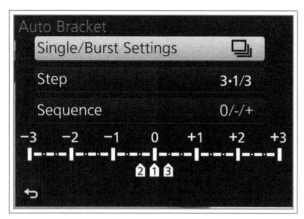

Figure 4-44. Auto Bracket Menu Options Screen

To set the single or burst option, select the Single/Burst Settings item at the top of the menu. If you select Burst, the camera will take the specified number of exposures (three, five, or seven) with one press of the shutter button. If you select Single, the camera will take only one shot in the sequence with each press of the shutter button, so you can make any needed adjustments to the scene between exposures.

To control the order in which the shots are made, choose the Sequence option. If you select 0/–/+, the default option, the first exposure will be made at the normal exposure, the second will be at a reduced EV setting, and the next will be at an increased EV setting. If you choose –/0/+, the other option, the exposures will be made in increasing order of EV value.

I will discuss the other Auto Bracket menu options, for choosing the EV interval between the exposures and the number of exposures, in Chapter 5 in connection with the Drive Mode options.

## SELF-TIMER

The next menu option is another one that lets you adjust settings that are normally made through the Drive Mode menu after pressing the Down button from the shooting screen. With this option, you can set the self-timer to a delay of two seconds or ten seconds for a single shot, or to a delay of ten seconds with a series of three shots. In Chapter 5, I will discuss how to make these settings from the Drive Mode menu.

## HIGHLIGHT SHADOW

This menu option gives you a tool for adjusting the highlights and shadows in your images. When you select this menu option, the camera displays a screen

like that shown in Figure 4-45, with seven small icons at the bottom available for selection.

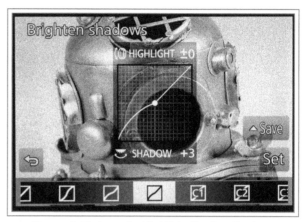

Figure 4-45. Icons for Highlight Shadow Settings

(For this illustration I have scrolled to the fourth icon, so all seven icons are visible.) Each small icon represents a different curve shape for the larger graph in the center of the screen, which includes a line that represents the adjustments to highlights and shadows for your images. When the line is a straight diagonal, no adjustments are present. When the upper part of the line bulges to the left, highlights are increased. When it bulges to the right, the brightness of highlights is lowered. Similarly, the lower part of the line bulges to the left or right to increase or decrease the brightness of shadow areas.

The first four icons are presets for standard (no adjustments), higher contrast (highlights brighter and shadows darker), lower contrast (highlights darker and shadows brighter), and brighten shadows. The last 3 icons represent custom settings 1, 2, and 3.

If you want to use one of the four presets, just select it. If you want to make other adjustments, you can select any one of the seven icons and make adjustments to the settings. To make the highlights brighter, turn the control ring to the right; to make them darker, turn it to the left. To make the shadows brighter, turn the rear dial to the right; to make them darker, turn it to the left. You also can adjust the curves by moving the graph lines on the touch screen. When you have adjusted the curves as you want, press the Up button to save the settings. You will then see the screen shown in Figure 4-46, prompting you to select custom 1, 2, or 3 as the slot in which to save your settings.

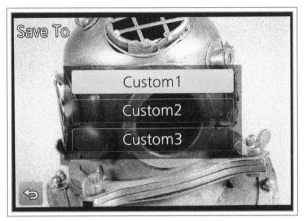

Figure 4-46. Screen to Save Custom Highlight Shadow Setting

Highlight any one of those and press the Menu/Set button to save the settings. Then, whenever you want to recall those settings, go to the Highlight Shadow menu option and select the custom 1, 2, or 3 icon, depending on which slot you used to save your custom settings.

This option can be useful if you are often faced with situations with your subject partly in shadow and partly in bright light. It can be particularly helpful because you can see the effects of the adjustments you make on the live view, as you turn the dials to adjust highlights and shadows. Of course, the ZS100 also has other options to deal with that situation, such as the HDR setting, discussed later in this chapter, and the Intelligent Dynamic setting, discussed next.

## INTELLIGENT DYNAMIC

The last option on screen 3 of the Recording menu is shown as i.Dynamic, which I will refer to here as Intelligent Dynamic. This option gives you another way to accomplish what the Highlight Shadow option does—that is, to deal with a situation in which there is considerable contrast between the dark and bright areas of the scene. This option, unlike the previous one, does not let you make precise adjustments to the shadow and highlight curves. Instead, it adjusts contrast and exposure generally; it lets you set the intensity of the camera's adjustments to a level of Low, Standard, or High. You also can leave the option turned off, or you can set it to Auto and let the camera make the adjustments based on its analysis of the scene.

Figure 4-47 is a composite image with 2 views of the same outdoor scene, partly in sunlight and partly in deep shade.

Figure 4-47. i.Dynamic Composite Image

As you can see, in the top image, with Intelligent Dynamic turned off, the contrast is quite stark. In the bottom image, with Intelligent Dynamic set to High, the contrast is evened out and the shadowed areas are brightened noticeably. This is a good setting to use when you are taking photos in an area with both sunlight and shade.

The next items to be discussed are on screen 4 of the Recording menu, shown in Figure 4-48.

Figure 4-48. Screen 4 of Recording Menu

## INTELLIGENT RESOLUTION

The first setting on the next screen of the menu is shown as i.Resolution, which I will call Intelligent Resolution. This option can be set to Off, Extended, Low, Standard, or High, as shown in Figure 4-49.

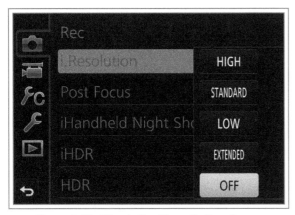

Figure 4-49. i.Resolution Menu Options Screen

This setting increases the apparent resolution in images by providing additional sharpening through in-camera digital manipulation. It does seem to improve image quality somewhat in certain situations. I recommend that you try shooting with it turned on and off to see if it provides actual benefits for your shots. I do not often use it myself, because I prefer to shoot with Raw quality and add sharpening with my editing software.

## POST FOCUS

This next menu option represents a powerful feature of the ZS100. As its name indicates, this feature lets you choose the focus point of an image after it was captured. In order to accomplish this feat, the camera activates 4K video recording and records a short video sequence adjusting the focus for different parts of the scene throughout the recording. When the recording is finished, you can select a frame from the video sequence that has the sharpest focus on the area you are most interested in, and the camera will save a JPEG image from that frame.

The only setting for Post Focus is to turn the feature on or off. You can do that with this menu option, or with the Fn2 button, if that button remains assigned to its default setting of Post Focus. (Of course, you also could assign a different button to activate this feature, though it makes sense to leave the Fn2 button with this assignment, if you expect to use the feature.) You can use this option in any shooting mode except Creative Video and Panorama.

Once Post Focus is turned on, either through the menu option or by pressing a function button, aim the camera at the subject and press the shutter button halfway. Because the camera is using 4K video mode, which crops

the frame somewhat, you will see that the camera has zoomed in slightly. You may have to adjust the framing of the image to account for the increased focal length.

If the camera finds a focus point, it will display a steady green circle in the upper right corner. If it cannot find a focus point, the green circle will blink. When you are ready, hold the camera as still as possible and press the shutter button all the way down and release it. The camera will record a video sequence for several seconds, during which it will change the focus to every focus point it can find throughout the scene.

When the recording has finished, press the Play button to enter playback mode. You will see a screen like that in Figure 4-50, with a Post Focus icon in the upper left corner.

Figure 4-50. Post Focus Sequence Ready to Play

Press the Up button or touch that icon, and you will see a screen like that in Figure 4-51, with various icons including a plus sign, a return arrow, Fn2, and an icon in the lower right corner for saving an image from the sequence. On this screen, move your finger to any point where you would like focus to be fixed. If the camera is able to show an image with that focus point, it will display a green frame at that point and change the focus to that location. For example, in Figure 4-52, after I touched the Egyptian figurine in the foreground of the scene, the camera displayed an image with sharp focus at that point.

Figure 4-51. Post Focus Sequence After Pressing Up Button

Figure 4-52. Focus Point on Foreground Subject

In Figure 4-53, after I touched the mannequin head in the background of the scene, the camera displayed a frame with focus fixed on the head.

Figure 4-53. Focus Point on Background Subject

To adjust the focus at any point in more detail, press the magnifying glass icon with the plus sign, or move the zoom lever to the right, to enlarge the image. The camera will then display a sliding scale at the bottom of the screen, as seen in Figure 4-54. Slide your finger along that scale, or use the Left and Right buttons or the rear dial, to adjust the focus point in small

increments until you have adjusted the focus location as precisely as possible. Then touch the return arrow in the lower left corner of the screen, or move the zoom lever to the left, to return the image to normal size.

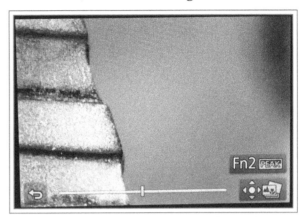

Figure 4-54. Enlarged View with Sliding Scale

You also can press the Fn2 button or its on-screen icon, which causes the camera to turn on its peaking display, placing colored pixels at the areas of sharpest focus to help you determine where focus is sharp. Successive presses of that button or icon cycle through various levels of peaking.

When you have focus adjusted as you want it, touch the icon in the lower right corner of the screen, or press the Menu/Set button, and the camera will display the message shown in Figure 4-55, asking if you want to save this image. If so, highlight and select Yes, and the camera will save a JPEG image with the focus point set as you have selected.

Figure 4-55. Message to Save Post Focus Image

Post Focus cannot be used with several settings of Scene mode and Creative Control mode, or when Multiple Exposure, Time Lapse Shot, or Stop Motion Animation is being used. The camera cannot use the Raw setting for Quality, and the image will be limited to a size of 8 megapixels. The camera will use the electronic shutter with a limited range of shutter speeds. However, you still can adjust many settings, and this feature is very useful in situations where focus is critical or uncertain, such as macro photography. In a sense, it acts for focus as the Raw format does for white balance and exposure, which can be adjusted after the fact.

### iHandheld Night Shot

This setting is available for selection only when the camera is set to Intelligent Auto mode. This option is designed to minimize the motion blur that can result from taking a handheld shot at the slow shutter speed that is likely to be needed to get a sufficient exposure at night. If the camera detects darkness and senses that it is handheld, the camera will raise its ISO setting in order to permit the use of a faster than normal shutter speed. Also, because using a higher ISO can increase the visual "noise" or grainy look in an image, the camera will take a burst of several shots and combine them internally into a final image. By blending the contents of several images together, the camera can reduce the noise in the final, composite result. This setting is a useful one to activate when shooting in low-light conditions without flash or a tripod.

You cannot decide when to capture an image with this feature yourself—all you can do is turn it on and see if the camera determines that conditions call for it to be used.

### iHDR

The next menu option, iHDR, is another one that is available only when Intelligent Auto mode is in use and only when the camera determines that its use is called for. In this case, the option is triggered when the camera detects a scene with strong contrast between the dark and light areas. When the camera makes that determination, the ZS100 will take a burst of shots and combine them internally to create a final result. In this situation, the camera will place on the screen a message saying HDR Shutters 3 to let you know that the shutter will fire three times. You should try to hold the camera steady while it takes the burst of shots.

I will discuss high dynamic range, or HDR photography, further in the next section of this chapter. Essentially, with HDR, the camera combines the most normally exposed parts of multiple images in order to achieve

a final result that appears to be properly exposed throughout most or all of its various areas. This setting can be useful when you are taking photographs in highly contrasty conditions.

### HDR

The option discussed directly above, iHDR, is activated only when the camera determines that it is needed, in Intelligent Auto mode. If you want to use the ZS100's built-in HDR capability on your own terms, you can set the camera to one of the PASM modes and choose this HDR option on screen 4 of the Recording menu.

HDR photography was developed because cameras, whether using film or digital sensors, cannot record images that retain clear details when the scene includes wide variations in brightness. If part of the scene is in dark shadows and another part is brightly lighted, the scene has a "dynamic range" that may exceed the ability of the camera to expose both the dark and the bright areas in a way that looks good to the human eye.

A few years ago, the primary way to deal with this issue was to take multiple shots of the scene using different exposure settings, so the photographer would have a range of shots, some exposed to favor dark areas, and some for bright areas. The photographer would merge those images using Photoshop or special HDR software to blend differently exposed portions from all of the shots. The end result is a composite HDR image that can exhibit clear details in all parts of the image.

More recently, camera makers have incorporated some degree of HDR processing in their cameras to help the cameras even out areas of excessive brightness and darkness to preserve details, without the need to use software to merge multiple shots. With the ZS100, Panasonic provides several settings that, to one degree or another, attempt to process shots of scenes with wide dynamic range to produce a pleasing result. I discussed earlier the Highlight Shadow, Intelligent Dynamic, and iHDR options. The HDR option is the most direct approach to using traditional HDR techniques. It lets you set up the camera to take a burst of shots at different exposure levels, and the camera combines the multiple images internally to create a composite image with overall exposure that attempts to even out the areas of heaviest contrast.

To use this option, first select the Set item from the sub-menu for HDR. You will then see a menu with choices of Dynamic Range and Auto Align. Select Dynamic Range, press the Menu/Set button, and you will see the screen shown in Figure 4-56, letting you choose the exposure interval among the three shots the camera will take.

Figure 4-56. HDR Exposure Interval Selection Screen

You can choose Auto, which causes the camera to choose an interval, or you can choose a specific EV interval of one, two or three stops. Use the higher settings for scenes involving relatively large degrees of contrast, such as a view including a shaded area next to an area in bright sunshine.

When you have set the interval, go back to the Auto Align option on the menu and set it either on or off. If it is turned on, the camera will do its best to align the three shots automatically when it processes them internally. However, in doing so, it will crop them slightly in order to delete the outer edges of areas that are not in alignment. This setting is useful for handheld shots. If you are using a tripod, it is better to leave Auto Align turned off.

When the settings are all made, go back to the main HDR menu and set HDR to On. Then aim at the subject and press the shutter button. You will hear the shutter fire three times and a composite image will be saved to the memory card.

To test this feature, I took several shots of a fruit plate in conditions with bright light and shadows. In Figure 4-57, I took a shot with HDR turned off. In Figure 4-58, I used the HDR setting at an interval of EV1, and in Figure 4-59 I used an interval of EV3. Then, for Figure 4-60, I took a series of images using Manual exposure

mode at various exposure levels, and combined them using Photomatix Pro HDR software.

Figure 4-57. HDR Turned Off

Figure 4-58. HDR Set to EV1

Figure 4-59. HDR SEt to EV3

Figure 4-60. HDR Image from Photomatix Software

As you can see, the camera's HDR menu option did a fairly good job of reducing the heavy contrast, with more even exposure at the higher HDR setting. The composite image from the HDR software did a better job, but that is to be expected. The in-camera HDR option is a useful one when you are confronted with a scene with sharp contrast between light and dark areas.

Next, I will discuss the options on screen 5 of the Recording menu, shown in Figure 4-61.

Figure 4-61. Screen 5 of Recording Menu

## MULTIPLE EXPOSURE

The Multiple Exposure option is more in the category of creative photography than control of normal image-making. It lets you create double, triple, or quadruple exposures in the camera. The steps to take are a bit unusual, because you actually carry out the picture-taking through the Recording menu system.

On the Recording menu, highlight Multiple Exposure, then press the Right button (or touch the menu option on the screen), which takes you to a screen with the word Start highlighted, as shown in Figure 4-62.

Figure 4-62. Multiple Exposure Main Options Screen

Unless you want to overlay new images on an existing Raw image, as discussed below, make sure the Overlay option is set to Off. Then press the Menu/Set button to select Start. The screen will have the word End displayed; you can press the Fn1 button to end the process if you have had second thoughts.

If you are going to proceed, then compose and take the first picture. At this point the screen will display the image you just took along with the choices Next, Retake, and Exit. If you're not satisfied with the first image, scroll to Retake and select that option with the Menu/Set button, then retake the first image. If you're ready to proceed to taking a superimposed image, leave Next highlighted and press the shutter button halfway down, or, if you prefer, press the Menu/Set button to select Next. Either action produces the interesting effect of leaving the first image on the screen and making the screen live at the same time to take a new image, as shown in Figure 4-63.

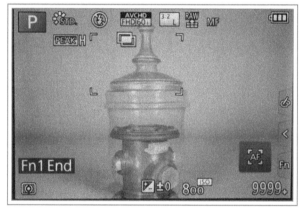

Figure 4-63. Multiple Exposure Screen After First Shot

Compose the second shot as you want it while viewing the first one, and press the shutter button fully to record that image. You can repeat this process to add a third image, retake the second image, or exit the whole process. You can then add a fourth image if you want. When you are done, you will have a single image that combines the two, three, or four superimposed images you recorded.

Before you take the images using the Multiple Exposure procedure, the menu gives you the option of setting Auto Gain on or off. If you leave it on, the camera adjusts the exposure based on the number of pictures taken; if you turn it off, the camera adjusts the exposure for the final superimposed image. In my experience, the On setting produces results with clearer images of the multiple scenes; Off produces images that may have excessive exposure.

You also have the option of starting with a Raw image that was taken earlier by this camera. It has to be a Raw image, not a JPEG one, and it has to have been taken in a mode in which Multiple Exposure is available, which means one of the PASM modes.

To use this option, set the Overlay option of the Multiple Exposure menu item to On. Then, from the Multiple Exposure screen, highlight Start and press the Menu/Set button. The camera will display your images in playback mode. Scroll through them until you find the Raw image you want to use as the first image in the multiple exposure series. When it is displayed, press the Menu/Set button to select it as the first image of the series. Then line up the next image, with the Raw image displayed on the screen, and press the shutter button to take the next image; it will be overlaid over the existing Raw image. You can then proceed with the rest of the sequence, as before.

Figure 4-64. Final Image for Multiple Exposure

Figure 4-64 shows the final result of using the Multiple Exposure feature to include a shot of a model hydrant and a shot of a glass jar in a single composite image.

I have found that the Multiple Exposure feature usually works best if you remove the first item from the scene before taking the next shot. For example, in making the image shown here, I first photographed the glass jar, then removed it from the scene before photographing the fire hydrant. If you leave the first item in place, it is likely to overwhelm the other objects because it will be photographed more than once.

## TIME LAPSE SHOT

The Time Lapse Shot option lets you shoot a time-lapse series of photographs. You probably have seen sequences in the movies or on television in which an event that takes a fair amount of time, such as a sunset, a flower opening, clouds moving across the sky, or a parking lot filling up with cars, is shown in a speeded-up series of images, so it appears to happen in a few seconds.

The ZS100 can use its time-lapse feature with any shooting mode, including Intelligent Auto. If you use the more advanced shooting modes, you have access to all of the major settings for your images, including Raw quality, white balance, ISO, and others.

To use this feature, highlight Time Lapse Shot on the Recording menu and press the Right button to move to the setup screen, shown in Figure 4-65.

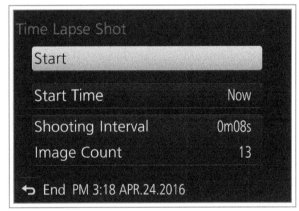

Figure 4-65. Time Lapse Shot Setup Screen

On that screen, use the direction buttons (or the touch screen) to navigate through the various options. Select a start time, the interval between shots, and the total number of shots. The interval can be set to any value from one second to 99 minutes 59 seconds. One point to bear in mind when setting the interval is that, if the lighting is very dim, the camera may need to set a long shutter speed. For example, if the camera is set to use a shutter speed of one minute, which requires a long time for in-camera processing after the exposure is made, this system will not succeed if the interval between shots is set to less than two minutes. The total number of shots can be any number up to 9,999.

When you have made all of the settings as you want them, press the Menu/Set button, then select Start from the main options screen. The camera will display a message prompting you to press the shutter button when you're ready to start the sequence.

When you press the shutter button, the camera will take the images at the specified intervals and will repeat the process until the total number of images has been recorded. Of course, if the battery runs down or the memory card fills up, the process will end prematurely. (You can use the optional AC adapter to avoid a power issue; see Appendix A.) At any time, you can press the Fn1 button and the camera will display a screen asking if you want to continue, pause, or end the process.

When the sequence is complete, either after the full series has been taken or after an interrupted series, the camera will display a message asking if you want it to create a movie using the recorded images. If you say yes, it will take some time to process the movie, which you can then play like any movie.

If you say no to creating the movie, assuming you have a detailed display screen selected in playback mode, the first image in the series will be displayed with indications like those in Figure 4-66, showing that you can press the Up button to play back the sequence quickly, like a short movie.

Figure 4-66. Playback Screen for Time Lapse Shot

If you press the Down button, you will see a sub-menu that gives you the options of displaying the images sequentially one by one or uploading them by Wi-Fi. (The uploading process is discussed in Chapter 9.)

If you don't create a movie from the shots at this point, you can do so later using the Time Lapse Video option on screen 2 of the Playback menu, as discussed in Chapter 6.

## STOP MOTION ANIMATION

This next feature is similar to the Time Lapse Shot option, because it involves taking a series of still images that the camera combines into a movie. The difference is that this option is intended for use in animating objects, such as clay figures or puppets. You also can use it to make an animated movie based on drawings, as is done for cartoons and animated feature films. You need to move the figure or change the drawing very slightly for each new shot. You will need a large number of images to create a movie of any length. For example, if the final movie is to be shown at 30 frames per second, you will need to take 30 images for every second of the movie, changing the position or other aspect of the subject slightly for each successive image.

When you select this option, you will see a screen with options for Start, Auto Shooting, and Shooting Interval. The interval option will not be available unless you first select Auto Shooting. If you select Auto Shooting, the camera will capture images on its own at the interval you specify, from one second to 60 seconds. Otherwise, you will have to trigger the camera yourself when you are ready for each shot. Because it is critical to keep the camera absolutely still throughout the image-taking process, it is advisable to use the Auto Shooting option so you will not have to touch the camera to take each shot. If you do not use Auto Shooting, you can control the camera from a smartphone or tablet by remote control, as discussed in Chapter 9.

You also may want to use the optional AC adapter, discussed in Appendix A, to make sure the camera does not lose power during the shooting. (However, if the camera does turn off, you can resume the series of shots when it is turned back on. It will prompt you to do so if the series has been interrupted.)

While the shooting is in progress, the camera will display an icon showing a series of frames at the right side of the display with the cumulative number of shots taken so far, as shown in Figure 4-67. It also will display an overlaid image of the previous 2 shots, to help you line up the next shot properly with the figure or drawing in the proper position.

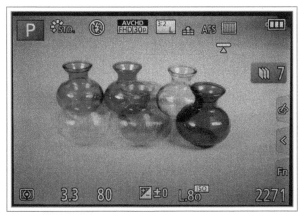

Figure 4-67. *Shooting Screen During Stop Motion Animation*

When you have finished your series of shots, press the Menu/Set button and go back to the Stop Motion Animation menu item. Press Menu/Set when that item is highlighted, and the camera will ask whether you want to stop the shooting series. If you say yes, it will ask if you want to create the video now. If so, it will prompt you for the settings to use, including recording quality, frame rate, and whether to run the sequence forward (normal) or in reverse. For the best quality, you should select 30 frames per second for the frame rate (in the United States), but 15 frames per second will still provide a reasonably smooth flow of action. Select OK when the settings are made as you want, and the camera will create the video. You can play it back in the camera by pressing the Up button.

If you don't create a movie from the shots at this point, you can do so later using the Stop Motion Video option on screen 3 of the Playback menu, as discussed in Chapter 6. As with the Time Lapse Shot option, you can view the shots in playback mode as a quick sequence using the Up button or individually from the sub-menu called up by the Down button.

## Panorama Settings

The next menu option, which is available only when the Mode dial is set to Panorama mode, has two sub-options that let you select the direction and image size for panoramic shots.

With the Direction sub-option, you can choose right, left, up, or down as the direction in which you will move the camera when shooting panoramas. The Picture Size sub-option lets you choose Standard or Wide for the size of your panoramic images. With Standard, the camera records the image at a higher pixel density,

but in a smaller area. With Wide, the camera records a larger image but with fewer pixels in a given area.

With the Standard setting, a horizontal panorama has a width of 8176 pixels and a height of 1920 pixels. With the Wide setting, a horizontal panorama has a width of 8176 pixels and a height of 960 pixels, but it covers a much wider area than a Standard panorama. So, if you want the highest quality, choose Standard; choose Wide only if you need to include a very wide panorama in the image. (Similar considerations apply for vertically oriented panoramas.)

I discussed the procedure for panorama shooting in Chapter 3.

## Shutter Type

The ZS100 is equipped with two different types of shutter—electronic and mechanical. With this menu option, you can set the camera to choose the shutter type automatically, or you can select one or the other shutter type for use. The three options for this setting are Auto, MSHTR, and ESHTR. With Auto, the camera will choose the shutter type based on the current settings and conditions. With MSHTR or ESHTR, it will use only the mechanical or electronic shutter, depending on your selection.

For most purposes, the mechanical shutter is the better option. With that choice, the camera operates a physical iris with leaves that open and close to allow light to pass through to the sensor. With the electronic shutter, the circuitry in the camera starts and stops the exposure, with no mechanical parts involved. Therefore, the electronic shutter can produce faster shutter speeds than the mechanical one. Also, because of the lack of moving parts, the camera can remain silent when the electronic shutter is activated. However, using the electronic shutter can result in a "rolling" effect that distorts images or videos, especially if the camera or subject is moving horizontally.

If you select Auto or ESHTR, the shutter speed can be set as fast as 1/16000 second; with MSHTR, the fastest speed available is 1/2000 second. However, even if you select MSHTR, if you then select burst shooting and set the burst rate to SH for super high, the camera will use the electronic shutter to achieve the high speed for that shooting.

I almost always leave this setting at Auto so the camera will use the electronic shutter when needed, but will use the mechanical shutter in most cases. One reason to turn on the ESHTR option would be if you want the camera to remain completely silent for a particular shooting session. Another way to make the camera silent is to select the Silent Mode option on screen 1 of the Custom menu. In that case, the camera will automatically activate the electronic shutter, even if the MSHTR option had been selected on the Recording menu.

Next, I will discuss the items on screen 6 of the Recording menu, shown in Figure 4-68.

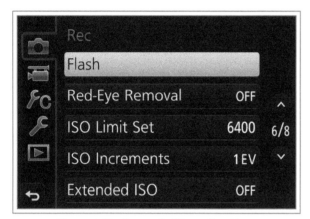

Figure 4-68. Screen 6 of Recording Menu

# FLASH

The first item on screen 6 of the Recording menu, simply called Flash, is the gateway to several options for using the built-in flash unit. The Flash item does not appear on the menu in Intelligent Auto mode. In that shooting mode, the camera will make its flash settings based on its programming, with no input from you. (In Intelligent Auto Plus mode, the camera skips over the entire screen 6 of the Recording menu, because all items on that screen are unavailable in that mode.)

When you highlight Flash on the menu and press the Right button or the Menu/Set button (or press the menu item on the touch screen), the camera will display the screen shown in Figure 4-69. That screen has three sub-options: Flash Mode, Flash Synchro, and Flash Adjustment.

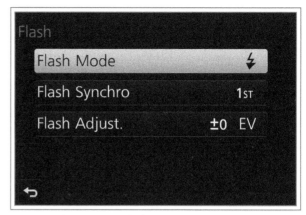

Figure 4-69. Flash Menu Options Screen

## Flash Mode

This first sub-option lets you set the flash mode for your shot. There are four options for this setting: Forced On, Forced On with Red Eye, Slow Sync, and Slow Sync with Red Eye.

If you choose Forced On, sometimes referred to as fill-flash, the flash will fire every time you press the shutter button, if the flash is operating properly and no other settings interfere. This is the mode to choose when you are certain you want the flash to fire, such as when you are taking snapshots in a dimly lighted area. It also is the mode to choose when you want to use flash to soften the shadows or brighten the scene slightly when you are taking a shot, especially a portrait, outdoors. A bit of fill-flash can offset the harsh shadows and highlights from direct sunlight, and even can provide a different look for a shot taken under a cloudy sky. For example, Figure 4-70 consists of two images I took outdoors on a cloudy day.

Figure 4-70. Fill-flash Example

For the left image, I left the flash turned off; for the right one, I used the Forced On setting. The right image has more even lighting, because the on-camera flash filled in the shadows that were cast on the subject, even through the clouds.

The next option, Forced On with Red Eye, is for use when you are aiming the camera with flash directly at a person's face. In that situation, the flash can bounce off the person's retinas and light up blood vessels, resulting in the unpleasant "red eye" effect that is common in flash snapshots. With this setting, the camera will fire a pre-flash before the main flash, to narrow the subject's pupils before the image is captured and thereby reduce the risk of the red eye effect.

The next setting, Slow Sync, is for use in dark conditions when you want to give the ambient light time to illuminate the background. With a normal flash shot, the exposure may last only about 1/60 second, enough time for the flash to illuminate the subject in the foreground, but not enough time for natural lighting to reveal the background. So, you may end up with an image in which the subject is brightly lit but the background is black. With Slow Sync, the camera will use a relatively slow shutter speed so that the ambient lighting will have time to register on the image.

Figure 4-71. Slow Sync Example

For example, Figure 4-71 is a composite with 2 images taken at the same time and in the same conditions except for the flash mode. I took the top image with the shutter speed set at 1/60 second, in normal flash mode (Forced On). The background is quite dark, because the exposure was too short to light up the area beyond the mannequin. I took the bottom image using Slow Sync

flash mode, which caused the camera to use a shutter speed of 1/5 second, allowing time for the ambient lighting to illuminate the room so the background showed up more clearly.

The Slow Sync option is not available for selection on the Recording menu when the camera is set to Shutter Priority or Manual exposure mode, because you set the shutter speed in those modes, so the camera cannot select a slow one. In Intelligent Auto mode, the camera may use the Slow Sync option, but you cannot select the setting yourself in that mode.

Slow Sync with Red Eye is the same as Slow Sync, except that the camera fires a pre-flash to try to reduce the red eye effect. In Scene mode, Slow Sync with Red Eye is the only flash mode setting available when the Clear Night Portrait setting is selected. When the Monochrome setting is selected, you can select any one of the four flash mode settings, including either of the two Slow Sync settings.

### Flash Synchro

The next sub-option for the Flash menu item, Flash Synchro, is one you may not have a lot of use for unless you encounter the particular situation it is designed for.

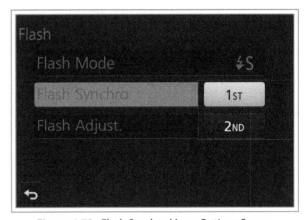

Figure 4-72. Flash Synchro Menu Options Screen

The Flash Synchro menu option, as shown in Figure 4-72, has two settings—1st and 2nd. Those terms are references to 1st-curtain sync and 2nd-curtain (also known as rear-curtain) sync. The normal setting is 1st, which causes the flash to fire early in the process when the shutter opens to expose the image. If you set it to 2nd, the flash fires later, just before the shutter closes.

The 2nd-curtain sync setting can help you avoid a strange-looking result in some situations. This issue arises when you are taking a relatively long exposure, such as 1/4 second, of a subject with taillights, such as a car or motorcycle at night, that is moving across your field of view. With 1st-curtain sync, the flash will fire early in the process, freezing the vehicle in a clear image. However, as the shutter remains open while the vehicle continues on, the camera will capture the moving taillights in a stream that seems to extend in front of the vehicle. If, instead, you use 2nd-curtain sync, the first part of the exposure will capture the lights in a trail that appears behind the vehicle, while the vehicle itself is not frozen by the flash until later in the exposure. Therefore, with 2nd-curtain sync in this particular situation, the final image is likely to look more natural than with 1st-curtain sync.

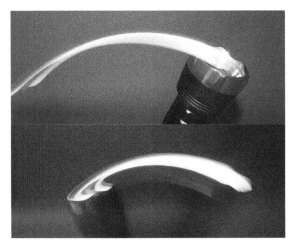

Figure 4-73. Flash Synchro Example

Figure 4-73 illustrates this concept with a composite image showing a flashlight in motion from right to left. Both pictures were shot with the ZS100's built-in flash, using an exposure of 1/2 second in Shutter Priority mode. In the top image, the flash fired quickly, and the light beam continued on during the long exposure to make the streak of light appear to move in front of the flashlight's motion.

In the bottom image, using the 2d setting, the flash did not fire until the flashlight had moved to the left, overtaking the place where the light had made its streak visible. If you are trying to convey a sense of natural motion, the 2d setting for Flash Synchro is likely to give you better results than the default setting.

A good general rule is to always use the 1st setting unless you are sure you have a need for the 2nd setting. Using the 2nd setting makes it harder to compose and set up the shot, because you have to anticipate where

the main subject will be when the flash finally fires late in the exposure process.

The Flash Synchro setting is available for selection only in the PASM shooting modes. When the 2d setting is turned on, you cannot use either of the Red Eye Reduction settings for flash mode.

## Flash Adjustment

The Flash Adjustment sub-option lets you adjust the intensity of the flash. If the exposure with flash seems too bright or too dark, you can use this setting to adjust it downward or upward in small increments. The adjustment screen for this item is shown in Figure 4-74.

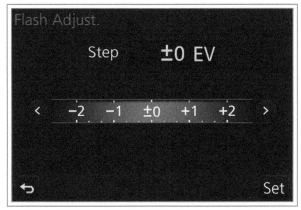

Figure 4-74. Flash Adjustment Setting Screen

Use the rear dial or the Left and Right buttons (or the touch screen) to dial in the amount of positive or negative EV adjustment you want. Of course, you also have the option of using regular exposure compensation, causing the camera to adjust the exposure using settings other than flash. This choice is up to you; it depends on what effect you are looking for. I rarely find a reason to increase the flash output, but I find that it can be useful to decrease the flash output to reduce the harshness of the lighting for a portrait in some cases.

## RED-EYE REMOVAL

This second setting on screen 6 of the Recording menu is not to be confused with Red-eye Reduction, which is an aspect of how the flash fires. As I noted earlier, "red eye" is the unpleasant phenomenon that crops up when a flash picture is taken of a person, and the light illuminates his or her retinas, causing an eerie red glow to appear in the eyes. One way the ZS100 (like many cameras) deals with this problem is with the Red-eye Reduction setting for the flash mode, which causes the flash to fire twice: once to make the person's eyes contract, reducing the chance for the light to bounce off the retinas, and then a second time to take the picture.

The ZS100 has a second line of defense against red eye, called Red-eye Removal. When you select this option, which can be turned either on or off, then, whenever the flash is fired and Red-eye Reduction is activated, the camera also uses a digital red-eye correction method, to actually remove from the image the red areas that appear to be near a person's eyes. This option operates only when flash mode is set to one of the two options with Red-eye Reduction.

I do not usually use this option, because I process my images using Photoshop or other software, and it's easy to fix red eye at that stage. But I did test it, and it did a good job of removing red areas from a mannequin's eyes on which I had pasted red dots to simulate red eye.

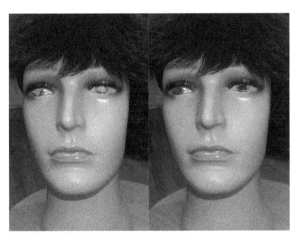

Figure 4-75. **Red-eye Removal Composite Image**

Figure 4-75 shows how the eyes looked with and without the Red-eye Removal option activated. So, for snapshots at a party, for example, this option can be quite useful.

## ISO LIMIT SET

ISO Limit Set, whose setting screen is shown in Figure 4-76, lets you set an upper limit for the value the camera will choose for ISO, when you have selected either Auto ISO or Intelligent ISO, as discussed earlier in this chapter. The choices for this setting are 200, 400, 800, 1600, 3200, 6400, 12800, or Off. If you choose Off, then the ISO limit is automatically set to 3200.

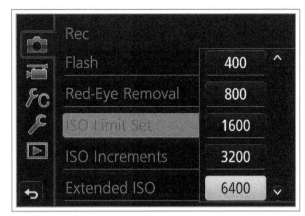

Figure 4-76. **ISO Limit Set Menu Options Screen**

This option does not have any effect for motion picture recording. If you want to make sure the camera will use a relatively low ISO to preserve image quality, you can set this value down to 200, 400 or 800. If you are shooting in dark conditions and your priority is to make sure you can capture the image even if image quality suffers, you might want to set a high limit, such as 12800.

## ISO INCREMENTS

Using this option, whose setting screen is shown in Image 4-77, you can expand the range of values available for the setting of ISO.

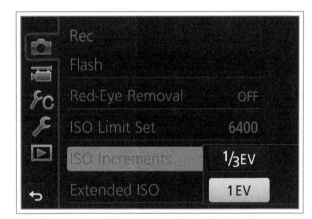

Figure 4-77. **ISO Increments Menu Options Screen**

Normally, when you set ISO to a numerical value, you can use only 125, 200, 400, 800, 1600, 3200, 6400, or 12800. However, if you select the increment of 1/3 EV instead of the normal 1 EV for this menu option, then several interpolated values for ISO are added, such as 250, 320, 500, 640, 1000, 8000, and others. You can then set these values from the Sensitivity item on screen 2 of the Recording menu.

Note that this menu option applies only to the settings you make yourself. Even if the ISO Increments option is set to 1 EV, the camera can still set intermediate ISO values when Auto ISO or Intelligent ISO is in effect and the camera is choosing the ISO value. I have never found a need to use the 1/3 EV option, so I leave this setting at its default value of 1 EV.

## EXTENDED ISO

The third ISO-related option on the Recording menu, Extended ISO, can be turned either on or off. When it is turned on through this menu item, you get access to the lowest ISO levels of 80 and 100, and to the highest value of 25600, which are not available otherwise. If you have set the ISO Increments option, discussed above, to 1/3 EV, then you will also get access to the ISO settings of 16000 and 20000.

The additional ISO values of 80, 100, and those above 12800 are considered "extended" because they are not values that are native to the sensor. Therefore, using one of them does not increase the dynamic range or improve the image quality; it just acts to change the light sensitivity of the sensor. Using a low value such as 80 ISO can be useful when you need to reduce the light sensitivity so you can use a slower shutter speed or wider aperture than you could otherwise. Using one of the very high values can be helpful when light is very low, as long as you don't mind the increased noise from using such a high value.

The items on screen 7 of the Recording menu are shown in Figure 4-78.

**Figure 4-78.** Screen 7 of Recording Menu

## LONG SHUTTER NOISE REDUCTION

When you take a picture using a shutter speed of several seconds, the image sensor may generate an excessive amount of visual noise because of the way its circuitry reacts to long exposures. If you turn on the Long Shutter Noise Reduction menu option, the camera will use noise-reduction processing that lasts as long as the exposure itself to reduce the noise. For example, if your exposure lasts for 12 seconds, the camera will continue processing the image for another 12 seconds after the exposure ends. This action will delay your ability to take another shot, and the processing can reduce the details in your image. If you don't want to experience this delay or if you want to deal with the possibility of noise some other way (such as using software to reduce it), turn this option off.

This option is available only in the PASM, Scene, and Creative Control shooting modes. It is not available for motion picture recording, for burst shooting at the SH rate, when Post Focus is active, when recording with the 4K Photo feature, or with the electronic shutter.

## DIFFRACTION COMPENSATION

When the camera uses a narrow aperture such as f/8.0, the diffraction effect comes into play and can cause distortion in the image. If you set the Diffraction Compensation option to Auto, the camera uses its processing to counteract that effect, when needed. If you would rather deal with that issue with your post-processing software or leave it untouched, choose Off. This option is available with all shooting modes except Intelligent Auto.

## INTELLIGENT ZOOM

The Intelligent Zoom, or i.Zoom, option is related to the i.Resolution feature, discussed earlier, although you do not have to turn on i.Resolution in order to take advantage of i.Zoom. When i.Zoom is turned on, the camera automatically takes advantage of i.Resolution processing in the zoom range to improve the appearance of the image, so you can zoom to a higher level of magnification without image deterioration, using either normal optical zoom or Extended Optical Zoom. (As discussed earlier in this chapter, Extended Optical Zoom is available when Picture Size is set to Medium or Small, because extra pixels are available for enlarging the image.)

For example, without the i.Zoom setting, the limit for the optical zoom is 10x; with i.Zoom turned on, the maximum is 20x. The question of image quality in this situation is a matter of judgment; as with i.Resolution, I recommend that you try this setting to see if you are satisfied with the quality of the images. If so, you can then use an effective zoom range up to 500mm, rather than the 250mm of the optical zoom alone. (The range can be even greater if combined with Digital Zoom and Extended Optical Zoom, although the quality of the image will suffer with excessive zoom range in effect.)

The i.Zoom feature is not available in conjunction with certain types of shooting that involve special processing, including panorama shots, shots with the Raw format, Multiple Exposure, shots involving bursts with burst rate set to SH, shots using the HDR option, or shots using the filter effects of Impressive Art, Toy, or Toy Pop.

## DIGITAL ZOOM

With Digital Zoom, unlike Intelligent Zoom and Extended Optical Zoom, the camera produces what Panasonic calls "decreased" picture quality. As with many digital cameras, Digital Zoom is available on the ZS100 as a way of enlarging the pixels that are displayed so the image appears larger; there is no additional resolution available, so the image can quickly begin to appear blocky and of low quality. Experts often recommend not using this sort of zoom feature.

As with Extended Optical Zoom and Intelligent Zoom, this option can help you in viewing a distant subject. Digital Zoom has a maximum power of four times the normal lens's magnification, or 1000mm. When you combine all of the zoom options, including Digital Zoom and using a smaller picture size for Extended Optical Zoom, there is a maximum total zoom power of eight times normal, or 2000mm. Digital Zoom is not available in Intelligent Auto or Panorama mode or with some other settings, including Raw quality, Post Focus, super high-speed burst shooting, or with the filter effects of Impressive Art, Toy, Toy Pop, or Miniature.

## COLOR SPACE

With this option, you can choose to record your images using the sRGB "color space," the more common choice and the default, or the Adobe RGB color space. The sRGB color space has fewer colors than Adobe RGB;

therefore, it is more suitable for producing images for the web and other forms of digital display than for printing. If your images are likely to be printed commercially in a book or magazine or it is critical that you be able to match a great many different color variations, you might want to consider using the Adobe RGB color space. I always leave the color space set to sRGB, and I recommend that you do so as well unless you have a specific need to use Adobe RGB, such as a requirement from a printing company that you are using to print your images.

If you are shooting your images with the Raw format, you don't need to worry so much about color space, because you can set it later using your Raw-processing software. This menu item is available in all shooting modes except the basic Intelligent Auto mode, Creative Video mode, and Creative Control mode.

The eighth and final screen of the Recording menu is shown in Figure 4-79.

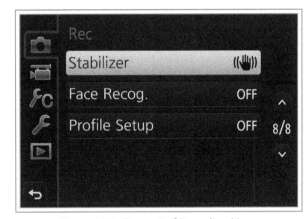

Figure 4-79. Screen 8 of Recording Menu

## STABILIZER

The ZS100 is equipped with an optical image stabilization system that counteracts the effects of camera shake on the image. This system has three possible settings, as shown in Figure 4-80, from top to bottom: Normal, Panning, and Off.

With the Normal setting, the camera corrects for both horizontal and vertical motion. With the Panning setting, the camera assumes that you are moving the camera from side to side in order to pan over the scene, so it does not attempt to correct for horizontal motion, only vertical. I generally leave this setting at Normal when I am hand-holding the camera. If I have the camera on a tripod, the setting is unnecessary and possibly could cause some distortion as the camera tries to correct for camera movement that does not exist.

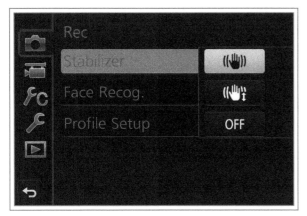

Figure 4-80. Stabilizer Menu Options Screen

The Normal stabilization setting is not available when you are shooting panoramas. The Panning setting is not available when recording movies or using 4K Photo or Post Focus. The Stabilizer menu option is not available for selection in the basic Intelligent Auto mode or in Creative Video mode.

## FACE RECOGNITION

With the Face Recognition option, you can register the faces of up to six people so the camera will recognize them when Face Recognition is turned on. Here are the essential steps to follow. First, go to the Face Recognition menu item and select the third option, Memory, as shown in Figure 4-81.

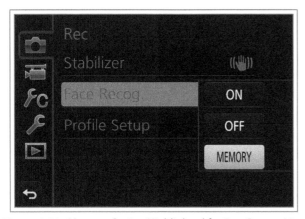

Figure 4-81. Memory Option Highlighted for Face Recognition

Press Menu/Set (or use the touch screen) to go to the screen with six blue blocks, shown in Figure 4-82. Move the yellow highlight to the first available blue block that says New, and press Menu/Set; you will see the screen shown in Figure 4-83, which prompts you to position the face to be registered in the yellow frame.

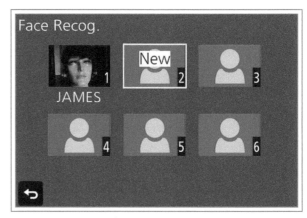

Figure 4-82. Blocks for Registering New Face to Recognize

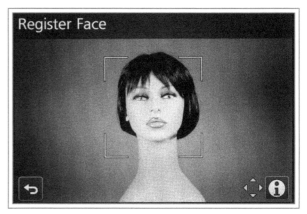

Figure 4-83. Screen for Registering New Face

When you have the face properly positioned, press the shutter button to take a picture. If the registration fails, you will see an error message. If it succeeds, you will see a screen like that in Figure 4-84. You can then proceed to enter data for the person, including name and birthdate.

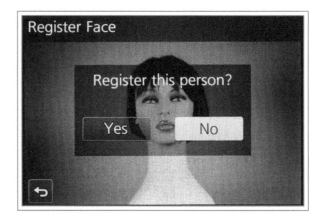

Figure 4-84. Message for Successful Face Registration

Once you have one or more faces registered, you can turn Face Recognition on through this item on the Recording menu whenever you want the camera to try to recognize those faces. You also have to have AF Mode set to Face/Eye Detection on screen 2 of the Recording menu.

When the camera recognizes a face, it will place a frame over the face and display the name, if one was entered into the camera's memory, as shown in Figure 4-85.

**Figure 4-85.** Shooting Screen with Recognized Face

The camera will adjust its focus and exposure for the recognized face or faces. It can recognize up to three faces at a time. When the image is played back, the camera will display the name and age of the person briefly, though that information does not become part of the image.

If you want, you can add additional images for any person, taken from different angles and in different lighting, to increase the camera's ability to recognize that person. To do that, choose the Memory option and then select the person for whom you want to add images. You also can edit the person's information, including name and birthdate.

I do not often use this feature, but I can appreciate how useful it could be if, for example, you are taking photos at a school event and you want to make sure the camera focuses on your child when you are aiming at a group of children.

If you don't want the camera to use face recognition, just turn this menu item off.

### PROFILE SETUP

This final option on the Recording menu lets you set up profiles for two babies and one pet, so the camera will display the name and age of the baby or pet when you take a picture of him or her. For example, you can enter

a profile for a baby named Charles, born April 7, 2016. Then, whenever you take a picture of Charles, you can recall that profile and the camera will display his name and his age as of the date the picture is taken. So, if you take his picture on December 20, 2017, the camera will display: Charles 1 year 8 months. This information will be recorded with the image, and it will display in playback mode with the detailed information screen, but it will not become a permanent part of the image unless you take further steps.

One way to imprint the information in the image is to use the PHOTOfunSTUDIO software provided with the camera, though it is available only for Windows-based computers. Another way to imprint the information is to use the Text Stamp option on the Playback menu, as discussed in Chapter 6.

This menu option does not cause the camera to recognize a pet or baby; it just lets you call up the profile you have entered for Baby 1, Baby 2, or Pet. So, you actually could enter any name and birthdate in any of those three profiles. When you call up the profile and take a picture with the profile activated, the camera will record the name and age, regardless of the actual subject matter of the image.

## Quick Menu

The ZS100 has another menu system with settings for recording images and videos. (I will discuss the menu for movie settings in Chapter 8.) This menu system is called the Quick Menu. It is not part of the regular menu system; instead, you get access to it by pressing the Q.Menu button, located at the extreme lower left of the control area on the camera's back. When you press the Q.Menu button while the camera is in recording mode, a mini-version of the camera's menu system opens up, with several options in two lines, one at the top of the screen and one at the bottom, as shown in Figure 4-86.

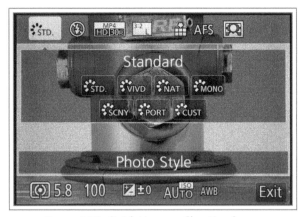

**Figure 4-86.** Quick Menu on Shooting Screen

Navigate through these menu options by pressing the Left and Right buttons, by turning the rear dial, or by touching icons on the screen until you find the category you want. The name of the setting that is currently active will appear near the top of the screen for items in the bottom row, and near the bottom of the screen for items in the top row. For example, in Figure 4-86 the Photo Style icon is highlighted at the top of the screen, and its name appears near the bottom of the screen. The highlight will wrap around between the bottom and top of the screen, so you can keep turning the rear dial or pressing the Left and Right buttons to cycle through all of the items continuously.

If the item you highlighted is at the top of the screen, you can then press the Down button to move down to the row or rows of icons with settings for that item. If the highlighted item is at the bottom of the screen, press the Up button to move to the row or rows of icons with settings. For example, Figure 4-87 shows the white balance item highlighted at the bottom of the screen. To move to the icons with settings for white balance, you would press the Up button to move the highlight into the area in the middle of the screen with those icons.

Once you have highlighted the icons with settings, move left and right through the sub-menu with the direction buttons, rear dial, or touch screen. When you have highlighted the setting you want to make, you can then move to another item in the Quick Menu to make another setting. When you have finished making settings, press the Menu/Set button, the Q.Menu button, or the Exit icon in the lower right corner of the screen to exit from the Quick Menu to the recording screen. You also can press the shutter button halfway to return to that screen.

The menu options vary according to what mode the camera is in; not surprisingly, the Quick Menu offers the largest variety of choices when the camera is in Program, Aperture Priority, Shutter Priority, or Manual mode. It offers a smaller variety in Intelligent Auto mode, though it still offers several choices.

The Quick Menu is a useful alternative to the Recording menu. This system lets you make certain settings very efficiently that otherwise would require a longer time, in part because you can see all available options at the same time on the screen as soon as you press the Q.Menu button.

For example, I find that the Quick Menu is an excellent way to select Raw or Fine quality for still images. Access to the feature is very fast this way, and, even better, when you later press the Q.Menu button again to go back to change the Quality setting again, the Quality option is still highlighted, and it takes just a couple of button presses or touches of icons on the screen to change from Raw to Fine or vice-versa.

You can customize the settings included on the Quick Menu using the Quick Menu item on screen 7 of the Custom menu. I will discuss that process in Chapter 7.

**Figure 4-87.** White Balance Setting on Quick Menu

# Chapter 5: Physical Controls

Not all settings that affect the recording of images and videos are on the Recording menu. Several important functions are controlled by physical buttons and switches on the ZS100. In addition, the camera is equipped with a versatile touch screen, which is helpful for quick and efficient focusing as well as for controlling camera settings.

I have talked about many of these controls in previous chapters. But to make sure all information about physical controls is included in one place, I'll discuss each control. I'll start with the items on top of the camera as shown in Figure 5-1.

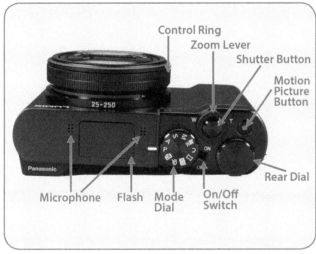

Figure 5-1. Controls on Top of Camera

## Items on Top of Camera

### Shutter Button

This control is the most important one on the camera. With the default settings, you press it halfway to check focus and exposure, and press it the rest of the way to record the image. You can press it halfway to wake the camera up from Sleep Mode, or to return to recording mode from a menu screen or from playback mode. You can press this button to take a still image while recording a video sequence, in most situations. When the camera is set for burst shooting or auto bracketing,

you hold this button down to fire a burst of shots. When the shutter speed is set to T, for time exposure, in Manual exposure mode, you press this button once to open the shutter, and press it a second time to end the exposure. When you have turned on the 4K Photo option through screen 3 of the Recording menu, pressing the shutter button starts and stops a 4K video recording. When that option is in use, you cannot use the shutter button to take still images. When the Mode dial is at the Creative Video position, pressing this button starts or stops a video recording; you cannot take still pictures with the camera in that mode.

You can change the behavior of this button in a couple of ways using options on the Custom menu. With the Shutter AF item on screen 1 of that menu, you can disable the function of focusing when the button is pressed halfway. With the Half Press Release item on screen 2 of that menu, you can set the camera so a half-press of the shutter button will release the shutter. I will discuss those options in Chapter 7.

### Zoom Lever

The zoom lever is the ring with a small handle that encircles the shutter button. The lever's basic function is to change the lens's focal length to various values ranging between wide-angle, by pushing it to the left, toward the W indicator, and telephoto, by pushing it to the right, toward the T indicator. You can set the lever to zoom in specific increments (step zoom) using the Zoom Lever item on screen 7 of the Custom menu. When you are viewing pictures in playback mode, the lever enlarges the image on the LCD screen when pushed to the right, and selects different arrangements of thumbnail images to view when pushed to the left. Also, you can use this lever to speed through the menus a full page at a time, either forward or backward.

## ON/OFF SWITCH

The on/off switch is at the rear of the camera's top, next to the Mode dial. Slide it forward to turn the camera on and pull it back to turn it off. If you leave the camera unattended for a period of time, it automatically powers off, if the Sleep Mode option is turned on through the Economy option on screen 2 of the Setup menu. I'll discuss the Setup menu in Chapter 7, but this option can be set to be off altogether so the camera never turns off just to save power, or to turn the camera off after 1, 2, 5, or 10 minutes of inactivity. You can cancel the Sleep Mode shutdown by pressing the shutter button halfway.

## MODE DIAL

The Mode dial is marked with icons or letters representing each of the camera's shooting modes, including Intelligent Auto, Shutter Priority, Scene, and the others. Just turn this dial to select the mode you want. That mode controls what features are available for shooting and how the camera's controls behave. You can shoot still images by pressing the shutter button with the dial set to any position other than Creative Video (M with movie camera icon). With the mode dial at that position, if you press the shutter button the camera will start (or stop) recording a movie. You can record a movie with the Mode dial set to any position except Panorama, by pressing the red motion picture button on top of the camera.

For the most automatic settings, turn the dial to the iA icon, for Intelligent Auto, and make sure the Intelligent Auto item, the top icon on the list of menu icons, is set to the iA selection, rather than iA+.

## MOTION PICTURE BUTTON

The red motion picture button is located to the right of the shutter button. Press this button once to start recording a movie, and press it again to stop recording. As noted above, you can use this button to record a movie in any shooting mode except Panorama. In Chapter 8, I will provide details about how the various menu and control settings affect the recording of movies.

## REAR DIAL

Although this dial is located on top of the camera, Panasonic calls it the rear dial. This name makes sense, because you are likely to move this dial with your thumb at the rear of the dial while holding the camera. However, because it is located on top of the camera, I will discuss it in this section.

This dial has default functions very similar to those of the control ring—the large, ridged ring that surrounds the lens. I will discuss that ring later in this chapter. (As I will discuss later, you can change the default functions of both the control ring and the rear dial through the Custom menu.)

The default function of the rear dial varies according to the shooting mode that is currently set. Table 5-1 lists the default assignments of the dial for each shooting mode.

Table 5-1.    **Default Assignments for Rear Dial in Various Shooting Modes**

| Shooting Mode | Function of Rear Dial |
| --- | --- |
| Intelligent Auto | No Function |
| Program | Program Shift |
| Aperture Priority | Adjusts Aperture |
| Shutter Priority | Adjusts Shutter Speed |
| Manual Exposure | Adjusts Shutter Speed |
| Panorama | Selects Picture Effects |
| Scene | No function, with two exceptions below |
| Scene–Appetizing Food Setting | Adjusts Aperture |
| Scene–Artistic Nightscape | Adjusts Shutter Speed |
| Creative Control | Selects Picture Effects |
| Creative Video | Adjusts Aperture or Shutter Speed if Exposure Mode Permits |

The functions I have just outlined for the rear dial are the default functions programmed at the factory. You can change the function of the rear dial through the Ring/Dial Set option on screen 8 of the Custom menu. If you use that menu option to select a setting other than the default, the dial will control a single setting, such as ISO, white balance, Drive Mode, or filter effects. The following list shows the possible assignments for the rear dial.

° Default (see Table 5-1, above)

° Exposure Compensation

° ISO Sensitivity

° White Balance

- AF Mode

- Focus Mode

- Drive Mode

- Photo Style

- Filter Effect

- Aspect Ratio

- Highlight Shadow

- i.Dynamic

- i.Resolution

- Flash Mode

- Flash Adjustment

If you select an option other than Default, that setting will take effect for all recording modes. If you select Highlight Shadow for the rear dial, it will also be assigned to the control ring, and vice-versa. (Highlight Shadow is the only setting for which that situation exists.)

Apart from its main functions, this dial has a few other uses. You can turn it to move through menu screens by one item at a time. You can turn the dial to adjust the size of the focus frame when the focus mode permits that adjustment, or to adjust the size of the frame used for the Miniature setting of the filter effects. You can also use it to adjust the size of the light source for the Sunshine effect. This dial is also used to adjust the settings for the Highlight Shadow option on screen 3 of the Recording menu and to set the interval for white balance bracketing. In playback mode, turning this dial moves through your recorded images, and it is used to adjust the audio volume during a slide show or motion picture playback.

## Built-in Flash Unit

The ZS100's built-in flash is stored inside the top of the camera. In order to use it, you have to press the flash release button, at the top center of the camera's back. In most shooting modes, you can control the operation of the flash using the Flash item on screen 6 of the Recording menu.

## Microphone

The camera's built-in stereo microphone receives sounds through the small openings on either side of the built-in flash unit. Be sure not to cover up these openings when recording a movie, so as not to block the recording of sounds. This camera does not have any jack for plugging in an external microphone.

# Controls on Back of Camera

Figure 5-2 shows the controls on the camera's back.

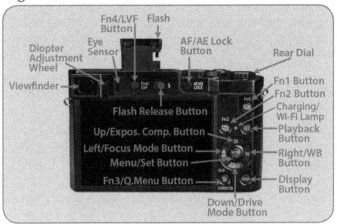

Figure 5-2. Controls on Back of Camera

## Viewfinder, Eye Sensor, LVF Button, and Diopter Adjustment Wheel

The viewfinder window at the top left of the camera's back is where you can see the recording display and playback display when the viewfinder is in use. The vertical slot to the right of the window is the eye sensor. That device senses when your head is near the viewfinder window, and switches the display from the LCD screen to the viewfinder, if the camera is set for automatic switching of the view.

To change the way the view is switched between the viewfinder and the LCD screen, you can use the LVF button, labeled Fn4/LVF, to the right of the eye sensor. Each time you press that button, it selects a different setting. If you press it to select LVF/Monitor Auto, then the view switches between the viewfinder and the LCD screen automatically when your head (or something else) approaches the eye sensor. Otherwise, it can be set to LVF or Monitor, to keep the viewfinder or LCD screen permanently activated. These functions work only if the LVF/Fn4 button remains set to its default function. If you don't need this switching function, you can reassign that button to carry out some other operation using the Function Button Set option on screen 7 of the Custom menu.

You also can control the switching between the viewfinder and monitor using the LVF/Monitor Switch menu option, a sub-option of the Eye Sensor item on screen 8 of the Custom menu. You can control the sensitivity of the eye sensor using the Sensitivity sub-option of the Eye Sensor menu item.

You also can set the camera so it will use its autofocus mechanism to focus on the scene when your eye approaches the eye sensor. That option is controlled using the Eye Sensor AF option on screen 2 of the Custom menu.

You can adjust the view in the viewfinder for your eyesight using the diopter adjustment wheel between the viewfinder and the eye sensor. If you wear glasses, you may be able to adjust this dial so you can see clearly through the viewfinder without your glasses.

The information displayed in the viewfinder is controlled by pressing the Display button. There are four different screens with various information; I will talk about those screens in the discussion of the Display button, later in this chapter.

## Flash Release Button

This button, at the top center of the camera's back, has just one purpose—to release the built-in flash unit so it will pop up. If you don't pop up the flash with this button, the flash cannot be used. To release the flash, slide this button to the left. When you are done with the flash, press it gently back into the camera until it clicks into place.

## AF/AE Lock Button

The AF/AE Lock button is located at the upper right of the camera's back, just below the Mode dial. Using the AF/AE Lock item on screen 1 of the Custom menu, you can set this button to lock both autofocus and autoexposure, or just one or the other. Then, you can press this button to lock whichever of those settings have been selected through the menu option. With the same menu option, you also can select AF-On. If you turn on that option, pressing this button operates the camera's autofocus system. That option gives the camera

a capability for "back button focus," so named because you can press a button on the camera's back to focus the lens. If you want to turn off the shutter button's focusing function, you can do that by turning off the Shutter AF option on screen 1 of the Custom menu.

You cannot lock exposure with the AF/AE Lock button when the camera is set to Manual exposure mode, and the button does not function at all in either variety of Intelligent Auto mode. When manual focus is in use, the button cannot lock focus. Zooming the lens cancels either type of lock. You can set the button to hold its setting without keeping it pressed, using the AF/AE Lock Hold item on screen 1 of the Custom menu.

## Playback Button

This button, located to the upper right of the group of cursor buttons, is marked by a small triangle. You press this button to put the camera into playback mode. Press it again to switch back into recording mode. When the camera is placed into playback mode, the lens barrel will retract automatically after about 15 seconds, because the lens is not needed during playback operations.

## Display Button

The Display button is at the bottom right of the camera's back, to the lower right of the group of cursor buttons. It has several functions, depending on the context. Its primary function is to switch among the several available display screens for the LCD screen or the viewfinder, in both recording mode and playback mode.

In recording mode, following are the screens you see on the LCD monitor from repeated presses of the Display button, when the Monitor Display Style option on screen 6 of the Custom menu is set to its bottom option, for the monitor style layout. The items displayed are slightly different if that menu option is set to the other setting, for live viewfinder style display layout. I will not include the touch screen icons in describing these screens, because the touch screen can be turned off, removing all such icons from the display.

1. As shown in Figure 5-3, full display, with battery status, Picture Size, Quality, aspect ratio, Photo Style, flash status, ISO (if set to a specific value), exposure compensation amount, movie quality and format, recording mode, metering mode, autofocus mode, number of pictures or length of video that

can be shot with the remaining storage, and the histogram (discussed later), if it is turned on through screen 4 of the Custom menu. The aperture and shutter speed also will display briefly after exposure is evaluated, and one or both of those values will remain on the screen in some shooting modes.

Figure 5-3. Recording: Full Information Display

2.  Blank display except for the focus area (if using a focus mode that displays a focus frame, such as 1-Area AF or AF Tracking). The aperture, shutter speed, ISO value, and exposure compensation scale also will display briefly after exposure is evaluated.

3.  As shown in Figure 5-4, full information with level gauge, as well as histogram and focus frame if applicable.

Figure 5-4. Recording: Full Information with Level Gauge

4.  As shown in Figure 5-5, level gauge with focus frame if applicable.

5.  Blank screen (black, with no information) (not shown).

Figure 5-5. Recording: Level Gauge Display

In the basic Intelligent Auto mode, the Display button produces the screens listed above, but the histogram does not appear even if it was turned on through the Custom menu. There also are other items that will appear on the information screens, such as the Guide Line grid if selected on screen 4 of the Custom menu, and icons for items such as the self-timer when they are activated.

The viewfinder uses the same display screens as those discussed above, except that it does not include the blank screen. The items displayed are affected by the LVF Display Style option on screen 6 of the Custom menu.

If the camera is set for playback, repeated presses of the Display button produce the following screens.

Figure 5-6. Playback: Full Information Display

1.  As shown in Figure 5-6, image with battery status, Picture Size, Quality, flash status, recording mode, aperture, shutter speed, exposure compensation, ISO, white balance, and icon showing that you can press the Down button to upload images via Wi-Fi. (As with the recording mode displays, I am not

including touch icons, because the touch screen may be turned off).

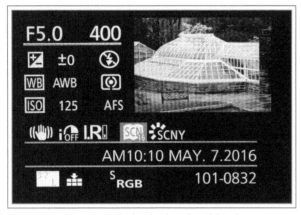

Figure 5-7. Playback: Thumbnail Display

2. As shown in Figure 5-7, a smaller image with the same information, plus date and time of image capture, image number, and some other settings, including metering mode and Photo Style.

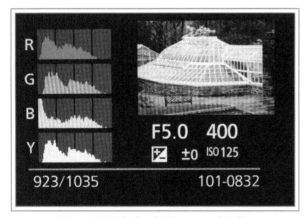

Figure 5-8. Playback: Histogram Display

3. As shown in Figure 5-8, the smaller image with basic recording information and the histogram, which is discussed in Chapter 7. Basically, the histogram is a graphic display that shows the brightness of the image through peaks and dips. A normal histogram should have most peaks in the middle portion of the graph, for each color.

4. Just the recorded image, with no other information, but flashing the highlights in areas that are overexposed. (This screen appears only if the Highlight option is turned on through screen 5 of the Custom menu. The highlights also will flash on the detailed information screens; this screen is added so you can see the overexposed areas without interference from information items.)

5. Just the recorded image with no other information, and with no flashing highlights.

If you are playing back a motion picture, the display is similar, except for some added information that applies to that mode, including an icon showing that you can press the Up button to start the motion picture playing.

After about one minute of no activity with the controls, the camera removes the playback information from the screen. To restore it, press the Playback button or the Display button.

The Display button also has several other functions. You can press it to restore the focus frame to normal after you have moved it off center or resized it when using the 1-Area focus mode or one of the other modes that allows you to move or resize the focus point or points. If you need a reminder of the current date and time, with the camera in recording mode, press the Display button enough times to cycle back to the screen with the most recording information, and the date and time will appear on the lower left of the screen for about five seconds. Also, when you are viewing a menu screen, you can press the Display button to cycle through the menu by a full screen at a time, the same way you can by pressing the zoom lever to the right.

## MENU/SET BUTTON AND DIRECTION BUTTONS

An important control group on the ZS100 is the set of five buttons on the back of the camera, arranged in a circular pattern. Each of the buttons is marked with an icon that indicates its primary function. In the center of the pattern is a fifth button, labeled Menu/Set. I generally refer to the four outer buttons as direction buttons or cursor buttons (Left, Right, Up, and Down), and to the center button as the Menu/Set button.

### Direction Buttons

The direction buttons act as cursor keys do on a computer keyboard, letting you navigate up and down and left and right through menu options. However, the buttons' functions do not stop there. Each of the four direction buttons performs at least one additional function, as indicated by the icon or label on the button. I will discuss those functions for each button in turn.

## Up Button: Exposure Compensation

The Up button doubles as the exposure compensation button. This control gives you a way to adjust the brightness of images in all shooting modes except Manual exposure mode and the basic Intelligent Auto mode.

Here is an example of how to control exposure to account for an unusual, or non-optimal, lighting situation. Suppose you have the ZS100 set to Program mode and you are photographing a fairly dark subject, such as a pair of fabric balls, in front of a white background, as shown in Figure 5-9.

Figure 5-9. Exposure Compensation Example - Before

The camera will do a good job of averaging the amount of light coming into the lens, and will expose the picture accordingly. The problem is, the very light background will likely "fool" the camera into closing down the aperture, because the overall picture will seem quite bright. But your subject, which is not nearly as light as the background, will seem too dark in the picture. One solution to this problem is to use exposure compensation. (Another is to use spot metering.)

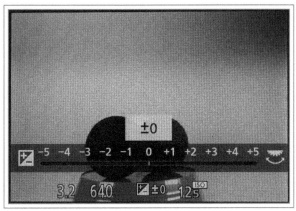

Figure 5-10. Exposure Compensation Scale on Display

First, compose the image as you want. Then, press the Up button to place the exposure compensation scale on the display, as shown in Figure 5-10. Use the rear dial, the Left and Right buttons, or slide your finger along the touch screen to select the desired setting. The values range from –5 to +5 EV, with one-third steps in between. EV stands for exposure value, a standard measure of brightness. If you move the value down to -5, the picture will be much darker than the automatic exposure would produce. If you move it to +5, the picture will be much brighter.

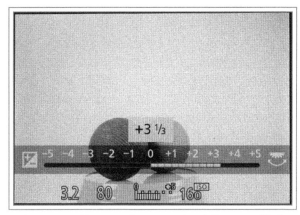

Figure 5-11. Exposure Compensation Adjustment Made

The camera's screen shows you how the exposure is changing, before you take the picture, as shown in Figure 5-11. In this case, after 3 1/3 EV of exposure compensation is added, the image becomes brighter and the fabric balls can be seen more clearly. The small EV scale at the bottom center of the display shows the amount of exposure compensation that has been applied after the exposure compensation screen has been dismissed, as shown in Figure 5-12.

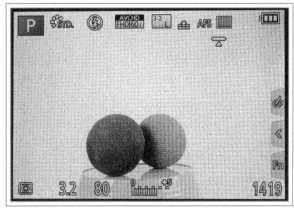

Figure 5-12. Exposure Compensation Icon on Display

Once you've taken the picture, you should reset the EV compensation back to zero so you don't unintentionally affect the pictures you take later.

In basic Intelligent Auto mode, the Up button calls up the defocus control option. In Intelligent Auto Plus mode, the button calls up that option as well as the exposure compensation option, with successive presses of the button.

In playback mode, the Up button is used to start playing a motion picture, a panorama, or a burst of SH shots when the initial frame is displayed on the screen. The button also serves as a play/pause button once a movie has started playing, and it has various duties to move among settings on certain screens, such as the screen for saving Highlight Shadow values on the Recording menu, the screen for setting a custom white balance setting, and the screen for saving a Custom Multi frame for AF Mode.

### Right Button: White Balance

The Right button has the important duty of calling up the menu for selecting the camera's setting for white balance. The white balance menu option is needed because cameras record the colors of objects differently according to the color temperature of the light source that illuminates those objects.

Color temperature is a value expressed in Kelvin (K) units. A light source with a lower K rating produces a "warmer," or more reddish light. A source with a higher rating produces a "cooler," or more bluish light. Candlelight is rated about 1,800 K, indoor tungsten light (ordinary light bulb) is rated about 3,000 K, outdoor sunlight and electronic flash are rated about 5,500 K, and outdoor shade is rated about 7,000 K. If the camera is using a white balance setting that is not calibrated for the light source that illuminates the scene, the colors of the recorded image are likely to be inaccurate.

The ZS100, like most digital cameras, has an Auto White Balance setting that attempts to set the proper color correction for any given light source. The Auto White Balance setting works well, and it will produce good results in many situations, especially if you are taking snapshots whose colors are not critical.

If you need more precision in the white balance of your shots, the ZS100 has settings for common light sources, as well as options for setting white balance

by color temperature and for setting a custom white balance based on the existing light source.

You get access to this setting by pressing the Right button, which calls up the white balance menu screen at the bottom of the display, as shown in Figure 5-13.

Figure 5-13. White Balance Menu Screen

This menu includes the following choices for the white balance setting, most of them represented by icons: Auto White Balance (AWB); Daylight (sun icon); Cloudy; Shade; Incandescent; Flash; White Set 1; White Set 2; White Set 3; White Set 4; and Color Temperature. (Only the first six options are shown in Figure 5-13; you need to scroll to the right to reach the others.)

Most of these settings are self-explanatory. You may want to experiment to see if the named settings (Daylight, Shade, Incandescent, etc.) produce the results you want. If not, you'll be better off setting the white balance manually. To do that, you can use any one of the four White Set options, which let you measure the white balance based on the light that is actually illuminating your subject, and save a custom setting to that numbered slot in the camera's memory. Then, you can use that custom setting whenever you are faced with the same lighting situation in the future.

To set white balance manually, press the Right button to activate the white balance menu and scroll to highlight one of the four White Set icons, as shown in Figure 5-14. Press the Up button, and a yellow rectangle will appear in the middle of the display, as shown in Figure 5-15.

Figure 5-14. White Set Icon Highlighted

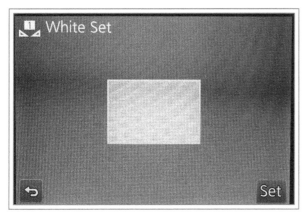

Figure 5-15. Yellow Frame for Setting Custom White Balance

Figure 5-16. Color Temperature Option Highlighted on White Balance Menu

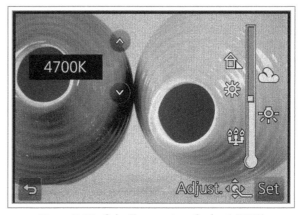

Figure 5-17. Color Temperature Scale at 4700K

Aim the camera at a white or gray surface illuminated by the light source you will be using, and fill the rectangle with the image of that surface. Then press the Menu/ Set button (or you can press the shutter button if you prefer) to lock in that white balance setting. The camera will display a Completed message if the setting was successful. Now, until you change that setting, whenever you select that preset value (White Set 1 or another slot, as the case may be), it will be set for the white balance you have just set. This system is useful if you often use a particular light source and want to have the camera set to the appropriate white balance for that source.

To set the color temperature directly by numerical value, choose the Color Temperature option from the white balance menu, as shown in Figure 5-16.

Then press the Up button to pop up a screen with a value such as 2500K displayed. You then can press the Up and Down buttons, turn the rear dial, or slide your finger on the touch screen to adjust that value anywhere from 2500K to 10000K in increments of 100K, as shown in Figure 5-17, where the value is set to 4700K.

With this approach, you have to know the color temperature of your light source in order to make this setting. One way to find that value is to use a color temperature meter like the Sekonic Prodigi meter shown in Figure 5-18.

Figure 5-18. Sekonic Prodigi Color Meter

That meter is helpful when you need accuracy in your white balance settings, but it is fairly expensive, and you may not want to use that option. In that case, you can still use the Color Temperature option, but you will have to do some guesswork or use your own sense of color. For example, if you are shooting under lighting from incandescent bulbs, you can use 3,000

K as a starting point, because, as noted earlier, that is the approximate color temperature of that light source. Then you can try setting the color temperature figure higher or lower, and watch the camera's display to see how natural the colors look. As you lower the color temperature, the image will become more "cool" or bluish; as you raise it, the image will appear more "warm" or reddish. Once you have found the best setting, leave it in place and take your shots.

Once you have made the white balance setting, either using one of the preset values such as Daylight, Incandescent, or Cloudy, or using a custom-measured setting or a color temperature, you can still fine-tune the setting to an additional degree.

To make this further adjustment, after you make your white balance setting, before pressing the Menu/Set button to return to the recording screen, press the Down button, and you will be presented with a screen for fine adjustments, as shown in Figure 5-19.

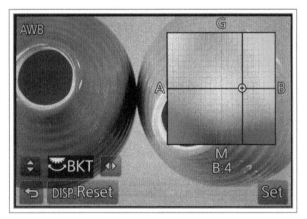

Figure 5-19. Screen with Color Axes to Adjust White Balance

You will see a box containing a pair of axes that intersect at a zero point, marked by a circle with a plus sign inside it. The four ends of the axes are labeled G, B, M, and A, for green, blue, magenta, and amber.

You can use all four direction buttons, or just slide your finger over the colored square, to move the circle away from the center toward any of the axes, to adjust these four values until you have the color balance exactly how you want it. The camera will remember this value whenever you select the white balance setting that you fine-tuned. When you have fine-tuned the setting using this screen, the white balance icon on the camera's display changes color and/or adds an indicator to indicate what changes you have made along the color

axes. If there was an adjustment to the amber or blue side, the icon changes color accordingly. If there was an adjustment to the green or magenta side, the icon will have a plus sign added for green or a minus sign added for magenta.

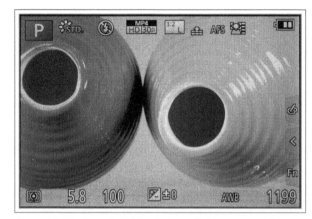

Figure 5-20. Icon for White Balance Adjustment on Screen

For example, Figure 5-20 shows the icon, in the bottom right corner of the screen, after the white balance setting was adjusted toward the blue side of the axes. If you want to reset the adjustment axes to the zero point, press the Display button (or touch the Reset icon) while the axes are displayed, and the circle will return to the center of the adjustment area.

One more note: If you're shooting with Raw quality, you don't have to worry about white balance so much, because, once you load the Raw file into your software, you can change the white balance however you want. This is one of the advantages of using Raw. If you had the camera's white balance setting at Incandescent while shooting under a bright sun, you can just change the setting to Daylight in the Raw software, and no one need ever know about the error of your shooting.

Before I discuss white balance bracketing, I am going to include a chart in Figure 5-21 that shows how the different white balance settings affect the images taken by the ZS100. The images in this chart were taken under artificial light balanced for daylight, with the camera set for each available white balance setting, as indicated on the chart. In my opinion, the best results were obtained with the Auto White Balance, Daylight, Color Temperature, and White Set settings. The Flash setting also appeared to match the actual color temperature quite closely, and the Cloudy and Shade settings did not do badly. The Incandescent setting is the only one that yielded a result that clearly is incorrect.

## Panasonic Lumix ZS100 White Balance Chart

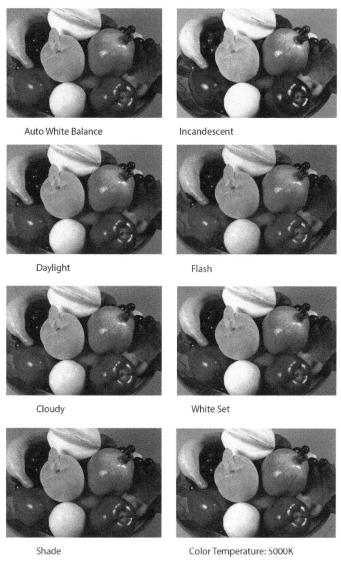

Auto White Balance · Incandescent

Daylight · Flash

Cloudy · White Set

Shade · Color Temperature: 5000K

**Figure 5-21.** White Balance Comparison Chart

There is one other aspect of white balance that needs to be discussed. Later in this chapter I'll discuss exposure bracketing, also known as Auto Bracket, a feature by which the ZS100 automatically takes several pictures at varying exposure settings, so you can have multiple options to choose from. You can do something similar with white balance—set the camera to take three images at once with different white balance settings, to give you a better chance of having one image with perfect color balance. I'm discussing this option here rather than in the section on Auto Bracket, because this option is accessed from the white balance setting screen.

Here is how to set up white balance bracketing. After pressing the Right button to select white balance,

highlight the icon for a main setting, such as Daylight, Incandescent, White Set 1, or any other choice. Then press the Down button to move to the fine adjustment screen, which I discussed above. First, make any adjustments you want to make, such as tweaking the white balance to the blue side by pressing the Right button a few times. (Of course, you may not need to make any such adjustments.)

Then, you need to decide on which axis to set the bracketing: the amber-blue axis, or the magenta-green axis. If you want to use the amber-blue axis, turn the rear dial to the right; if you want to use the magenta-green axis, turn the dial to the left. As you turn it in either direction, you will see small circles appear on the chosen axis. The circles will spread apart as you continue to turn the dial. The final positions of those circles indicate the differences among the three shots that the camera will take. If you have also set an adjustment to the white balance setting using the adjustment screen, the white balance bracketing will take the adjustment into account and bracket the exposures with the adjustment factored in.

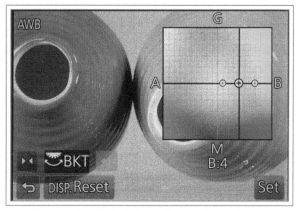

**Figure 5-22.** White Balance Bracket Setup Screen

For example, Figure 5-22 shows white balance bracketing set up to take three shots with the greatest possible differences along the amber-blue axis.

Once the circles are set up as illustrated here, press the Menu/Set button, and the camera will return to the white balance screen. Then press that button again or press the shutter button halfway to return to the live view.

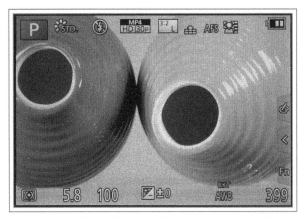

Figure 5-23. White Balance Bracket Icon on Shooting Screen

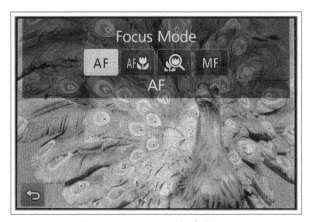

Figure 5-24. Focus Mode Menu

As shown in Figure 5-23, the display will then show the BKT icon just above the icon for the white balance setting, in the lower right corner of the display. Now, when you press the shutter button, the camera will take three pictures with different white balance adjustments, from more amber to more blue. You will only hear the sound of the shutter once, though; the camera alters the white balance settings electronically. To cancel the bracketing, return to the adjustment screen and press the Display button.

This function does not work in Intelligent Auto mode or Panorama mode. It also does not work with Raw images or with certain other settings, including HDR, Post Focus, burst shooting, and Time Lapse Shot.

Besides giving access to white balance settings, the Right button has some miscellaneous functions. For example, when playing movies and slide shows, the Right button acts as a navigation control to move through the images, and it is used to navigate among the various portions of screens with settings, such as the Highlight Shadow and Photo Style screens. When you have selected a filter effect in Creative Control mode or with the Filter Settings menu option, you can press the Right button to get access to a screen for making an adjustment to that setting.

### Left Button: Focus Mode

The Left button is marked with a flower icon and the letters MF, for manual focus. Pressing this button brings up the menu for selecting a basic focus mode, as shown in Figure 5-24. The four choices, from the left, are autofocus, autofocus macro, macro zoom, and manual focus.

### Autofocus

If you choose autofocus, the camera will use its autofocus mechanism, along with the settings you make for other focus-related options such as AF Mode, AFS/AFF/AFC, and others. The camera will use its normal autofocus distance range of 1.6 foot (50 cm) to infinity at the wide-angle setting, and 2.3 feet (70 cm) to infinity at the telephoto setting.

### AF Macro

If you choose AF macro, the camera can focus as close as about 2 inches or 5 cm, when the lens is zoomed back to its wide-angle setting. At the extreme telephoto setting, the lens can focus as close as 2.3 feet (70 cm), the same as with normal autofocus mode.

### Macro Zoom

If you choose macro zoom, you can focus at the same closeup distance as with AF macro, but the camera will let you use digital zoom, at a magnification factor of up to three times normal, while still focusing at the minimum focus distance, with the optical zoom at its wide-angle setting. The macro zoom setting is not available with certain other settings, including Multiple Exposure, Handheld Night Shot, Panorama mode, high-speed video recording, burst shooting using the SH rate, or with the HDR, Impressive Art, Toy Effect, Toy Pop, or Miniature Effect settings.

### Manual Focus

If you choose manual focus, you will need to adjust the focus manually using the control ring. The process for using manual focus involves several possible steps, which depend on the settings for several Custom menu options. I will discuss the details of those options in Chapter 7. For now, to discuss the basics of using manual focus, I will assume that the MF Assist option on screen 3 of the Custom menu is turned on, and that the Touch Screen is set to On under the Touch Settings item on screen 8 of the Custom menu. I will also assume that the MF Assist Display item on screen 4 of the Custom menu is set to PIP (picture-in-picture), and that the MF Guide and Peaking items on that screen are set to On.

With the above settings in place, press the Left button to bring up the Focus Mode menu. Select the MF option at the right by highlighting it and pressing the Menu/Set button or by half-pressing the shutter button to return to the shooting screen. Now, start turning the control ring (the large ring around the lens) to adjust the focus.

Figure 5-25. Enlarged Screen with MF Assist

As soon as you start turning the ring, you should see a screen like that in Figure 5-25, with an enlarged block inset in the display, with yellow arrows at its sides. You can move that block around the screen with your fingers, and you can pinch or pull on the screen or turn the rear dial to change the enlargement factor to anywhere between 3.0x and 6.0x normal. You also can use the direction buttons to move the block. When you have the enlarged block sized and located where you want it, turn the control ring to get the focus as sharp as you can. The peaking feature will place an increasing density of colored pixels at the areas that are in sharpest focus.

You can press on the touch icon that looks like a rectangle with a small, solid rectangle in its upper right corner to switch the view from the PIP setting to a full view, with the entire display enlarged. In that case, the enlargement factor can vary between 3.0x and 10.0x normal. You can press on the small AF icon to cause the camera to use its autofocus on the area in the center of

the enlarged display. You can touch the DISP. RESET icon to make the focus point return to the center of the display. You can touch the EXIT icon to return to the normal-sized display. While you are adjusting focus, the MF Guide will appear near the bottom of the display, showing roughly where the focus point is located between the minimum focus distance and infinity.

I will discuss the options for assisting with manual focus further in Chapter 7.

### Down Button: Drive Mode

The last of the cursor buttons to be discussed, the Down button, provides access to Drive Mode, which includes settings for the camera's burst shooting, exposure bracketing, and self-timer options.

When you press the Down button, you will see a line of icons, as shown in Figure 5-26.

Figure 5-26. Drive Mode Menu

Scroll through them with the rear dial, the Left and Right buttons, or by touching the icons on the touch screen. As you highlight each one, the camera places a label underneath it listing its function. From left to right, these icons have the following functions: burst shooting off; single shooting; burst shooting on; 4K Photo; Auto Bracket; and self-timer. I will discuss all of these functions below.

The first two icons on the Drive Mode menu have the same function—to turn off all burst shooting, including the self-timer. There is no functional difference between these icons; you can select either one when you want to make sure the camera is not set to use the burst, bracketing, or self-timer options. There are some camera settings, such as Intelligent Zoom, Digital Zoom, and Shutter Type, that do not function when one of the burst shooting options is selected. So, if you find a feature is not working, you may want to select the first or second Drive Mode icon to disable all burst features and see if that removes the conflict.

The third icon is used to activate burst shooting, which I will discuss now.

### Burst Shooting

With burst shooting, sometimes called continuous shooting, the camera takes a continuous series of images while you hold down the shutter button. This capability is useful in many contexts, from shooting an action sequence at a sporting event to taking a series of shots of a portrait subject to capture changing facial expressions. I often use this setting for street photography to increase my chances of catching an interesting image.

To activate burst shooting, press the Down button, then scroll to the third icon from the left. It looks like a stack of frames with the letters SH, H, M, or L beside it, for super-high, high, medium, or low speed bursts. Once this icon is highlighted, press the Up button (or touch the More Settings icon) to get access to more settings, and you will see icons with all four of those speed notations, as shown in Figure 5-27.

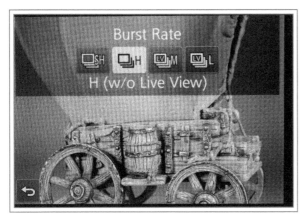

Figure 5-27. Burst Rate Options Screen

Scroll through those icons to select the one you want to use, then press the Menu/Set button to activate it and return to the recording screen. I will discuss these four options in turn.

If you select SH for super-high, the camera will take a very fast burst of shots at a speed of up to 50 frames per second (fps), but with several limitations. The images cannot be of Raw quality, they are limited to Small for the Picture Size setting, and the burst will stop after 60 images are taken. In addition, the only autofocus mode

available is AFS, for single autofocus, though you can use manual focus if you want. The focus, exposure, and white balance settings will be fixed with the first shot, and there will be no updated live view of the current scene on the camera's display. The camera will use the electronic shutter.

Despite these limitations, the SH setting for burst mode is quite powerful. The ability to take a burst of 60 shots, even at the relatively small size of about 5 MP, depending on aspect ratio, lets you do a high-speed study of a sports action such as a golf swing, or of any other fast-moving action. It also can let you freeze a speedy action. For example, Figure 5-28 is from a burst of SH shots I took of a very quick spaniel puppy as she ran up some outdoor steps with a ball in her mouth. This shot caught her suspended in mid-air.

Figure 5-28. Sample Image Taken in SH Burst Mode

When you take a burst of shots with the SH setting, the camera saves them in a group, so you do not have to scroll through as many as 60 images. When you press the Playback button, you will see a screen like that in Figure 5-29, showing that you can press the Up button to play the burst as a group, using Burst Play.

Figure 5-29. Initial Burst Mode Playback Screen

If you press that button, the camera will display the images rapidly, almost like a movie.

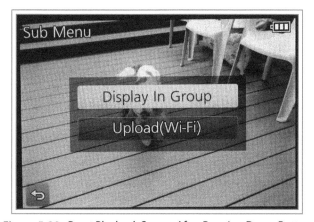

Figure 5-30. Burst Playback Screen After Pressing Down Button

If you press the Down button, you will see a screen like that shown in Figure 5-30, which gives you the option to display the images "In Group," which actually means to display them individually. If you select that option, you can then scroll through all of the images from the burst in normal playback mode. You also have the option to upload the images using Wi-Fi. I will discuss that process in Chapter 9.

The next burst option is H, for high-speed shooting. As you might expect, reducing the speed to this level increases the capability of the feature. With this setting, there still is no updating live view on the camera's display during shooting, but most of the other restrictions are lifted. So, you can shoot with Raw quality and the camera can adjust its focus during shooting. If the focus mode is set to AFS or MF, the exposure and white balance settings will be fixed with the first shot. However, if you set the focus mode to AFF or AFC, the camera can adjust focus, exposure and

white balance for each shot (depending on conditions), at the expense of a loss in speed of shooting. The maximum speed available is 10 fps with single autofocus or manual focus, and 5 fps with flexible or continuous autofocus.

With the next lower speed, M, for medium, the camera can provide an updating live view throughout the shooting, and otherwise can perform the same as with the H setting with respect to focus and exposure. The maximum speed drops to 5 fps with all types of focus.

Finally, with the lowest speed, L, for low, the speed drops to 2 fps with all focus modes.

With all burst shooting, the specifications for speed and numbers of images will vary according to conditions. When conditions are dark and the camera has to use a slower shutter speed, that factor alone will slow down the shooting. Other factors that affect shooting capacity and speed include image quality and the speed and capacity of the memory card in the camera. I carried out some indoor experiments with my ZS100 using a very fast card, the SanDisk Extreme PRO 512 GB SDXC card, rated in UHS Speed Class 3, the highest speed category currently available. I used Shutter Priority mode at 1/100 second in order to have consistent conditions. Table 5-2 gives the results of my tests.

Table 5-2.    **Results of Burst Shooting Tests with Panasonic Lumix DMC-ZS100 Camera**

| Burst Mode | Image Quality | Image Size | Focus Mode | No. Images Before Slowdown |
|------------|---------------|------------|------------|----------------------------|
| H | Raw & JPEG | L | AFS | 12 |
| H | Raw | - | AFS | 15 |
| H | Fine | L | AFS | 82 |
| H | Raw & JPEG | L | AFC | 14 |
| H | Fine | L | AFC | 200+ |
| M | Raw & JPEG | L | AFC | 15 |
| L | Raw & JPEG | L | AFC | 20 |

The results did not always agree with the expected results according to the specifications, though Panasonic makes it clear that results will be affected by shooting conditions. Based on these results, my recommendation is to use the slower speeds when you don't need super-fast shooting. For example, if you are taking a portrait and would like to capture changing expressions but don't need to freeze an action as you might at a sporting event, try using the L or M setting to increase your chance of getting usable shots, especially if you are using continuous autofocus.

If you are shooting sports or other fast-moving events, you should get good results with the H setting, especially if the action is at a constant distance and you can use single autofocus. I did not get great results with focus adjustments using the H setting, though the dim lighting for my shots probably was a contributing factor. Also, I was using the Release setting for the Focus/Release Priority option on screen 3 of the Custom menu. With that option, the camera uses predictive focusing and gives more priority to speed of shooting than to accuracy of focusing. With the Focus setting for Focus/Release Priority, focusing results may be better, depending on other conditions. With continuous autofocus, I got more shots before slowdown than with single autofocus, but at a slower maximum burst speed.

Of course, you also can use the SH setting when you need a really fast burst for a very limited time, with small image size.

The burst-shooting options are available in every shooting mode for still images, except for Panorama. However, there are several limitations on the use of burst shooting. You cannot use it with flash, or with the Rough Monochrome, Silky Monochrome, Miniature, Soft Focus, Star Filter, or Sunshine filter effect settings. You also cannot use it with some of the other special settings such as Multiple Exposure, White Balance Bracket, Time Lapse Shot, iHandheld Night Shot, Glistening Water, Glittering Illuminations, or Soft Image of a Flower settings, or during motion picture recording.

After shooting with any of the burst options, you are likely to see for at least a few seconds the red icon indicating that the camera is writing images to the memory card; while that icon is displayed, you should not try to take any more pictures, and you should not open the battery compartment cover or otherwise interfere with the camera's operation.

### 4K Photo

The fourth icon from the left for Drive Mode, labeled 4K, gives you access to the powerful 4K Photo features. The term 4K originated with 4K video recording, which is available with the ZS100 and other modern cameras. 4K is a video format that has about 4,000 (4K) pixels

in the horizontal dimension, as opposed to the more standard HD (high-definition) formats that have about 1,920 pixels in that dimension. The 4K format is sometimes referred to as Ultra-HD.

With the ZS100 camera, a single frame of 4K video has 3840 horizontal pixels and 2160 vertical ones, for a total of about 8.3 megapixels. So, a single frame of 4K video has about the same resolution as a still image taken with aspect ratio set to 16:9 and picture size set to M. Because of the relatively high resolution of each frame of 4K video, you can use the 4K capability of the camera as another alternative for taking a high-speed burst of single images. The difference from normal burst shooting is that, with 4K Photo, the camera actually records a video sequence at its normal rate of 30 frames per second, and it can continuously record at that fast rate for up to 15 minutes, rather than the relatively short time the camera can record at a fast rate with normal burst shooting. As a result, you can record thousands of medium-resolution still images and then select the best ones from that group.

In order to use this option, as with 4K video recording, you need to use a memory card that is rated in UHS Speed Class 3.

The 4K Photo option has three sub-options with somewhat different functions, as discussed below. You select these settings in the same way as for the normal burst settings of Drive Mode. After you highlight 4K Photo on the Drive Mode menu, press the Up button to move to the screen shown in Figure 5-31, with the three sub-options.

Figure 5-31. Options Screen for 4K Photo Burst

Highlight the one you want to select and press the Menu/Set button or select the icon on the touch screen.

You also can call up the 4K Photo Mode menu by pressing the FN1 button, assuming it remains assigned to its default setting as the 4K Photo button.

### 4K Burst

The basic option for the 4K Photo feature is called 4K Burst. With this option, the camera records a 4K video sequence while you press the shutter button and hold it down. This approach is useful when you are trying to capture a burst of shots of an activity with a fairly clear duration. For example, if a group of bicycle racers is approaching your position, when the cyclists get close, you can press the shutter button and hold it down until the racers have passed out of view. With this setting, the camera can record for up to 15 minutes at a time.

### 4K Burst S/S

The second selection is 4K Burst Start and Stop. With this option, the camera starts recording its 4K video sequence when you press and release the shutter button, and it records continuously until you press and release the button again. The idea with this approach is that you are letting the camera run so it can capture a burst of shots of an unpredictable activity. For example, if you are photographing a group of geese on a pond and you want to catch them in flight, you can start the camera recording and not stop it until they have actually taken off and flown away. Here, again, the camera can record a sequence for up to 15 minutes.

### 4K Pre-burst

With this final option, the camera actually records continuously, even before you press the shutter button. It retains only a short amount of action in its memory—about one second. When you press the shutter button fully down and release it, the camera records the scene for the one second that is already in its memory and for about one additional second, resulting in a sequence lasting about two seconds. You can use this option for a situation when you believe an action is about to happen, and you don't want to miss the beginning of it. For example, if you are watching a batter at a baseball game, you can press the shutter button as soon as the bat hits the ball, and you should catch the entire swing and impact.

With this option, because the camera records continuously even when you are not pressing the shutter button, the battery is run down more quickly

than usual. So, you should not activate this setting until you are ready to use it.

All of the 4K Photo options are available for use in all still-image shooting modes except Panorama. Therefore, you can shoot these high-quality bursts in the more advanced modes, including Shutter Priority and Manual exposure. It often may be useful to select one of those modes, because you can then set the shutter speed to a fast setting, such as 1/1000 second, to increase the chance of capturing an image that is free from motion blur. Of course, you can only use a shutter speed that fast when there is plenty of light, or the ISO setting is high. But, if you can do so, you should consider that possibility. If you use autofocus with any of these settings, focus will be adjusted continuously, regardless of the AFS/AFF/AFC setting on the menus. (This is because the camera is actually recording video, and in that mode, focus always is adjusted continuously when autofocus is in use.)

With the 4K Burst and 4K Pre-burst options, no audio is recorded. However, with the 4K Burst (S/S) option, audio is recorded through the camera's built-in microphone. This audio is not played back when you play back the sequence in the camera. However, if you copy the sequence's .mp4 file to a computer and play it back, the audio track will be present. So, if you want to capture both still images and video with audio for a scene, this option can be a useful one.

### Extracting a 4K Photo Still Image

Once you have recorded a 4K Photo sequence, you need to take further steps to extract a still image from it.

Figure 5-32. 4K Photo Playback Screen

When you press the Playback button and find the sequence, press the Up button to enter 4K Photo playback mode, as indicated in Figure 5-32. The camera will display a screen with a group of image icons stacked near the bottom center of the display. With your finger, swipe along that stack to drag through the series of images, or turn the rear dial to move through the stack. A vertical yellow line will move through the progress bar at the top of the display to show how far through the group of images you have moved. If there are more than 45 images in the group, you can touch the right or left arrow icon on the screen, on either side of the stack of image icons, to move to the next or previous group. (You also can press the Menu/Set button when the arrow pointing to the next or previous group is highlighted in yellow.)

If the sequence is long, you can play through it with DVR-like controls. To do that, press the Fn2 button and the camera will display a screen like that in Figure 5-33, with playback control icons.

Figure 5-33. Playback Icons After Pressing Fn2 Button

You can touch those icons (or press the button associated with each icon, as indicated by the yellow arrow next to each icon, to play or rewind, or to advance or go backward a frame at a time. (For example, to play through the frames at normal speed, press the Up button, or touch the play icon next to the upward-facing yellow triangle.)

Once you have found the single frame you want to extract from the 4K Photo sequence as a still image, press the Menu/Set button, or touch the icon at the far right of the bottom of the screen. The camera will display the message shown in Figure 5-34, asking if you want to save the image. If you highlight and select Yes, the camera will save that frame.

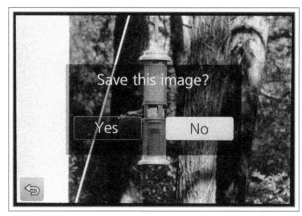

Figure 5-34. Message to Save 4K Still Image

I have found the 4K Photo feature to be of great use, especially when I am trying to capture an image of a bird at a birdfeeder. The birds come and go rapidly and unpredictably. With this option, I can set up the camera on a tripod, activate 4K Photo (S/S), and leave the camera alone for 15 minutes. When I return, the chances are good that I will have captured an image like that in Figure 5-35, showing a bird in flight.

Figure 5-35. Still Image from 4K Photo Burst

## Auto Bracket

The fifth icon from the left on the Drive Mode menu represents the Auto Bracket option, which sets up the camera to take multiple images with one press of the shutter button with different exposure settings. This option gives you an added chance of getting a usable image. If you're shooting with Raw quality, exposure is not so much of an issue, because you can adjust it later with your software, but it's always a good idea to start with an exposure that's as accurate as possible.

Also, you can use this feature to take several differently exposed shots that you can merge into a single HDR image, in which the images combine to cover a wider range of lights and darks than any single image could. This merging can be accomplished using software such as Photoshop (use the command File-Automate-Merge to HDR Pro) or a more specialized program such as PhotoAcute or Photomatix Pro. For HDR shooting, I suggest you set the interval between the exposures to the largest amount available, which is 1 EV (exposure value). If possible, you should use a tripod so all of the images will include the same area of the subject and can be easily merged in the software.

After you highlight the Auto Bracket icon, press the Up button (or touch the More Settings icon on the screen) to move the highlight to the screen for setting the number of exposures and the EV interval, as shown in Figure 5-36.

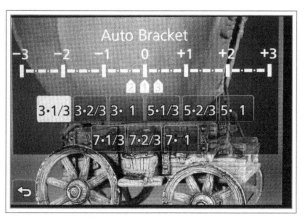

Figure 5-36. More Settings Screen for Auto Bracket

Then turn the rear dial, press the Left and Right buttons, or touch the screen icons to scroll through the nine possible options. These options let you choose three, five, or seven images, taken at EV intervals of 1/3, 2/3, or one. For example, if you select the 5•2/3 option, the camera will take five images with an interval of 2/3 stop between them. You will hear multiple shutter sounds as the exposures are recorded.

As I discussed in Chapter 4, you can use the Auto Bracket option on screen 3 of the Recording menu to set the options for Auto Bracket, including the number of images and the EV interval, as well as two other

options. With that menu item, you can set the camera to take the multiple shots either as a burst, as described above, or singly, if you want to have the camera pause after each exposure so you can evaluate the scene, adjust costumes or props, and the like. In that case, you have to press the shutter button to take each shot in the series. You also can specify the order of the images, choosing either the default order of normal exposure, followed by lower and then higher, or the order going from lowest exposure to highest.

The Auto Bracket procedure is not available with the basic Intelligent Auto mode or when shooting movies, nor with several other settings, the same as those specified earlier for burst shooting. Auto Bracket is not canceled when the camera is turned off, so be sure to cancel it when you have finished using the feature.

### Self-timer

The last icon in the line of Drive Mode options represents the self-timer. When you activate the self-timer, the camera delays for the specified number of seconds (ten or two) after you press the shutter button before taking a picture. The ten-second setting is useful when you need to place the camera on a tripod and press the shutter button, and then run around to join a group of people the camera is aimed at. The two-second setting is helpful when you need to avoid jiggling the camera by pressing the shutter button as the exposure is taken. This is the case when taking extreme closeups or other shots for which focus is sensitive.

To activate the self-timer, scroll to the last Drive Mode icon and press the Up button (or touch the More Settings icon) to select further settings. You will see the display shown in Figure 5-37, with three options.

Figure 5-37. Self-timer More Settings Screen

From left to right, these selections are ten-second self-timer; ten-second self-timer with three images taken; and two-second self-timer. Select the setting you want with the Left and Right buttons, by turning the rear dial, or by touching an icon on the screen. (You also can press the Up button repeatedly to cycle through the choices.) You can then press Menu/Set or half-press the shutter button to return to the recording screen.

The camera's display will have an icon in the upper right corner showing the current self-timer setting, as seen in Figure 5-38.

Figure 5-38. Self-timer Icon on Shooting Screen

Now you can wait as long as you want before actually taking the picture (unless the camera times out by entering Sleep Mode or you take certain other actions, such as turning on the 4K Photo option). Compose the picture and press the shutter button. The AF assist lamp, which does double duty as the self-timer lamp, will blink and the camera will beep until the shutter is automatically tripped at the end of the specified time. The beeps and blinks speed up for the last second as a warning, when the timer is set to ten seconds. For the two-second option, the camera beeps four times and blinks five times as it counts down. You can cancel the shot while the self-timer is running by pressing the Menu/Set button.

If you choose the option with which the camera takes three pictures after the ten-second timer runs, the three shots will be spaced about one second apart, so tell your subject(s) to maintain their pose until all three images have been captured.

You can choose the self-timer options from the Self Timer item on screen 3 of the Recording menu. However, to activate the self-timer, you still have to

select its icon from the Drive Mode menu. The self-timer can be set to remain active even after the camera has been powered off and back on. To make that setting, go to screen 4 of the Setup menu and set the Self Timer Auto Off option to Off. If, instead, you set that option to On, the self-timer will be deactivated when the camera is powered off. I use the two-second self-timer often, because I do a lot of shooting from a tripod and I like to avoid camera shake whenever possible. Therefore, I usually leave that menu option turned off, so the self-timer will be active when I turn the camera on for a new shooting session.

You cannot use the self-timer option with multiple images when the camera is set for White Balance Bracket, Post Focus, or Multiple Exposure, when the shutter speed is set to T for time exposure, or when Simultaneous Record Without Filter is turned on. You cannot use the self-timer at all when recording motion pictures or using the 4K Photo or Time Lapse Shot options.

Besides activating Drive Mode, the Down button has various other duties. For example, pressing this button takes you to the screen for fine-tuning a white balance setting, and it provides access to the screen with options for setting the location of focus areas from the AF Mode screen. When the camera is in playback mode, pressing the Down button initiates the process to upload images by Wi-Fi, as discussed in Chapter 9. When you are playing a slide show or a movie, the Down button acts like a Stop button on a DVR to stop the playback completely. When you use the Video Divide function from the Playback menu, the down button is used to "cut" a movie at your chosen dividing point. When you are viewing a group of images that were taken with the super-high burst, Time Lapse, or Stop Motion Animation options, you can press the Down button to view the images individually rather than as a group.

### Center Button: Menu/Set

The last button to discuss in the cursor buttons group is the button in the center of the pattern, labeled Menu/Set. You use this button to enter and exit the menu system, and to make or confirm selections of menu items or other settings. In addition, when you are playing a motion picture and have paused it, you can press the Menu/Set button to select a still image to be saved from the motion picture recording.

## Function Buttons

The ZS100 has four physical function buttons, labeled Fn1, Fn2, Fn3, and Fn4. (There also are five virtual buttons called Fn5 through Fn9 that can appear on the touch screen; I will discuss them in connection with the touch screen, later in this chapter.)

Each of the four physical buttons has an assigned function by default, and each button also can be programmed to handle any one of a large number of possible operations when the camera is in recording mode. Three of the buttons also can be assigned a function for use in playback mode.

To program a button for a new assignment, you use the Function Button Set option on screen 7 of the Custom menu, which is discussed in Chapter 7. You also can press and hold the button for a few seconds to pop up the menu for changing the button's assignment.

Some of the items that can be assigned to these buttons are not available through any menu or other control, while some of them are options that can also be selected through the menu system or through another control. I will discuss all of those possible assignments later in this chapter. First, I will discuss the pre-assigned duties of the buttons.

### Fn1/4K Photo Button

The Fn1 button, located at the far upper right of the camera's back, is assigned by default as the 4K Photo button. With that assignment, when you press the button the camera displays a menu for selecting one of the 4K Photo burst modes, or turning 4K Photo off. Ordinarily, you can reach this menu by pressing the Down button to bring up the Drive Mode menu, and then pressing the Up button when 4K is highlighted on the Drive menu.

The Fn1 button also has some other miscellaneous duties. For example, when you are using the Multiple Exposure or Time Lapse Shot option on screen 5 of the Recording menu, you can press this button to end the operation. When you are recording a 4K Photo sequence using the 4K (S/S) option, you can press the Fn1 button to add a marker to the sequence at any point. The button also is used to change the size or position of the crop frame in the 4K live cropping operation. In any of these cases, the Fn1 button will not be available for any other assigned function.

### Fn2/Post Focus Button

The Fn2 button is located to the left of the Playback button and to the upper left of the arrangement of cursor buttons. With its default assignment, pressing this button brings up the brief menu shown in Figure 5-39, allowing you to turn the Post Focus feature on or off. The other way to get access to this menu is through the Post Focus item on screen 4 of the Recording menu, which I discussed in Chapter 4.

Figure 5-39. Post Focus Menu from Pressing Fn2 Button

The Fn2 button also has some miscellaneous functions that are permanently assigned to it. When you are setting up the autofocus area using the Custom Multi option of AF Mode, in which you select one or more of 49 possible focus zones, you press this button to lock in your selections after highlighting the desired zones. When you are using the 4K burst playback screen to select a still image from a 4K Photo burst sequence, you can press the Fn2 button to display the slide view screen while the sequence is paused. When you are using the Post Focus feature, you can press this button to highlight the in-focus part of the image with focus peaking.

### Fn3/Delete/Q.Menu/Cancel Button

The Fn3 button, located to the lower left of the cursor buttons, has several functions. First, as indicated by the trash can icon on the button, it serves as the Delete button. When the camera is set to playback mode, press this button while an image is displayed, and you are presented with several options on the camera's display: Delete Single, Delete Multi, and Delete All, as shown in Figure 5-40.

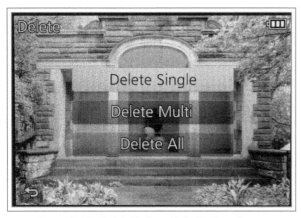

Figure 5-40. Delete Button Main Options Screen

Use the direction buttons, the rear dial, or the touch screen to navigate to your choice. If you select Delete Single, the camera will display a confirmation screen; if you confirm the action, the camera will delete the currently displayed image (unless it is protected, as discussed in Chapter 6).

If you select Delete Multi, the camera presents you with a display of recent pictures, up to nine at a time per screen, as shown in Figure 5-41.

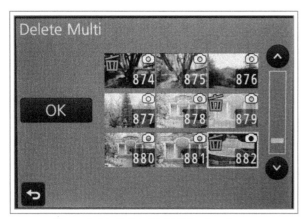

Figure 5-41. Delete Multi Selection Screen

You can scroll through these thumbnail images and press the Menu/Set button to mark any picture you want to be included in the group for deletion, up to 100 in total. You can press Menu/Set a second time to unmark a picture for deletion. When you have finished marking pictures for deletion, move the highlight to the OK block at the left of the display and press Menu/Set to start the deletion process; the camera will ask you to confirm, and one more press of Menu/Set will delete the marked images.

The Delete All option deletes all images on the memory card, unless you have marked some as Favorites and choose to delete all except Favorites (indicated by stars), as prompted by the camera. You can interrupt a deletion process with the Menu/Set button, though some images may have been deleted before you press the button.

The Fn3 button also serves as a Cancel button, as indicated by the backward-curving arrow below the button. When you are viewing menu screens, you can press this button to cancel out of a selection or other event, such as the use of the Format command on the Setup menu to erase and re-format a memory card. When the Fn3 button can be used to cancel an action and return to a previous screen, the camera displays the curving arrow, as shown in Figure 5-41, for example.

In addition, the Fn3 button acts as the Quick Menu or Q.Menu button, as indicated by the label below the button. In this capacity, the button has only one function—to activate the Quick Menu. I discussed that menu system in Chapter 4. Once you press this button while the shooting screen is displayed, you have instant access to several of the more important settings on the camera. You can customize the available choices using the Quick Menu option on screen 7 of the Custom menu, as described in Chapter 7. If you assign the Fn3 button to a new function through the Function Button Set option on screen 7 of the Custom menu, the button will no longer call up the Quick Menu.

### Fn4/LVF Button

The Fn4 button is located just to the right of the electronic viewfinder's eye sensor window. As indicated by its label, this button is assigned by default to control the operation of the electronic viewfinder. Pressing the button repeatedly calls up the three possible settings for the LVF/Monitor Switch setting, which is an option found under the Eye Sensor item on screen 8 of the Custom menu. The three settings for that item are LVF/Monitor Auto, LVF, and Monitor. With the first option, the camera automatically switches the view from the monitor to the viewfinder when your head (or another object) comes close to the eye sensor, located to the right of the viewfinder. With the LVF setting, the view stays in the viewfinder. With the Monitor setting, the view stays on the LCD monitor. It is convenient to be able to switch this setting just by pressing this button, rather than digging through the menu system to find it.

## Assigning Functions to Function Buttons

As I noted above, you can assign any one of numerous functions to any of the four physical function buttons, Fn1, Fn2, Fn3, and Fn4, using the Function Button Set option on screen 7 of the Custom menu. You also can bring up that menu option by pressing and holding any of the four physical function buttons for about two seconds.

The function you assign to a button will be carried out whenever you press the assigned button. Of course, the function will be carried out only if the present context permits. For example, if you assign the Fn1 button to activate the HDR option, and then press the Fn1 button while the camera is in Intelligent Auto mode, nothing will happen, because the HDR option is not available in that recording mode.

Similarly, if you assign the Fn1 button to activate the level gauge option, and then press that button while using the Time Lapse Shot option from screen 5 of the Recording menu, the level gauge will not appear, because the Fn1 button is permanently assigned to interrupt the Time Lapse Shot operation.

Each of these four buttons can be assigned an option for use when the camera is in recording mode. Three of the buttons—Fn1, Fn2, and Fn4—also can be assigned one of a few functions for use in playback mode. A button can have both assignments at the same time, though, of course, only one of the options can be used at a time because the camera has to be in recording or playback mode for the given function to operate. The following table lists the functions that can be assigned to each button for use in recording mode. The buttons listed in parentheses are the default assignments for the listed functions.

**Table 5-3.** **Possible Function Button Assignments for Recording Mode**

| Menu & Screen No./Normal Control Used for Function | Function |
| --- | --- |
| Recording 3 | 4K Photo Mode (Fn1) |
| Setup 1 | Wi-Fi (Fn5) |
| --- | Q.Menu (Fn3) |
| Custom 8 | LVF/Monitor Switch (Fn4) |
| Custom 1 | AF/AE Lock |
| Custom 1 | AF-On |
| --- | Preview |
| --- | One Push AE |
| Touch Screen | Touch AE |
| Display Button | Level Gauge (Fn6) |
| --- | Focus Area Set |
| --- | Cursor Button Lock |
| Recording 1 | Photo Style |
| Recording 1 | Filter Select |
| Recording 1 | Aspect Ratio |
| Recording 1 | Picture Size |
| Recording 1 | Quality |
| Recording 2 | Sensitivity |
| Recording 2 | AF Mode |
| Recording 2 | AFS/AFF/AFC |
| Recording 2 | Metering Mode |
| Recording 2 | Burst Rate |
| Recording 3 | Auto Bracket |
| Recording 3 | Self Timer |
| Recording 3 | Highlight Shadow |
| Recording 3 | i.Dynamic |
| Recording 4 | i.Resolution |
| Recording 4 | Post Focus (Fn2) |
| Recording 4 | HDR |
| Recording 5 | Shutter Type |
| Recording 6 | Flash Mode |
| Recording 6 | Flash Adjustment |
| Recording 7 | i.Zoom |
| Recording 7 | Digital Zoom |
| Recording 8 | Stabilizer |
| Up Button | Exposure Compensation |
| Right Button | White Balance |
| Recording | Focus Mode |
| Down Button | Drive Mode |
| --- | Restore to Default |
| Creative Video 1 | 4K Live Cropping |
| Creative Video 1 | Snap Movie (Fn8) |
| Creative Video 1,2 | Motion Picture Settings |
| Custom 1 | Silent Mode |
| Custom 4 | Peaking |
| Custom 4 | Histogram (Fn7) |
| Custom 4 | Guide Line |
| Custom 5 | Zebra Pattern |
| Custom 5 | Monochrome Live View |
| Custom 6 | Recording Area |
| Custom 7 | Zoom Lever |
| Custom 8 | Touch Screen |

There are three functions that cannot be assigned to the virtual function buttons, Fn5 through Fn9: LVF Monitor Switch, AF/AE Lock, and AF-On. Also, the virtual buttons cannot be used when the viewfinder is in use. The Fn9 button does not have a default assignment, unlike the other eight buttons.

Most of the settings in Table 5-3 are self-explanatory; they are options that also can be activated from one of the menus or with a dedicated control. For example, if a button is assigned to the Photo Style option, pressing the button calls up a menu or settings screen for that option from screen 1 of the Recording menu. The screen that is called up by pressing the function button may look different from the screen that is called up from the menu, but it will let you make the basic selection of the menu option. The level gauge is normally activated by pressing the Display button until a screen with that item appears. I will not discuss those assignments here; you can find details about those settings in the chapters that discuss the menu systems and physical controls.

However, there are several possible button assignments that are not found on the regular menus and are not normally activated by any control button. I will discuss those functions below.

### Preview

The first non-menu setting, Preview, lets you see the effects of the current aperture and shutter speed settings on the final image before you take a picture. Ordinarily, when you aim the camera at a subject, the live view on the camera's display is set to provide a clear view of the scene, without giving effect to the current settings.

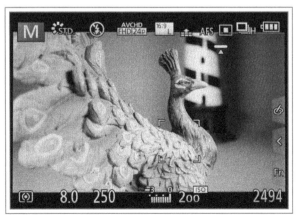

Figure 5-42. Preview Turned Off

For example, suppose you are using Manual exposure mode for an indoor shot of two objects at different distances. Suppose you have set the aperture to f/8.0 to keep both items in focus with a broad depth of field and you have set the shutter speed to 1/250 second. If you aim the camera at the subjects, you will see a view like that in Figure 5-42, which does not show the effects of these settings.

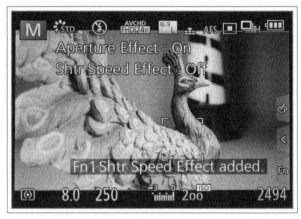

Figure 5-43. Preview After Fn1 Button Pressed Once

Now, if Preview is assigned to the Fn1 button, press that button once and you will see a screen like that in Figure 5-43. For this view, the Preview feature has caused the camera to close the aperture down to the actual setting of f/8.0, which shows the effect of the broad depth of field, bringing the background into sharper focus. The message on the screen, Fn1 Shtr Speed Effect Added, means that the camera is currently displaying the effect of the aperture setting; if you press Fn1 again, the camera will also display the effect of the shutter speed setting.

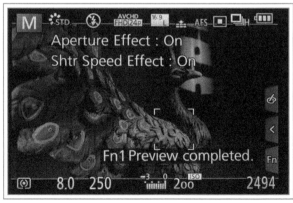

Figure 5-44. Preview After Fn1 Button Pressed Twice

After you press Fn1 the second time, the recording screen will look like Figure 5-44. In this case, the camera is displaying the effects of both the aperture and shutter speed settings. The recording screen is quite dark, which shows that using the current shutter speed and aperture would result in a dark image. In addition, the message on the screen indicates that you can press Fn1 to end the preview.

If you have turned on the Constant Preview option through screen 5 of the Custom menu, the Preview function will not work in Manual exposure mode, because the preview will already be in effect. (The Constant Preview option works only in Manual exposure mode.) You can change the settings while the preview screen is displayed, to see how the changes affect the image.

### One Push AE

This next setting gives you a quick way to set the camera to achieve a normal exposure. It is of use only when the camera has been unable to expose the image properly given the settings you have made, including the aperture and shutter speed. For example, if you are using Shutter Priority mode and have set the shutter speed to 1/640 second with ISO set to 80, if conditions are fairly dark the camera may not be able to expose the image within a normal range. In that case, the aperture and shutter speed values will blink red on the display. At that point, press the function button assigned to One Push AE and the camera will change its settings to correct the exposure problem. When I tried these settings in a fairly dark room, the camera changed the shutter speed to 1/13 second, which produced a normal exposure.

I find this setting to be somewhat odd, because it is difficult to think when it would be useful. If you want the camera to make the settings, you can always use a mode such as Intelligent Auto or even Program, and it very likely will be able to find settings that will expose the image properly. But, if you are just learning how to use the camera and feel it would be helpful to have this extra safety valve to rescue an image in a difficult lighting scenario, you might want to give it a try. It is available only in the PASM modes and Creative Video mode.

### Touch AE

This option can also be activated by touching the Touch AE icon on the touch screen tabs, as I will discuss later in this chapter. If you assign Touch AE to a function button, you can turn on this option with one button push. Then, just touch the LCD display on the subject you want the camera to optimize exposure for. The

camera will move a small blue cross over the area you touched, as shown in Figure 5-45.

Figure 5-45. Blue Cross for Touch AE

Then press the Set icon or press the Menu/Set button to accept the new exposure setting. You can press the Display button or touch the DISP. Reset icon to reset the exposure point to the center of the display.

### Focus Area Set

If you assign this option to a function button, when you press the button, the camera will immediately display a screen for adjusting the current focus setting. The actual result of pressing the button will depend on the current setting. For example, if you are using autofocus with the 1-Area AF Mode setting, pressing the assigned button will place the focus frame on the display with arrows, ready to be moved using the direction buttons. If the current AF Mode setting is Custom Multi, pressing the assigned button will call up the screen for selecting the pattern of focus zones. If you are currently using manual focus, pressing the button will call up a screen for adjusting the MF Assist area.

This option can be useful if you often adjust the area where the camera focuses, so you don't have to go through extra steps to reach the screen to adjust that area.

### Cursor Button Lock

When this function is assigned to a button, pressing that button locks out the operation of the four direction buttons and the Menu/Set button while the camera is in recording mode. You might want to use this feature if you don't want the current settings to be disturbed by the accidental press of a button. Once you have pressed this button, you will not be able to use the menu system in recording mode or make any settings using the buttons until you press the assigned function button again to cancel the lock. The camera will display a Cursor Button Lock message at the top of the screen if you press a locked button.

The lock remains in place even when the camera is powered off and then on, so, if you find you cannot use the Menu/Set button when the camera is first turned on, try pressing the function buttons to see if the direction buttons and Menu/Set button have been locked with this feature.

### Restore to Default

If you choose this option for a given function button, that button will be restored to its default setting. Those defaults are shown on Table 5-3.

#### Assigning Option to Function Button for Playback Mode

As I noted earlier, the camera also lets you assign a function to three of the function buttons—Fn1, Fn2, and Fn4—for use when the camera is in playback mode. The functions that can be assigned to any of those buttons are the following:

- Favorite
- Print Set
- Protect
- Delete Single
- Off
- Restore to Default

By default, the Fn2 button is assigned to Favorite, and the other two buttons are assigned to Off, which means they have no assignment. I have not found a need to use this capability, but it is available if you want to use it.

## LCD MONITOR

The ZS100 is equipped with an LCD monitor that has a diagonal dimension of three inches or 76mm, with a resolution of about one million dots. It does not have the ability to tilt or swivel, but it does have an excellent set of features as a touch screen. I will provide an overview of those features here. I will also discuss them as I cover the various menu options and other camera functions that rely on the touch screen.

### Using the Touch Screen

There are a few basic pointers that can be helpful in understanding the use of the touch screen. First, the Touch Settings menu option, on screen 8 of the Custom menu, controls several important touch screen settings. I will discuss the details in Chapter 7. If the Touch Screen sub-option of Touch Settings is turned off, there will be no touch screen functions available. If the Touch Tab sub-option is turned off, there will be basic touch options, but none of the special tabs that appear at the right edge of the shooting screen. In addition, the Touch AF and Touch Pad AF sub-options control other aspects of the camera's touch screen functions.

Second, watch for icons that appear to be touchable, and try them out. It can't hurt to experiment, and you will eventually come to realize which icons on the screen are responsive to your touch and which ones are there only to provide information.

Third, don't forget that the touch screen operates in playback mode and with menu screens, not just with recording functions. In this discussion, though, I will concentrate on using the touch screen in recording mode.

**Figure 5-46.** Touch Screen Icons in Program Mode

Figure 5-46 shows the shooting screen in Program mode, with the touch screen settings turned on. At the right edge of the screen are three icons. From the top, these are the touch icons for controlling filter effects, for activating the touch tab, and for getting access to the virtual function buttons. In this image, all three of those icons are white.

Figure 5-47. Shooting Screen After Touching Fx Icon

Figure 5-49. Shooting Screen with Touch Zoom Controls

If you touch the top icon, the icons change, as shown in Figure 5-47. You will now see a larger filter effect icon with an X beside it. That icon means that filter effects are turned off. If you touch that icon, the currently selected filter effect, in this case Impressive Art, turns on, and the icons change again. To change the effect, touch the IART icon, and the camera will display a screen for selecting a different filter effect. When you are done with filter effects, touch the top icon again to turn off the effect. Then touch the yellow filter effect icon to collapse the touch tab area.

The second of the three icons at the right of the screen is the left-facing arrow, which is the touch tab icon. When you touch that icon, the display changes as seen in Figure 5-48, to show various items in the touch tab area. From the top, these are the touch zoom icon, the touch shutter icon, the touch AE icon, and the peaking icon.

Figure 5-48. Shooting Screen After Touching Left Arrow

If you touch the touch zoom icon, it will turn yellow to show that it is active and the camera will display the touch zoom controls, as shown in Figure 5-49. You can then touch those controls to zoom the lens in or out.

Touch the yellow icon again to turn off touch zoom and get access to other items in the touch tab area.

The icon below the touch zoom icon is the touch shutter icon. If you touch it, it turns yellow to show that it is active. You can then touch the screen on any object you want the camera to direct its focus on, and the camera will take a picture without your having to press the shutter button. Touch the yellow icon to turn touch shutter off.

The next icon is the touch AE icon. When you touch that icon, a small blue cross appears on the display, as shown earlier in Figure 5-45. Move that cross with your finger over the subject where you want the exposure to be evaluated, or just touch that area, then touch the Set icon. Touch the touch AE off icon at the left of the screen to cancel touch AE.

Finally, you can press the Fn icon at the bottom of the touch tab area to open up the area for the virtual function buttons, Fn5 through Fn9.

Figure 5-50. Virtual Function Buttons on Shooting Screen

The display will then look like Figure 5-50, with the icons for those buttons visible. Touch any one of those icons to activate the function assigned to it. Earlier in this chapter I discussed how to assign a function to a function button. In this illustration, Fn5 is assigned to Wi-Fi, Fn6 to the level gauge, Fn7 to the histogram option, and Fn8 to snap movie. Fn9 is not assigned. When you have finished using the virtual function buttons, press the yellow Fn icon to collapse the Fn tab.

I will discuss the various other touch screen functions in connection with the appropriate menu items and camera operations as they come up in later chapters of this book.

## Items on Front of Camera

### CONTROL RING

The control ring, shown in Figure 5-51, is the unmarked ring around the lens. This control adds a great deal of convenience to the operation of the ZS100 through its ability to be customized according to your preferences.

Figure 5-51. Items on Front of Camera

Whenever the camera is set to manual focus mode, the control ring is used to adjust focus. Just turn the ring to adjust the distance at which the camera sets its focus. The display will vary according to settings you make for manual focus through the Custom menu.

When the camera is set to an autofocus mode, the control ring can control other options, according to how it is set through the Ring/Dial Set option on screen 8 of the Custom menu, as discussed in Chapter 7.

If you use the default setting, the ring controls various functions depending on the shooting mode. Table 5-4

lists the ring's default functions for each shooting mode.

Table 5-4.   **Default Functions of Control Ring**

| Shooting Mode | Control Ring Default Function |
|---|---|
| Intelligent Auto | Step Zoom |
| Program | Program Shift |
| Aperture Priority | Adjusts Aperture |
| Shutter Priority | Adjusts Shutter Speed |
| Manual Exposure | Adjusts Aperture |
| Panorama | Selects Filter Effects |
| Scene | No Function, with 2 exceptions below |
| Scene – Appetizing Food Setting | Adjusts Aperture |
| Scene – Artistic Nightscape Setting | Adjusts Shutter Speed |
| Creative Control | Selects Filter Effects |
| Creative Video | Adjusts Aperture or Shutter Speed if Exposure Mode Permits |

If you use the menu option to select a setting other than the default, the ring can control a single setting, such as ISO, zoom, white balance, or filter effects. The following list sets forth the possible assignments for the control ring.

- Default (see Table 5-4, above)
- Zoom
- Step Zoom
- Exposure Compensation
- ISO Sensitivity
- White Balance
- AF Mode
- Focus Mode
- Drive Mode
- Photo Style
- Filter Effect
- Aspect Ratio
- Highlight Shadow
- i.Dynamic

- ° i.Resolution
- ° Flash Mode
- ° Flash Adjustment
- ° Off (Not Set)

If you select an option other than Default, that setting will take effect for all recording modes, except when manual focus is in effect. With manual focus, the control ring always controls focus. If you select Highlight Shadow for the control ring, it will also be assigned to the rear dial, and vice-versa.

All of the settings that are available for the control ring are self-explanatory, except step zoom, which is discussed below.

### Step Zoom

With this feature turned on, when you turn the control ring the lens zooms, but only to a series of specific focal lengths: 25mm, 28mm, 35mm, 50mm, 70mm, 90mm, 135mm, 160mm, 200mm, and 250mm. (Additional values are available if any of the extended zoom settings are turned on.) This feature allows you to select one of these specific settings easily. If you want to zoom the lens continuously instead, you can use the zoom lever, which will select any focal length, not just the designated steps. (You can set the zoom lever to use step zoom through the Zoom Lever option on screen 7 of the Custom menu, if you want.)

## AF Assist/Self-timer Lamp

This small lamp gives off a bright reddish light when it carries out either of its two functions. First, when the camera is set to use autofocus, this light turns on when lighting is dim, in order to assist the autofocus mechanism in observing the scene and detecting focus points. You can control that behavior using the AF Assist Lamp item on screen 3 of the Custom menu. If you set that option to Off, the lamp will never turn on for autofocus assistance. You might want to make that setting in order to avoid disturbing a child or pet, or to avoid drawing attention to your camera. Even with that option set to turn the lamp off, the lamp will still illuminate when the self-timer is used. The lamp will blink several times during the self-timer countdown.

# Chapter 6: Playback

In this chapter I'll discuss the playback operations of the ZS100, including the features on the Playback menu and options for printing images directly from the camera to a printer.

## Normal Playback

First, you should be aware of the setting for Auto Review on screen 7 of the Custom menu. This setting determines whether and for how long the image stays on the screen for review when you take a new picture. If your major concern is to check images right after they are taken, this setting is all you need to use. As discussed in Chapter 7, you can leave Auto Review turned off or set it to one, two, three, four, or five seconds, or to Hold. If you choose Hold, the image will stay on the display until you press the shutter button halfway to return to recording mode.

To control how images are viewed later on, you need to use the options available in playback mode. For ordinary review of images, press the Playback button, marked by a small triangle, to the upper right of the cursor buttons. Once you press that button, the camera is in playback mode, and you will see the most recent image that was viewed in playback mode. To move back through older images, press the Left button or turn the rear dial to the left. To see more recent images, use the Right button or turn the rear dial to the right. To speed through the images, hold down the Left or Right button.

You also can use the touch screen to scroll through images and videos, if the Touch Settings item on screen 8 of the Custom menu has Touch Screen turned on. Just drag across the screen with your finger in either direction to scroll backward or forward through the images. You can adjust the speed of this scrolling using the Touch Scroll option on screen 8 of the Custom menu.

## Index View and Enlarging Images

When you are viewing an individual image in playback mode, as shown in Figure 6-1, press the zoom lever once to the left, and you will see a screen showing 12 images, one of which is outlined by a yellow frame, as shown in Figure 6-2. You also can touch the index screen icon, located above the trash can icon on the individual image.

Figure 6-1. Single Image on Screen in Playback Mode

Figure 6-2. Index Screen with 12 Images

Press the zoom lever to the left once more, or touch the index screen icon in the lower left of the index screen, to see an index screen with 30 images.

You can press the Menu/Set button to view the outlined image, or you can move through the images and videos on the index screen by pressing the four direction buttons or by turning the rear dial. You can also drag on the touch screen to scroll the images.

From the 30-image index screen, one more press of the zoom lever to the left or a touch of the CAL icon brings up a calendar display, as seen in Figure 6-3.

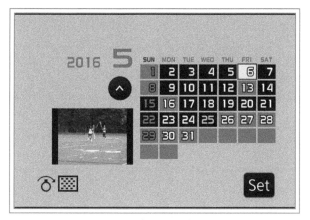

Figure 6-3. Calendar Index Screen

On that screen, you can move the highlight to any date with a dark background and press the Menu/Set button or touch the Set icon to bring up an index view with images from that date.

When you are viewing a single image or video, one press of the zoom lever to the right enlarges the image (or first video frame). You will briefly see a display in the upper right corner showing a green frame with an inset yellow frame that represents the area of the image that is filling the screen in enlarged view, as shown in Figure 6-4. When that inset frame disappears, you will just see the enlarged image with a few icons.

Figure 6-4. Enlarged Image in Playback Mode

If you press the zoom lever to the right repeatedly, the image will be enlarged to greater levels, up to 16 times normal. While it is magnified, you can scroll in it with the four direction buttons or by dragging on the touch screen. The yellow inset frame will reappear and will move around inside the green frame. To reduce the image size again, press the zoom lever to the left as many times as necessary or press the Menu/Set button to revert immediately to normal size. To move to other images while the display is magnified, turn the rear dial.

You can enlarge an image to two times normal size by tapping on the touch screen twice. If you tap twice again, an enlarged image returns to normal size.

## The Playback Menu

The Playback menu is represented by a triangle icon that turns green when highlighted. It is the last icon at the bottom of the line of menu icons at the left of the main menu screen, as seen in Figure 6-5.

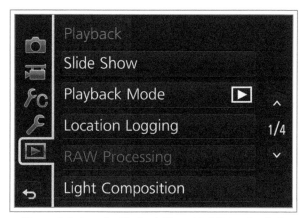

Figure 6-5. Icon for Playback Menu Highlighted at Left

This menu has four screens of options that control how playback operates and that give you access to special features. The first menu screen is shown in Figure 6-6.

Figure 6-6. Screen 1 of Playback Menu

## SLIDE SHOW

The first option on the Playback menu is Slide Show. Navigate to this option, then press Menu/Set or the Right button (or press the menu option on the touch screen), and you are presented with the choices All, Picture Only, Video Only, 4K Photo, Post Focus, Category Selection, and Favorite, as shown in Figure 6-7.

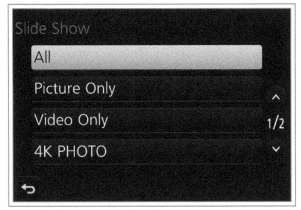

Figure 6-7. Slide Show Main Options Screen

(The Post Focus, Category Selection, and Favorite options are on the second screen of this menu item. The Favorite option is available for selection only if you have already marked some images as Favorites. That option is discussed later in this chapter.) Following are details for each of these choices.

### [Play] All

If you choose All from the Slide Show menu, you are taken to a menu with the choices Start, Effect, and Setup, shown in Figure 6-8.

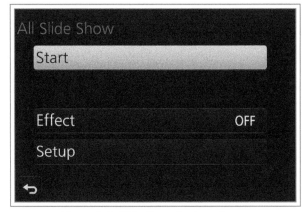

Figure 6-8. Slide Show Settings Screen

You can choose Start to begin the slide show, or you can select Effect or Setup first and make some selections. Setup lets you choose a duration of one, two, three, or five seconds for each still image, but you can only set the duration if Effect is set to Off. If you turn on any effect, the camera will automatically set the duration to two seconds per still image.

You can also choose to set Sound to Off, Audio, Music, or Auto, but only if some effect is selected. If no effect is selected, the Sound option can be set only to Audio or Off. With Off, no sound is played. With the Auto setting, the camera's music is played for still images, and motion pictures have their own audio played. The Music setting plays music as background for all images and movies, and the Audio setting plays only the movies' audio tracks.

Also, you can set Repeat On or Off. Note that you can set a duration even when there are videos included along with still images; the duration value will apply for the still pictures, but not for the videos, which will play at their normal, full length.

For effects, you have the following choice of styles: Natural, Slow, Swing, Urban, or turning effects off altogether. If you choose Urban, the camera not only plays "urban" music, it uses a somewhat more dramatic visual style, with a variety of transitions, including converting some color images to black and white. So choose Urban only if you don't mind having a slide show with altered images. If you choose Category Selection for your choice of images and videos to play, then the camera gives you another choice of effect: Auto, in which the camera chooses an appropriate effect according to the category of each given image or video. (Categories are discussed later in this chapter.)

Once the slide show has begun, you can control it using the direction buttons as a set of playback controls, the same as with playing motion pictures. The Up button controls play/pause; the Left and Right buttons move back or forward one slide; and the Down button is like a stop button; pressing it ends the slide show. The rear dial adjusts audio volume. A small display showing these controls appears briefly on the screen at the start of the show. After it disappears, you can press the Display button to make it appear again. You also can use touch screen icons to control playback.

### [Play] Picture Only/Video Only

These next two options for playing the slide show are self-explanatory; instead of playing all images and videos, you can play either just still images or just videos. If you select videos, the camera will also include photos recorded in 4K burst mode or with the Post Focus feature. For Post Focus, though, the camera will only include one, well-focused image for each group of images.

The only difference between the options for these two choices is that, as you might expect, you cannot select an effect or a duration setting for a slide show of only videos; the slide show will just play all of the videos on the memory card, one after the other. You can use the Setup option to choose whether to play the videos with their audio tracks or with the sound turned off.

### 4K Photo/Post Focus

With these two options, the camera plays back images taken in 4K Photo mode or Post Focus mode, as indicated. For Post Focus, the camera plays only a single well-focused image from each group.

### Category Selection

Rather than having the slide show play all of the pictures and/or videos available, with the Category Selection option you can set the camera to select the items for the show by category. You don't get to place your pictures and videos in categories of your own making; the camera has a pre-defined list of ten groups that it considers "categories," and it plays all of the images or videos in whichever single category you select. Note that some of the categories overlap with others—that is, an image might be in more than one category. Here are the categories:

- All images and videos that used Face Recognition; if you select this option, the camera will prompt you to select a particular person whose face was recognized.

- All images and videos taken with scene detection of Portrait, Night Portrait, or Baby, or with portrait-related Scene mode settings.

- All images and videos taken with scene detection of Scenery or Sunset or with scenery-related settings of Scene mode.

- All images and videos taken with scene detection of Night Portrait, Night Scenery, or Handheld Night Shot, or taken with night-related settings of Scene mode.

- All images and videos taken with the Clear Sports Shot setting of Scene mode.

- All images and videos taken with scene detection of Food, or with the food-related settings of Scene mode.

- All images with a Travel Date.

- All images taken with the SH burst shooting setting.

- All images taken with the Time Lapse Shot feature and videos created from them.

- All images taken with the Stop Motion Animation feature and videos created from them.

### Favorite

The final option for selecting the images to play in a slide show is to play all of the images and videos that you have marked as Favorites. In order to use this option, you have to have first used the Favorite setting on the Playback menu to mark one or more images or videos as Favorites. I will discuss that process later in this chapter.

## PLAYBACK MODE

The second option on the Playback menu, Playback Mode, is similar to the Slide Show option, in that it provides several choices for which images and videos are played. This option, though, controls which items are viewed when you are viewing them outside of a slide show. The ZS100 offers seven choices for this option:

Normal Play, Picture Only, Video Only, 4K Photo, Post Focus, Category Play, and Favorite Play.

Here are the details for these choices:

### Normal Play

Normal Play is the playback mode for ordinary display of your images. This mode is automatically selected whenever the camera is first turned on or switched into playback mode. With this mode, you scroll through the images individually using the Left and Right buttons, by turning the rear dial left and right, or by scrolling the touch screen with your fingers. Whenever an image is displayed on the screen, you can press the Fn3/Delete button to initiate the deletion process, and choose to delete a single image, multiple ones, or all images. You can press and hold the Left or Right button to speed through the images at a steady pace. You can control the speed of scrolling with the touch screen through the Touch Scroll option on screen 8 of the Custom menu.

You can enlarge an image by pressing the zoom lever repeatedly to the right, with magnification ranging from two times up to 16 times, as discussed earlier. Reverse the process by moving the lever to the left. If you then keep pressing the lever to the left, you will reach screens that display 12 images, then 30 images, then the Calendar display, from which you can select images from any date on which images were taken. You also can double-tap the screen to enlarge an image to two times normal, or to return it to normal size when enlarged. You also can use touch screen icons to reach the index and calendar screens.

### Other Playback Modes

The Picture Only, Video Only, 4K Photo, Post Focus, Category Play, and Favorite Play options work for playback just as they do for the Slide Show option, as discussed earlier.

## Location Logging

The next option on the Playback menu provides a way for you to add location information to the images saved to your memory card, using a smartphone. To do this, you have to first establish a Wi-Fi connection between the ZS100 and the smartphone; I discuss that process in Chapter 9. Essentially, to do that you need to use the Wi-Fi option on screen 1 of the Setup menu or press a button assigned to the Wi-Fi option. (The Fn5 virtual function button is assigned that option by default.) You

also need to download the Panasonic Image App to your smartphone. Once the Wi-Fi connection is established, follow the steps below.

1. Open the Panasonic Image App on the smartphone and, if the app is not on the Home screen, select the Home icon, on the left at the bottom of the screen, as shown in Figure 6-9. On the Home screen, shown in Figure 6-10, select Geotagging.

Figure 6-9. Home Icon at Bottom Left of Panasonic Image App

Figure 6-10. Home Screen of Panasonic Image App

2. On the Geotagging screen, shown in Figure 6-11, select the Time Sync option, which has an icon that looks like a clock.

Figure 6-11. Geotagging Screen of Panasonic Image App

3. When you select that icon and confirm by selecting Synchronize on the next screen, shown in Figure 6-12, the camera will synchronize its time with the smartphone so that the GPS data the phone receives will match up to the photos taken at the same time. Once the synchronization is complete, you can disconnect the camera from the smartphone by terminating the Wi-Fi connection.

Figure 6-12. Time Sync Screen of Panasonic Image App

Figure 6-13. Screen for Getting Location Data

4. On the smartphone, select the Start Geotagging option, as shown in Figure 6-11. The camera will display the screen shown in Figure 6-13, saying it is getting location data. Leave the smartphone in this status while you take photos with the ZS100. The smartphone will be recording location data that can later be synced with the images you are capturing at the same time.

5. After you have finished taking photos with the camera, select the Stop Geotagging option on the smartphone. Re-establish the Wi-Fi connection between the camera and the smartphone. Then go back to the Geotagging screen on the smartphone and select the Batch Send option, with an icon that looks like an arrow going to a camera, as shown in Figures 6-13 and 6-14.

6. When the app asks if it should send location data to the camera, as shown in Figure 6-14, say yes. After it sends the data, you can answer yes to the question whether the data can be erased. When the app asks if it should save the location information to the picture files, choose the Write option. The smartphone will display a screen saying Saving Location Data and the camera's display will say Writing Location Data. When that operation is complete, you can terminate the Wi-Fi connection.

Figure 6-14. Batch Send Option for Geotagging

7. When you load the images from your memory card into appropriate software, such as Adobe Bridge, you will see the latitude and longitude information recorded in the metadata for the images, as seen in Figure 6-15.

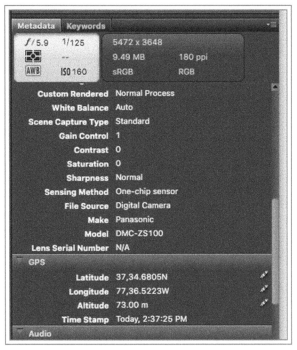

Figure 6-15. Latitude and Longitude Shown in Metadata for Image

8. You can use that information in mapping software, or in general-purpose software such as Adobe Lightroom, to map the locations of your images, or you can copy the GPS data into a resource such

as Google Maps to view the locations. Images that have had location data written to them will have the letters GPS at the top in playback mode, on the detailed display screen.

## RAW PROCESSING

The Raw Processing option gives you tools for processing your Raw files right in the camera. As I discussed in Chapter 4, the Raw format gives you great flexibility for adjusting settings such as exposure, white balance, sharpening, and contrast in post-processing software. But with the ZS100 you don't have to transfer your images to a computer to convert Raw files to JPEGs. You can adjust several settings in the camera and save the altered image as a JPEG, or just convert the Raw file to a JPEG with no alterations if all you need is a file that is easier to send by e-mail or view on another device.

If you're not certain whether a given image was shot with Raw image quality, press the Display button until one of the detailed information screens appears; the Raw label will appear next to the aspect ratio for all Raw shots, as shown in Figure 6-16.

Figure 6-16. Raw Label on Image Taken with Raw Quality

Once you have a single Raw image displayed on the screen in playback mode, highlight Raw Processing on the Playback menu, then press the Menu/Set button twice (or press the Set icon on the touch screen). The camera will display the Raw Processing screen, as shown in Figure 6-17, overlaid on the image you selected for processing.

Figure 6-17. Raw Processing Options Screen

At the left of the display will be a series of thumbnail images, each with a label displayed to the right. Scroll through those thumbnail images using the rear dial, the Up and Down buttons, or the touch screen, and press Menu/Set or the Set icon when the block for that thumbnail is highlighted with a yellow frame. Each of those thumbnail images represents an action you can take or a setting you can adjust.

For any setting other than Noise Reduction, Intelligent Resolution, and Sharpness, you can press the Display button to switch between the main setting screen, as shown in Figure 6-18, and a comparison screen, as shown in Figure 6-19, on which the camera displays several thumbnail images on the same screen so you can compare the effects of different settings as you scroll through them.

Figure 6-18. Main Adjustment Screen for Raw Processing Parameter

Also, for any setting, you can press the zoom lever to enlarge the image on the main setting screen so you can see the effects of the adjustment with a magnified view.

Figure 6-19. Comparison Screen for Raw Processing Parameter

Following are descriptions of the individual items you can adjust.

Setup. If you select this item, the camera will display a sub-menu with three items: Reinstate Adjustments, Color Space, and Picture Size. If you select Reinstate Adjustments, the camera will show you the image as it now stands with any adjustments you have made with the other settings. You can then proceed to cancel all of those adjustments if you want. The Color Space option lets you keep the color space setting the image was shot with, or change it to the other option, either Adobe RGB or sRGB. The Picture Size option lets you set the Picture Size to L, M, or S.

Begin Processing. If you select this block, the camera will process all of the adjustments you have set using the other blocks. Before it proceeds to make those changes, it will show you a preview of how the processed image will look before you confirm the operation, as shown in Figure 6-20.

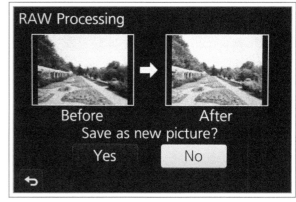

Figure 6-20. Begin Processing - Preview Screen

If you choose Yes, the camera will save a new JPEG image using all of the settings you have made. The new image will appear right after the existing Raw image on the camera's display, but it will have an image number at the end of the current sequence on the memory card.

White Balance. With this item, the camera will display the Raw image with the complete line of white balance adjustment icons at the bottom of the screen. (If you don't see that screen, press the Display button to make it appear.) As you scroll through those icons, the display will change to show how the image would look with the selected setting. If you select the color temperature option, you can press the Up button to select the numerical color temperature. For any setting, you can press the Down button to get to the screen with color axes for fine-tuning the white balance appearance.

Exposure Compensation. If you select this adjustment, you will be able to increase or decrease the exposure of the image, but only by up to plus or minus one EV level, in 1/3 EV increments.

Photo Style. With this item, you can change the Photo Style setting to any option you want. If you choose Monochrome, you will also be able to set the Color Tone adjustment and the Monochrome Filter Effect adjustment that simulates the use of a glass filter for black-and-white film. (Those two additional adjustments will appear later in the list of Raw Processing options.) If you select any other Photo Style setting, the Color Tone and Filter Effect adjustments will not be available. (The Saturation item will be available in place of the Color Tone adjustment.)

Intelligent Dynamic. The Intelligent Dynamic, or i.Dynamic screen lets you set this adjustment at a level of Off, Low, Standard, or High, regardless of how it was set when the image was captured.

Contrast. This adjustment is somewhat unusual because, ordinarily, it is made as part of the Photo Style adjustment. With the Raw Processing option, it is separated out. With this item, you can adjust the contrast of your Raw image by as many as five units positive or negative.

Highlight. On the Recording menu, the Highlight item is included as one aspect of the Highlight Shadow item. With the Raw Processing option, Highlight and Shadow are provided as two separate adjustments. If you select this item, you can alter the brightness of the highlights in the image by up to five units in either direction.

Shadow. This item is similar to the previous one, but deals with shadow rather than highlight adjustments.

Saturation. As noted earlier, this item is available for adjustment if you have selected a Photo Style other than Monochrome. If you selected Monochrome, the Raw Processing menu option includes Color Tone as an adjustment in place of Saturation.

Color Tone. As noted above, if you choose Monochrome for Photo Style, the camera presents this item for adjustment in place of Saturation.

Filter Effect. As discussed earlier, if you choose Monochrome for Photo Style, the Filter Effect item is available to adjust; otherwise, it does not appear.

Noise Reduction. With this item, you can adjust Noise Reduction up to five units positive or negative.

Intelligent Resolution. With the Intelligent Resolution, or i.Resolution item, you can set this feature to Off, Extended, Low, Standard, or High.

Sharpness. The last item in the line of boxes for adjustment is Sharpness, which, like Contrast and Resolution, is separated out from the Photo Style adjustment. You can change the level of this item up to five units in either direction.

## LIGHT COMPOSITION

This next menu option gives you a way to select and combine multiple frames from a sequence that was shot using 4K Photo mode. This feature lets you build a composition with dramatic areas of light in different locations, such as from a series of fireworks bursts. Figures 6-21 through 6-23 illustrate this effect. Figures 6-21 and 6-22 are two images from a 4K Photo burst; Figure 6-23 is a composite that resulted from combining those two images along with one other, using the Light Composition option.

To use this option, select it from the menu, and the camera will display any 4K Photo bursts on the memory card in the camera. Scroll through those choices and press the Menu/Set button or the Set icon on the screen to select an image. On the next screen, select Composite Merging or Range Merging. With Composite Merging, you can select any images from the 4K Photo burst. With Range Merging, you select the beginning and ending images of a range, and the camera includes all images within that range.

Figure 6-21.  First Component Image for Light Composition

Figure 6-22.  Second Component Image for Light Composition

Figure 6-23.  Final Composite Image for Light Composition

Then use the on-screen icons to select the images you want to include in the final composite. When you have finished, select Save, and the camera will display a message asking you to confirm, and telling how long it will take to produce the composite. If you confirm, the camera will create the composite image.

Apart from fireworks displays and similar light shows, I have not found situations in which this feature would be useful, though I'm sure a creative photographer

will find other applications for it. You should have the camera on a tripod to achieve good results, so the backgrounds of the combined images will blend together seamlessly. Also, note that the camera will create the image using only the brightest parts of the component images, so, if the parts you want to combine are not the brightest parts, they will not be included in the composite image. Of course, if you are shooting a fireworks display, the fireworks bursts almost certainly will be the brightest parts of the image, but in other contexts this feature may not work as expected.

The options on screen 2 of the Playback menu are shown in Figure 6-24.

Figure 6-24.  Screen 2 of Playback Menu

## CLEAR RETOUCH

This feature lets you erase parts of a recorded image by touching them with your finger on the camera's screen. It works only with normal JPEG images, not with Raw images, panoramas, movies, 4K burst shots, or shots taken with the Post focus option.

To use this option, select it from the Playback menu and scroll through your images until you find one to retouch. When that image is displayed, press the Menu/Set button or touch the Set icon on the screen. The camera will display a screen with Remove and Scaling icons at the right. Touch Remove and then drag or tap your finger on areas you want to erase from the image. The camera will color those areas, as shown in Figure 6-25.

Figure 6-25. Clear Retouch Screen - Showing Retouch Area

Touch Scaling if you want to enlarge the screen before designating areas to remove. After you touch Scaling, you can pinch the screen apart with your fingers to enlarge it. Then press Remove to activate the removal process.

Figure 6-26. Clear Retouch Example - Before

Figure 6-27. Clear Retouch Example - After

When you have finished touching areas to be removed, press the Set icon or press the Menu/Set button to finish the process. The camera will display a preview screen; touch the Save icon or press the Menu/Set button to save that version of the image. The camera will display a final confirmation screen for you to save

the image as a new picture. Figures 6-26 and 6-27 represent the before and after versions of an image that I edited with this option to remove one of the people from the scene.

This feature could be useful if you are preparing some images for a quick presentation and need to remove an object from one or two shots, but it is no substitute for editing with a program such as Photoshop using a computer.

## TITLE EDIT

This next option on the Playback menu lets you enter text, numerals, punctuation, and a fairly wide range of symbols and accented characters for a given JPEG image or group of images through a system of selecting characters from several rows.

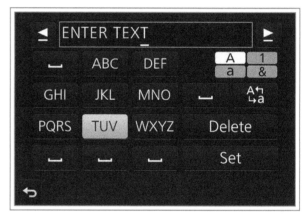

Figure 6-28. Title Edit - Screen for Entering Text

After you select this option from the Playback menu, choose one or more images to have text added and press Menu/Set or touch the Set icon to go to the screen with tools for entering text, shown in Figure 6-28. Navigate using the direction buttons to the block that contains the character to be entered. Then cycle through the choices in each block, such as ABC, using the Menu/Set button, and advance to the next space using the rear dial. You can toggle between displays of capital letters, lower case letters, and numerals and symbols using the Display button. You also can touch the letters and icons using the touch screen to select them.

The maximum length for your caption or other information is 30 characters. You can use the Multi option to enter the same text for up to 100 images. You cannot enter titles for motion pictures, images from 4K Photo bursts, Post Focus images, protected images (see discussion later in this chapter), or Raw images.

Once you have entered the title or caption for a particular image, it does not show up unless you use the Text Stamp function, discussed below, or the PHOTOfunSTUDIO software supplied with the camera. The title is then attached to the image, and it will print out as part of the image. There is no way to delete the title other than going back into the Title Edit function and using the Delete key from the table of characters, then deleting each character until the title disappears.

## TEXT STAMP

The Text Stamp function takes information associated with a given image and attaches it to the image in a visible form.

Figure 6-29. Text Stamp Option in Use

For example, if you have entered a title or caption using the Title Edit function discussed above, it does not become visible until you use this Text Stamp function to "stamp" it onto the image.

Once you have done this, the text or other characters in the title will print out if you send the picture to a printer. Besides the information entered with the Title Edit function, the Text Stamp function gives you the choice of making the following other information visible: year, month, and day; year, month, day, and time; age of subject (if set); travel date (if set); location (if set). Also, you can apply this function to information from pictures taken with names for Baby 1 or 2 and Pet, if you have entered a name for your baby or pet, and to pictures that have names registered with the Face Recognition function.

To use this function, highlight Text Stamp on the menu screen and press Menu/Set. On the next screen, choose Single or Multi, and then select the image or images you want to add text to. When you have selected one

or more images, press Menu/Set, highlight Set on the next screen, and press Menu/Set. You will then see the screen shown in Figure 6-30, where you can select the items to be imprinted on the image or images.

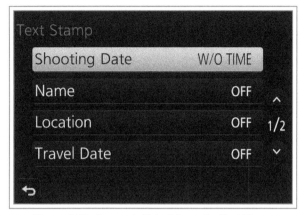

Figure 6-30. Screen to Select Items for Text Stamp

When you have made the selections, press the Q.Menu button to return to the previous screen, select OK, and press Menu/Set. The camera will ask if you want to save the stamped image as a new picture; select Yes and press Menu/Set to carry out the operation. The text will be set in small, orange characters in the lower right corner of the image, as shown in Figure 6-29.

This function cannot be used with Raw images, movies, 4K Photos, Post Focus images, or panoramas. The camera saves the text-stamped image to a new file, so you will still have the original. I have never found this function useful, but if you have an application that could benefit from it, it is available and ready to assist you.

## VIDEO DIVIDE

The Video Divide option gives you a basic ability to edit or trim videos in the camera. Using this procedure, you can, within limits, pause a video at any point and then cut it at that point, resulting in two segments of video rather than one. You can then, if you want, delete an unwanted segment.

To do this, highlight Video Divide on the Playback menu and press the Right button or Menu/Set to go to the playback screen. If the video you want to divide is not already displayed, scroll through your images using the Left and Right buttons or the rear dial until you locate it.

You can recognize videos because they display the length of the video in the upper right quarter of the screen and a movie camera icon with an up arrow in the upper left, as shown in Figure 6-31.

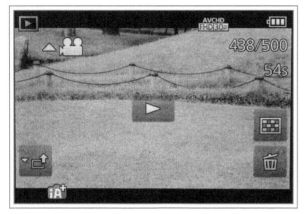

Figure 6-31. Movie File Showing Duration in Upper Right

The camera displays all your images here, including stills, so you may have to scroll through many non-videos until you reach the video you want. If you want to narrow the choices down to videos only, choose Video Only for Playback Mode on screen 1 of the Playback menu before selecting the Video Divide menu option.

With the desired movie on the screen, press Menu/Set to start it playing. When it reaches the point where you want to divide it, press the Up button to pause the video. While it is paused, move through it a few frames at a time using the Left and Right buttons, until you find the exact point where you want to divide it.

Once you reach that point, press the Down button to make the cut. You will see an icon of a pair of scissors in the display of controls at the bottom of the screen. After you press the Down button, the camera will display the message shown in Figure 6-32, asking you to confirm the cut.

Highlight Yes and press Menu/Set to confirm. Now you will have two new videos, divided at the point you chose.

As I noted above, this is a rudimentary form of editing. It can't be used to trim a movie too close to its beginning or end, or to trim a very short movie at all. But it's better than nothing, and it gives you some ability to delete unwanted footage without having to edit the video on your computer. Note, though, that this operation does not save a copy of the original video, so use it only if you are sure you want to divide the video file.

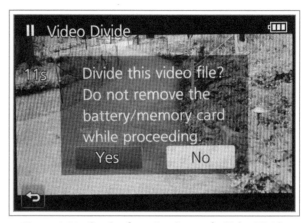

Figure 6-32. Cut Confirmation Screen for Video Divide

## TIME LAPSE VIDEO

This option lets you create a movie from a series of shots you took using the Time Lapse Shot feature on screen 5 of the Recording menu. As I discussed in Chapter 4, when you use that feature, the camera will ask at the end of the process if you want to create a movie from the group of time-lapse shots. If you say no, you can use this option on the Playback menu at a later time to create the movie.

When you select this option, the camera will display any groups of images that were taken with the Time Lapse Shot option. Scroll through those and select the one you want to make into a movie. Then press the Menu/Set button, and the camera will display the screen shown in Figure 6-33, where you can set the recording quality, frame rate, and whether to play the sequence normally or in reverse. Make your choices and press Menu/Set; the camera will then create the video.

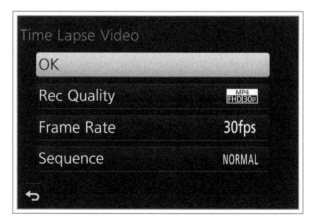

Figure 6-33. Time Lapse Video Creation Settings Screen

The options on screen 3 of the Playback menu are shown in Figure 6-34.

Figure 6-34. Screen 3 of Playback Menu

Figure 6-35. Resize Screen with Prompts for Size Options

## STOP MOTION VIDEO

This option, similar to the previous one, is for creating a video from images you took using the Stop Motion Animation feature discussed in Chapter 4. As with the Time Lapse Video option, select this option, scroll to the group of shots you want to use to create the video, and select your desired options from the screen that appears, which has the same options as in Figure 6-34.

## RESIZE

This function from the Playback menu is useful if you don't have access to software that can resize an image, and you need to generate a smaller file that you can attach to an e-mail message or upload to a website. After selecting this menu item, on the next screen you choose whether to resize a single image or multiple ones. Then navigate to the image you want to resize, if it's not already displayed on the screen.

Once an image to be resized is on the screen, press the Menu/Set button or touch the Set icon to start the resizing process. Following the prompts on the screen as shown in Figure 6-35, highlight the size to reduce the image to. The choices may include M and S for Medium and Small, or just S for Small, depending on the size of the original image. When the option you want to use is highlighted in yellow, press Menu/Set to carry out the resizing process. The camera will ask you to confirm that you want to save a new picture at the new size.

As with the Text Stamp function, resizing does not overwrite the existing image; it saves a copy of it at a smaller size, so the original will still be available. The new image will be found at the end of the current set of recorded pictures. Raw images, 4K Photo or Post Focus images, panoramas, protected images, and motion pictures cannot be resized, nor can pictures stamped with Text Stamp. If you want to convert up to 100 images at the same time, select the Multi option and follow the same procedure.

## CROPPING

This function is similar to Resize, except that, instead of just resizing the image, the camera lets you crop it to show just part of the original image. To do this, select Cropping from the Playback menu and navigate to the image to be cropped, if it isn't already displayed, and press the Menu/Set button or touch the Set icon. Then use the zoom lever or touch the zoom icon to enlarge the image, and use the direction buttons or scroll with the touch screen to position the part of the image to be retained.

Figure 6-36. Image Ready to Crop in Camera

When the enlarged portion is displayed as you want, as shown in Figure 6-36, press Menu/Set or the Set icon to lock in the cropping, and select Yes when the camera asks if you want to save the new picture. Again, as with Resize, the new image will be saved at the end of the current set of recorded images, and it will have a smaller size than the original image, because it will be cropped to include less information (fewer pixels) than the original image. The Cropping function cannot be used with Raw images, motion pictures, 4K Photo or Post Focus images, panoramas, or pictures stamped with Text Stamp.

## ROTATE

When you take a picture in a vertical (portrait) orientation by holding the camera sideways, you can set the camera to display it so it appears upright on the horizontal screen, as in Figure 6-37.

Figure 6-37. Vertical Image Displayed on Horizontal Screen

The setting to make such images appear in this orientation is the Rotate Display option, which is discussed next. If you have that option turned on, then the Rotate option becomes available, so you can manually rotate the image back to the way it was taken. If the Rotate Display option is not turned on, then the Rotate option is dimmed and unavailable for selection.

To use this option, select it from the menu and scroll to the image you want to rotate. Then press Menu/Set and the camera will display two arrows, as seen in Figure 6-38. Select the top arrow to rotate the image 90 degrees clockwise or the bottom one to rotate it 90 degrees counter-clockwise and press Menu/Set to do the rotation.

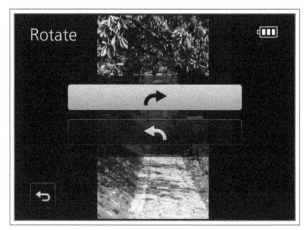

Figure 6-38. Two Arrows for Rotate Option

## ROTATE DISPLAY

As I noted above in connection with the Rotate option, when the Rotate Display option is turned on, images taken with the camera turned sideways are automatically rotated so they appear upright on the horizontal display. If you want to rotate such an image so you can see it at a larger size, taking up the full display, use the Rotate menu option, discussed above.

The options on screen 4 of the Playback menu are shown in Figure 6-39.

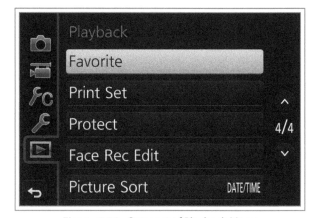

Figure 6-39. Screen 4 of Playback Menu

## FAVORITE

I have mentioned this function a couple of times before, because you have the option of viewing just your Favorite pictures or videos in some of the playback modes. You also can delete all images on the memory card except the Favorites.

To use this feature, choose Favorite from the Playback menu, and then choose the images to mark as Favorites, either single or multiple images (up to 999), using the same selection process as for other operations discussed above. The camera will display your images, either singly or as thumbnails, and you can mark any image as a Favorite by pressing the Menu/Set button or touching the Set/Cancel icon when the image or its thumbnail is displayed. A star will appear on the marked image, as shown in Figure 6-40.

Figure 6-40. Star on Image Marked as Favorite

Once the star appears, press the Q.Menu button or the Cancel icon to exit from this screen. (Don't press Menu/Set on this screen; if you do, the star will be removed.)

When you later display an image or video that was marked as a Favorite, a star appears in its upper left corner if you are viewing the playback screen that displays full information and the full-sized image. You cannot mark Raw images as Favorites.

## PRINT SET

The next option on the Playback menu, Print Set, lets you set your images for Digital Print Order Format (DPOF) printing. DPOF is a process developed by the digital photography industry to allow users of digital cameras to specify, on the camera's memory card, which pictures to print and other details, then take the card to a commercial printing shop to have them printed according to those specifications.

With the ZS100, you select this option from the Playback menu and then select Single or Multi. If you select Multi, the camera displays six images at a time on the screen. Using the four direction buttons, the rear dial, or the touch screen, navigate through the images. When you arrive at one you want to have printed, press the Menu/Set button or the Set icon, and you will then see a box with the word "Count" followed by a number

and up and down arrows. Use the Up and Down buttons or the screen icons to raise (or, later, lower, if you change your mind) the number of copies of that image you want to have printed, as shown in Figure 6-41.

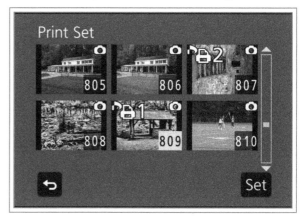

Figure 6-41. Print Set Option Showing Number of Copies to Be Printed

In addition, if you press the Right button or the Date icon, the word "Date" is added to the thumbnail image, and the date will be printed on that picture. You can follow the above procedure for a single image by selecting "Single" when you first choose the DPOF option.

The DPOF settings cannot be used for Raw images, videos, or 4K Photo or Post Focus images. Once you have set one or more images to print using this menu option, you can use the Cancel option from the Print Set menu to go back and cancel the printing setup.

## PROTECT

The next option on screen 4 of the Playback menu is Protect, which is used to lock selected images or videos against deletion. The process is essentially the same as that for the Favorite function: Select the Protect option, and then select Multi or Single. You mark the files you want to protect using the Menu/Set button. When a picture or video is protected in this way, a key icon appears on the left side of the display, as shown in Figure 6-42.

Figure 6-42. Protected Image with Key Icon

The Protect function works for all types of images, including Raw files and motion pictures. Note, however, that all images, including protected ones, will be deleted if the memory card is re-formatted.

## Face Recognition Edit

This Playback menu option is of use only if you have previously registered one or more persons' faces in the camera for face recognition. If you have, use this option to select the picture in question, then follow the prompts to replace or delete the information for the person or persons you select. Once deleted, this information cannot be recovered.

## Picture Sort

With this option, you can choose the order in which the camera displays your images from the memory card. If you choose the default option, File Name, then the camera arranges them in order by folders and then by numbers within the folders. For example, the file names of your images might include entries such as P1000003, P1000010, P1020023, P1030425, etc. If you have taken all of your images with the same camera, all of these images should also appear in chronological order according to when they were taken. However, if you have taken images with several different cameras you may have multiple images with the same file names, or with file names that do not match the order in which the images were taken. In that case you can choose the other option for this menu item, Date/Time. In that case, the images will be displayed in order by the dates and times they were taken.

# CHAPTER 7: THE CUSTOM MENU AND THE SETUP MENU

In Chapters 4 and 6 I discussed the many options available to you in the Recording and Playback menu systems. The next menu systems to discuss are the Custom and Setup menus, which include options for controlling things such as focus, zoom, and the appearance of the display, as well as date, time, formatting, and audio options. As a reminder, you enter the menu system by pressing the Menu/Set button on the camera's back.

## The Custom Menu

After pressing Menu/Set, press the Left button to move the highlight into the left column of menu choices, then use the Up and Down buttons or the rear dial to move to the wrench icon with the letter C, as shown in Figure 7-1. (You also can use the camera's touch screen features to navigate through the menu system.)

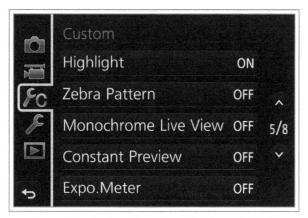

Figure 7-1. Custom Menu Icon Highlighted at Left

Once that icon is highlighted, navigate to the list of menu options, which occupy eight menu screens, discussed below. (If the camera is set to the basic Intelligent Auto mode, the Custom menu displays only one screen with three items.) If necessary, navigate to the top of the menu's first screen.

If you have to move forward or backward through several menu screens, you can press the zoom lever to move through them a screen at a time in either direction, or press the Display button to move a screen at a time in the forward direction only.

I will discuss all of the Custom menu items below, starting with the first screen, shown in Figure 7-2.

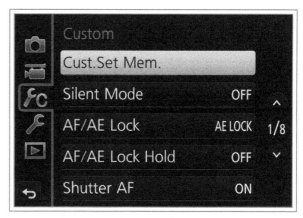

Figure 7-2. Screen 1 of Custom Menu

### CUSTOM SET MEMORY

This feature gives you a way to quickly change several shooting parameters without having to remember them or use menus or physical controls to set them. The camera lets you save three different groups of settings, each of which can be recalled instantly using the Custom (C) position on the Mode dial.

Here is how this works. First, you need to have the camera set to recording mode rather than playback mode, so if it's in playback mode, press the shutter button halfway or press the playback button to exit to recording mode. Then, set the camera to Program, Aperture Priority, Shutter Priority, Manual exposure, Scene, Panorama, Creative Control, or Creative Video mode (You can't use the Custom Set Memory feature in Intelligent Auto mode.)

Next, make all of the menu settings that you want to have stored for quick recall, such as Photo Style, ISO, focus mode, exposure metering method, i.Dynamic, and the like. Your custom set can include all of the items on the Recording Menu except Face Recognition and Profile Setup; all items on the Custom Menu; and all items on the Creative Video menu. You cannot include any items from the Setup menu. You can include white balance and Drive Mode, even though they are not set from the menu. Of course, you cannot add inconsistent settings. For example, you cannot adjust white balance if you have selected a filter effect. So, if you try to add both a white balance setting and a filter effect setting to a saved group, only the filter effect setting will be effective.

Once you have all of the settings as you want them, leave them that way and go to the Custom menu. Navigate to Custom Set Memory and select it, which gives you choices of C1, C2, and C3, as shown in Figure 7-3.

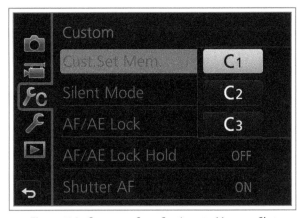

Figure 7-3. Screen to Save Settings to Memory Slot

Highlight the slot you want to save your settings in and press Menu/Set. The camera will display a message asking you to confirm this action; highlight Yes and select it to confirm.

When, at a later time, you want to use your set of saved settings, turn the Mode dial to the C position and press the Menu/Set button. On the sub-menu that appears, shown in Figure 7-4, select C1, C2, or C3. Once you have selected the custom mode you want, you are still free to change the camera's settings, but those changes will not be saved into the Custom Set Memory unless you go back to the Custom menu and save the changes there with the Custom Set Memory option.

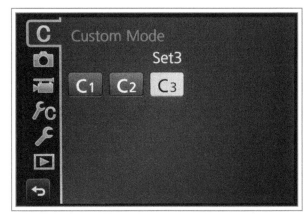

Figure 7-4. Screen to Select Memory Slot for Shooting

Although it has some limitations, Custom Set Memory is a powerful capability, and anyone who has or develops some favorite groups of settings would be well advised to experiment with this option and take advantage of its power.

## SILENT MODE

The Silent Mode option gives you a quick way to turn off the lights and sounds made by the camera that might distract a subject or cause a disturbance in a quiet area. When you turn this option on, the camera switches to using the electronic shutter, which is quieter than the mechanical shutter; silences all beeps and other sounds for matters such as focus and shutter operation; forces the flash off; and turns off the AF assist lamp. However, the lamp will still light up to indicate use of the self-timer, and the red Wi-Fi connection lamp will illuminate if you start a Wi-Fi connection. If you will often use Silent Mode, you can include it as part of a group of saved settings with the Custom Set Memory option, or you can assign it to a function button.

## AF/AE LOCK

This menu item lets you choose the function of the AF/AE Lock button, which is located beneath the Mode dial on the back of the camera. You can use this option, shown in Figure 7-5, to control how that button locks autofocus (AF) and autoexposure (AE) settings.

If you select AE Lock or AF Lock, the camera locks only the one designated setting. If you choose AF/AE Lock, the camera locks both settings at the same time.

Figure 7-5. AF/AE Lock Menu Options Screen

The camera will place icons on the recording display to indicate which of the values are locked, once you press the AF/AE Lock button and the values are locked in. The AF Lock icon will appear in the upper right corner and the AE Lock icon in the lower left corner. Figure 7-6 shows the display when both values are locked.

Figure 7-6. Shooting Screen with AF and AE Both Locked

It is not possible to lock exposure using the AF/AE Lock button in Manual exposure mode. None of the button's settings functions in Intelligent Auto mode.

If you select the final option, AF-On, pressing the AF/AE Lock button will cause the camera to use its autofocus system to focus on the subject, using whatever AF Mode setting is in effect to determine what area to focus on. If manual focus is in effect, the camera will still use the autofocus system when you press this button. This is a useful option as backup when you are using manual focus. You also can use it if you have set the Shutter AF option to Off, as discussed below, so pressing the shutter button halfway does not cause the camera to use its autofocus. You will then be able to press the AF/AE Lock button when you need to get the camera to focus again quickly. The ability to

use a button on the back of the camera for focusing is sometimes called "back button focus."

## AF/AE Lock Hold

This next menu option determines how the AF/AE Lock button operates. If you set AF/AE Lock Hold to On, then, when you press this button and release it, the camera retains the locked value(s). If you set this option to Off, then you have to hold the button down to retain the value(s); when you release it, the locked value(s) will be released. This option is dimmed and unavailable for selection when AF/AE Lock is set to AF-On. With that setting, pressing the AF/AE Lock button causes the camera to use its autofocus, but not to lock focus, so it is not possible to "hold" the locked setting.

## Shutter AF

This option lets you choose whether the camera will use its autofocus when you press the shutter button halfway, or not. With the default setup, with Shutter AF turned on, when the camera is set to an autofocus mode, it will evaluate the focus when you half-press the shutter button. With single autofocus (AFS), the focus will be locked as long as you hold the button in that position; with flexible autofocus (AFF), the camera will refocus if it detects movement, and with continuous autofocus (AFC), the camera will continue to adjust focus as movement occurs.

If you use this menu option to turn Shutter AF off, then the camera will not use its autofocus at all when you half-press the shutter button. There are several reasons why you might choose that setting. First, if you are taking a series of shots at the same distance, such as when you have the camera on a tripod and are taking shots of flat objects for auctions, you might focus once and then have no need to keep focusing. You can avoid using up the camera's battery for repeated uses of the autofocus system by turning Shutter AF off.

Another reason for using this option is if you prefer using the AF/AE Lock button to adjust autofocus. To do that, go to screen 1 of the Custom menu and set the AF/AE Lock menu option to AF-On. Then, when you press the AF/AE Lock button, the camera will adjust autofocus. With this setup (back button focus), you can adjust the focus whenever you want, and once you have it set as you want it, you can compose your shot and have the camera evaluate exposure without worrying that the camera will reset the focus to a different subject. You will be able to trigger the shutter to take another shot at any time.

Some photographers use this system with the autofocus mode set to AFC for continuous autofocus. Then, they can adjust focus at any time using the AF/AE Lock button, and press the shutter at any time without being concerned about focus. It's probably a good idea to give this setup a try and see if it works well for your type of shooting.

The next items to be discussed are on screen 2 of the Custom menu, which is shown in Figure 7-7.

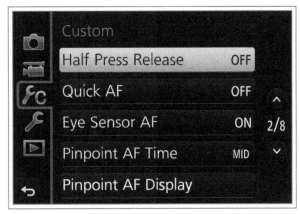

Figure 7-7. Screen 2 of Custom Menu

## HALF PRESS RELEASE

This option lets you set the camera to capture an image when the shutter button is pressed halfway down, rather than requiring a full press, as is the normal situation. If you turn this setting on when Shutter AF is turned on, the camera will still adjust focus just before the image is captured, so the half-press of the button carries out both the autofocus operation and the image capture. If you have Shutter AF turned off, then you would have to use the AF/AE Lock button to adjust autofocus, with the AF-On option turned on for that button. (Or, of course, you could use manual focus.)

Using the Half Press Release option can speed up your shooting, because you don't have to go through the sequence of half-press followed by full press of the shutter button; you can just touch the button lightly to capture an image, or a burst of images if the camera is set for burst shooting. This system can work well if you won't be needing to make adjustments to focus or exposure after half-pressing the shutter button. When you are shooting in predictable, steady lighting at a

constant distance and you need to shoot quickly, this option can be useful. Also, the ability to trigger the shutter with a light touch can help reduce the risk of motion blur from camera shake.

## QUICK AF

This next option on the Custom menu, Quick AF, can be turned either on or off. If you turn this setting on, the camera will focus on the subject whenever the camera has settled down and is still, with only minor movement or shake. You do not need to press the shutter button halfway down to achieve focus; the camera focuses on its own, as long as an autofocus mode is in use.

The advantage of turning Quick AF on is that you will have a slight improvement in focusing time, because the camera does not wait until you press the shutter button (or the AF/AE Lock button, if it is set for focusing) to start the focusing process. The disadvantage is that the battery will run down faster than usual. So, unless you believe a split second for focusing time is critical, I would stay away from this setting, and leave this menu option turned off. The camera will still focus automatically when you press the shutter button halfway down; it just will take a little bit longer to bring the subject into focus.

## EYE SENSOR AF

When this option is turned on and the camera is set to an autofocus mode, the camera will automatically use its autofocus mechanism to adjust focus as soon as your head approaches the eye sensor and turns on the electronic viewfinder. However, the autofocus system will work only once with this system, even if the camera is set for continuous autofocus. So, when you first put the camera up to your eye, the focus will be adjusted for whatever subject the camera is aimed at at that instant. The camera will not readjust the focus unless you then press the shutter button halfway or use the AF/AE Lock button, if that button is set up to adjust focus. The camera does not beep when focus is set with this feature.

This option can give the autofocus system a head start by bringing the scene into focus with an approximate setting, so it can quickly reach an exact focusing position when you press the shutter button halfway or use the AF/AE Lock button to make the final focus adjustments. I generally leave it turned off, but for snapshots it can be useful to have an approximate first cut at focusing take place as soon as you use the viewfinder.

This option works only when the viewfinder is turned on, either permanently or as your eye approaches it, through use of the LVF button or the Eye Sensor option on screen 8 of the Custom menu.

## PINPOINT AF TIME

As I discussed in Chapter 4, one of the options for AF Mode is Pinpoint AF, with which you can set a precise point for the focus area. Then, when you press the shutter button halfway to evaluate focus, the camera focuses at that point and enlarges the display briefly with that point centered, so you can judge the sharpness of the focus. The Pinpoint AF Time menu option controls how long the display stays enlarged when you press the shutter button halfway. The choices are Short (0.5 second), Medium (1.0 second), or Long (1.5 second). If you release the shutter button before the specified time has passed, the display will revert to normal size. Because of that behavior, I prefer to set this option to Long. Then, the display will stay enlarged for a long enough time to let me judge the focus, but I can always release the shutter button early to revert the display to its normal size.

## PINPOINT AF DISPLAY

This setting lets you choose one of two options for the size of the enlarged display that appears when you use the Pinpoint option for AF Mode—Full or PIP (picture-in-picture). With Full, the entire display is enlarged by a factor of between three and ten times; with PIP, only the central part of the display is enlarged, by a factor of between three and six times. You can vary the enlargement factor by turning the rear dial when the enlargement is active as you are setting the focus point. That enlargement factor will then take effect when you half-press the shutter button to focus using the Pinpoint AF option.

The next items to be discussed are on screen 3 of the Custom menu, shown in Figure 7-8.

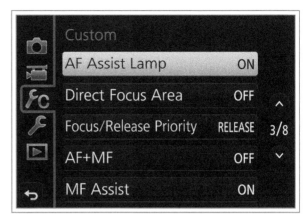

Figure 7-8. Screen 3 of Custom Menu

## AF ASSIST LAMP

The autofocus (AF) assist lamp is the reddish light on the front of the camera, near the lens below the Mode dial. The lamp illuminates when the ambient lighting is dim, to help the autofocus mechanism work by providing enough light to define the shape of the subject. Ordinarily, this option is left turned on for normal shooting, because the light only activates when it is needed in low-light conditions. However, you have the option of turning it off using the AF Assist Lamp menu option, so it will never turn on to help with autofocus. You might want to do this if you are trying to shoot your pictures without being detected, or without disturbing a subject such as a sleeping animal.

In Intelligent Auto mode, you cannot turn off the AF assist lamp using this menu option, but you can use the Silent Mode option on screen 1 of the Custom menu to turn off the lamp, along with the flash and camera sounds. The lamp does not illuminate when you are using manual focus (unless you have set up the AF/AE Lock button to use the AF-On option and you press that button to cause the camera to use its autofocus).

The AF assist lamp also serves as the self-timer lamp. Even if you set the AF Assist Lamp menu option to Off, the lamp will light up when the self-timer is used; there is no way to disable the lamp for that function.

## DIRECT FOCUS AREA

This is another option that can be turned either on or off; it is off by default. If you turn it on, then, in recording mode, if you press any of the four direction buttons, the camera immediately displays a screen for adjusting the position of the autofocus area. For example, if AF Mode is set to 1-Area, Pinpoint AF, or

Face/Eye Detection, then, when you press, say, the Left button, that button immediately activates the focus frame and starts moving it across the display. If you have AF Mode set to 49-Area or Custom Multi, then, when you press a direction button, the camera immediately displays the screen for selecting the focus zones to be included in the focus area. You can then keep pressing any of the direction buttons to adjust the area or use other controls to make other adjustments.

This option could be useful if you were in a situation when you need to adjust the focus area often, particularly with the 1-Area or Pinpoint AF options. I would not recommend using it with the 49-Area or Custom Multi options, because you need to do considerable adjusting with those options, and a split second of added speed will not be of that much use.

I do not use this option myself, because it is so easy to adjust the focus area without it. If you turn on Touch AF through the Touch Settings option on screen 8 of the Custom menu, you can just touch the screen to activate a movable focus area. Also, if you turn on Direct Focus Area, you lose the other functions of the direction buttons while this option is in effect. If you wanted to set white balance or ISO, you would have to use the Quick Menu, assign those functions to another button or to the control ring, or turn off this menu option before making that adjustment.

## Focus/Release Priority

You can set this option to Focus, the default option, or Release. If it is set to Focus, then the camera will not take a picture until focus has been confirmed, when autofocus is in effect. So, if you aim the camera at a subject that is difficult for the autofocus system to bring into sharp focus, such as an area with no sharp features in dim lighting, the camera may display a red focus frame and beep four times, indicating focus was not achieved. In that situation, if this menu option is set to Focus, the camera will not take the picture when you press the shutter button. If you set this option to Release, then the camera will take the picture even if it is not in focus. If you are using manual focus, then the camera will take the picture regardless of focus, even if you set the priority to Focus.

The use of this option is a matter of personal preference and the situation you are faced with. If you are taking images of a one-time event, you may want to use the Release option so you don't miss a shot just because focus is slightly off. It's much better to get an image that is slightly out of focus than no image at all. But if you have time to make sure focus is sharp, you can use the Focus option to make sure you have focus properly adjusted before you capture an image.

This option also has an impact on the speed of burst shooting. As I discussed in Chapter 5, if this option is set to Focus, shooting may be slowed down as the camera attempts to adjust focus before recording each image, when you are using a burst setting with continuous focus adjustments.

## AF+MF

This is an on-or-off option that is turned off by default. If you turn it on, then, when the autofocus mode is set to AFS, for single autofocus, once you have pressed the shutter button halfway to lock focus, while holding the button in that position, you can turn the control ring to fine-tune the focus manually. Features such as MF Assist and peaking will operate if they are turned on through the Custom menu. This option also takes effect if you have locked focus with the AF/AE Lock button, when that button is set to lock autofocus or to the AF-On setting through screen 1 of the Custom menu.

This option is useful when, for example, you have locked focus on a group of small objects, and you want to make sure the focus is precisely set on one of those objects, such as on an object behind the others, or on a portion of one of them. Once the autofocus system has locked on the group, just start turning the control ring while keeping the shutter button pressed halfway (or the AF/AE Lock button pressed, if applicable) to adjust the focus manually until you have it set exactly as you want.

## Manual Focus (MF) Assist

The MF Assist option, together with the MF Assist Display option, discussed next, lets you set whether and how the recording screen display is magnified when you're using manual focus. This option can be turned either on or off.

If you leave MF Assist turned off, there is no magnification when you turn the control ring to adjust manual focus. If you turn MF Assist on, then, when you start turning the control ring to focus, the screen will immediately be magnified to help you adjust the focus. Also, before you start turning the control ring, you can tap on the screen twice to activate the MF Assist function. The display will be enlarged, and you can move the focus point by dragging the screen with your finger or by using the four cursor buttons. You can change the enlargement factor with the rear dial or by pinching or squeezing the screen with your fingers. You can press the Display button or the DISP. Reset icon to return the focus point to the center.

The MF Assist option is not available for recording motion pictures, with the 4K Photo Pre-burst setting, or when Digital Zoom is activated.

The next options are on screen 4 of the Custom menu, shown in Figure 7-9.

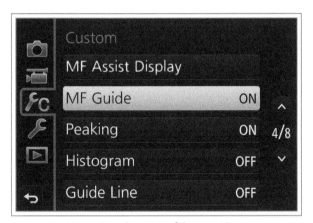

Figure 7-9. Screen 4 of Custom Menu

## MF ASSIST DISPLAY

The MF Assist Display menu option lets you set the area of magnification with MF Assist to Full or PIP (picture-in-picture). If you choose Full, the magnification takes up the whole display and varies between three and ten times normal. If you choose PIP, the magnification appears in a smaller window and the enlargement factor varies between three and six times normal.

As soon as you tap the touch screen twice or turn the control ring to start the magnification, the display will appear similar to Figure 7-10, which shows the MF Assist display when the Full setting is in effect.

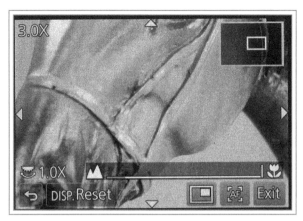

Figure 7-10. Screen Enlarged with MF Assist

You can use all four direction buttons or the touch screen to move the enlarged area around the display, and you can turn the rear dial or pinch the touch screen to change the magnification factor. To reset the focus point to the center of the display, press the Display button. To dismiss the MF Assist display, press the shutter button halfway or press the Menu/Set button. Or, if you turned the control ring to start the magnification, the screen will return to normal size on its own after about ten seconds. You can then turn the control ring to bring the MF Assist display back on the screen if you want, or you can just press the shutter button to take the picture. You can switch between the full-screen and PIP views by touching the rectangular icon at the bottom of the display with a small inset white rectangle in its upper right corner.

## MF GUIDE

If this option is turned on, then, when you are turning the control ring to adjust manual focus, the camera displays a scale at the bottom of the screen with an indicator that shows the approximate focus distance along the scale from far to near, with no numerical value for the distance. With this option turned off, the scale does not appear. An example of the scale is shown in Figure 7-10.

## PEAKING

This menu option controls another feature for assisting with manual focus. The peaking feature, when it is turned on, places colored pixels on the screen at areas that the camera determines are in sharp focus. As you turn the control ring to adjust focus, watch for the colored areas to reach their maximum intensity. When you see the largest areas of glowing pixels, focus will be sharp for the areas where those pixels appear.

Figure 7-11. Peaking Menu Options Screen

The peaking menu item has three main options: On, Off, and Set, as shown in Figure 7-11. In most cases, I leave it turned on, because it operates only when manual focus is in effect and I find it helpful for most manual focusing situations. The Set option has two sub-options: Detect Level and Display Color, as shown in Figure 7-12.

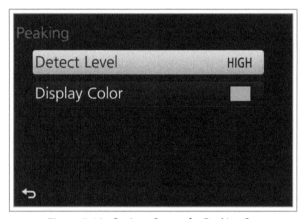

Figure 7-12. Options Screen for Peaking Set

The Detect Level can be set to High or Low. If you set it to High, the camera will require a higher degree of sharpness before it places pixels at a given focus area. With that setting, there will be fewer peaking pixels displayed than with the Low setting. You may find that it is easier to gauge the focus with fewer pixels, because you can adjust focus until those few pixels appear. However, in some situations, such as with objects that are lacking in straight lines or sharp features, you may find that it is preferable to set Detect Level to Low, so there will be more peaking pixels visible.

With the Display Color sub-option, you can choose light blue, yellow, yellow green, pink, or white for the peaking color if Detect Level is set to High, and you can choose dark blue, orange, green, red, or gray if the level is set to Low. It is a good idea to choose a color that contrasts with the scene you are photographing, so you can distinguish the peaking pixels from other parts of the image.

Figure 7-13. Peaking Composite Image

Figure 7-13 is a composite image that illustrates the use of this feature. The left side shows the view with peaking turned off, and the right side with peaking turned on with Detect Level set to Low.

As noted above, peaking operates only when the camera is set to manual focus. If you set the AF/AE Lock button to the AF-On function on screen 1 of the Custom menu, peaking pixels will appear when you press that button to cause the camera to use autofocus, if manual focus is in effect. Peaking also operates if you adjust manual focus using the AF+MF option, discussed earlier in this chapter. Peaking does not operate when the Rough Monochrome filter effect setting is in use.

## Histogram

The next menu option, Histogram, controls the display of the histogram in recording mode. A histogram is a graph showing the distribution of dark and bright areas in the image that is being viewed on the camera's screen. The darkest blacks are represented by vertical bars on the left, and the brightest whites by vertical bars on the right, with continuous gradations in between.

If an image has a histogram in which the pattern looks like a tall ski slope coming from the left of the screen down to ground level in the middle of the screen, that means there is an excessive amount of black and dark areas (tall bars on the left side of the histogram), and very few bright and white areas (no bars on the right). The histogram in Figure 7-14 illustrates this situation.

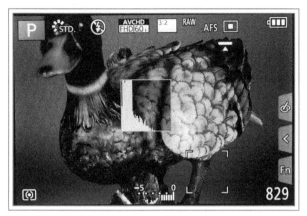

Figure 7-14. HIstogram for Underexposed Image

A pattern moving from the middle of the graph up to peaks at the right side of the graph would mean just the opposite—too many bright and white areas, as in the histogram shown in Figure 7-15.

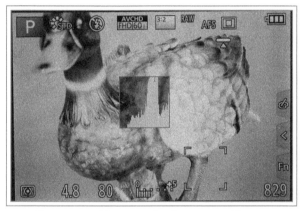

Figure 7-15. Histogram for Overexposed Image

A histogram that is "just right" would be one that starts low on the left, gradually rises to a medium peak in the middle of the graph, then moves gradually back down to the bottom at the right. That pattern indicates a good balance of whites, blacks, and medium tones. An example of this type of histogram is shown in Figure 7-16.

In playback mode, the ZS100 includes one display screen with a histogram for the image being displayed. The camera does not, by default, display the histogram for the live view in recording mode. To turn on the histogram when you are shooting, you need to use this menu option.

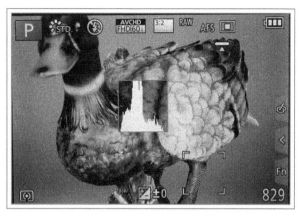

Figure 7-16. Histogram for Normally Exposed Image

The Histogram menu option has only two choices: On or Off. If you turn the histogram on, it will appear on the camera's display in recording mode, if a detailed display screen has been selected using the Display button, as shown in Figures 7-14 through 16.

The histogram does not display in Intelligent Auto mode. When the histogram is first activated, it appears in a yellow frame with arrows indicating that you can move it to any position on the display, as shown in Figure 7-17.

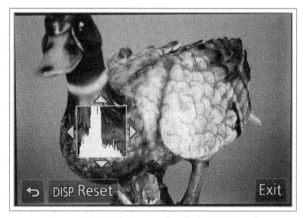

Figure 7-17. Histogram Ready to Be Moved

You can move it with the cursor buttons or by dragging it on the touch screen. Once you have it located where you want it, press the shutter button halfway down to lock it in place. While it is movable, press the Display button to reset it to the center of the display. If you need to move it after it has been locked in place, you can touch it on the screen to reactivate it for moving. Or, you can go back to this menu option and select On for the Histogram item.

The histogram is an approximation, and you should not rely on it too heavily. It provides some information as to how evenly exposed your image is likely to be. (Or, for playback, how well exposed it was.) If the histogram is displayed in orange, that means the recording and playback versions of the histogram will not match for this image, because the flash was used, or in a few other situations.

## GUIDE LINE

This option lets you set grid lines to be displayed on the LCD screen (or in the electronic viewfinder) to assist you with the composition of your pictures. Once you select Guide Line from the Custom menu, you get to a screen with four options: Off, and three patterns of lines, as shown in Figure 7-18.

Figure 7-18. Guide Line Menu Options Screen

If you choose Off, no grid lines will be displayed. If you choose the top option, the camera will display a grid that forms nine equal rectangles on the screen. This choice can help you line up subjects, including the horizon, along straight lines. The second option is a pattern of 16 rectangles along with a pair of intersecting diagonal lines, which can help you locate your subject along diagonals as well as along horizontal or vertical lines. Finally, with the third option, the camera displays just two intersecting lines, one horizontal and one vertical, and lets you set their positions using the direction buttons or the touch screen. This option can be useful if you need to compose your shot with an off-center subject.

When any of the Guide Line options is turned on, the grid lines will display whenever the camera is in recording mode, regardless of the shooting mode. They will not display when you select the display screen that is blank. An example of the second option as displayed in shooting mode is shown in Figure 7-19.

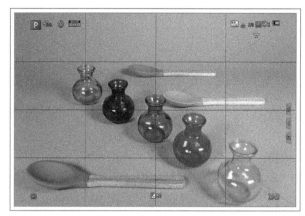

Figure 7-19. Second Guide Line Option in Use

The next menu options are on screen 5 of the Custom menu, shown in Figure 7-20.

Figure 7-20. Screen 5 of Custom Menu

## HIGHLIGHT

This feature produces a flashing area of black and white on areas of the image that are oversaturated with white, indicating they may be too bright. The flashing effect takes place only when you are viewing the pictures in Auto Review or Playback mode. That is, you will see the Highlight warning only when the image appears briefly on the screen after it has been recorded (Auto Review) or when you view the picture in Playback mode. This feature alerts you that the image may be washed out (overexposed) in some areas, so you may want to reduce the exposure for the next shot. If you find that sort of warning distracting, just turn this feature off. The flashing does not occur on one playback screen that shows the image only, with no information. So, even if this option is turned on, you can see your image without the flashing, by pressing the Display button to view that screen.

## ZEBRA PATTERN

This feature helps you gauge whether your image or video will be overexposed by setting the ZS100 to display a black-and-white-striped "zebra" pattern on the screen in recording mode. You can select either left-slanting or right-slanting stripes to match the scene as well as possible, and you can set either type of stripes to a numerical value from 50% to 105% in 5% increments. Those numbers are a measure of relative brightness or exposure, with 0 representing black and 100 representing bright white.

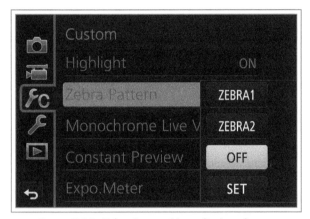

Figure 7-21. Zebra Pattern Menu Options Screen

To make the settings, select the menu option and pop up the menu with sub-options of Zebra1, Zebra2, Off, and Set, as shown in Figure 7-21.

Zebra1 generates stripes that slant from lower left to upper right and appear to move down to the right; Zebra2 generates stripes in the opposite direction. Use the Set option to set a numerical level for either Zebra1 or Zebra2, and then choose Zebra1 or Zebra2 from the menu to display that pattern on the screen.

When you turn this option on to any level less than about 90, you very likely will see, on some parts of the display, the "zebra" stripes that give this feature its name. When you see the stripes, that means the part of the image where the stripes appear is at or above the brightness level that was set for the stripes. For example, if you select stripes set to the 75% level and aim the camera at the scene, the stripes will appear on any part of the display where the brightness level reaches 75% of bright white.

There are various approaches to using these stripes, which originated as a tool for professional videographers. Some photographers like to set the

zebra function to 90% and adjust the camera's exposure so the stripes just barely start to appear in the brightest parts of the image. Another recommendation is to set the option to 75% for a scene with Caucasian skin, and expose so that the stripes appear in the area of the skin.

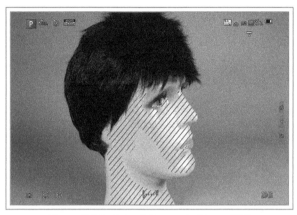

Figure 7-22. Zebra1 Pattern in Use at 75%

In Figure 7-22, I set the pattern to Zebra1 at 75% and exposed to have the stripes appear on the mannequin's face.

Zebra Pattern is a feature to consider, especially for video recording, but the ZS100 has an excellent metering system, including both live and playback histograms, so you can manage without this option if you don't want to deal with its learning curve.

## MONOCHROME LIVE VIEW

When you turn this feature on, the camera converts the display to a black-and-white view of the scene it is aimed at. This feature might help you concentrate on composition and geometry in your image, without being distracted by colors. You also might find it easier to adjust manual focus with this view, because you can turn on peaking with a color that contrasts clearly with all parts of the display. The monochrome view does not affect the recorded image, which will be in color unless you have also selected a monochrome setting for the final image using the Photo Style menu option or one of the Scene mode or Creative Control mode settings that produce monochrome images.

## CONSTANT PREVIEW

This option lets you see a preview of the effects of your exposure settings when the camera is in Manual exposure mode. When you turn this option on with the camera in that recording mode and then adjust shutter speed, aperture, or ISO, the display will grow darker or brighter to show how the settings would affect the final image. The display also will show how the aperture setting would affect the depth of field.

For example, if you set shutter speed to 1/125 second, aperture to f/8, and ISO to 1600 in a moderately lighted room with this option turned off, the camera's display will appear normal, showing the scene clearly. If you then press the shutter button halfway (assuming default settings for focus and shutter behavior), the display will grow dark and you will see more items in focus, reflecting the effects of the current settings. If you then turn this menu option on, you will see the same view you did when you pressed the shutter button halfway, even before pressing that button.

This setting can help if you need to see exactly what effect the current settings will have. However, in some situations it is better to leave this option turned off. For example, if you are shooting an image using an off-camera optical slave flash in Manual exposure mode, the camera will not realize that you are using the external flash, and the display screen may be quite dark with the settings you are using. In that situation, you might not be able to see the display to compose your image with this option activated, so you should leave Constant Preview turned off.

If you have a function button set to the Preview option and have the Constant Preview option turned on, pressing the function button in Manual exposure mode will not activate the Preview function, because it is already in effect through this menu option.

## EXPOSURE METER

This feature gives you the option of having the camera display its Exposure Meter feature, which is a set of two graphical dials that appear when you are adjusting shutter speed, aperture, exposure compensation, or Program Shift, as shown in Figure 7-23.

I find this display distracting and not all that helpful, so I leave it turned off, but you might want to try using it to see if it is useful in some situations.

Figure 7-23. Exposure Meter Dials on Display

Screen 6 of the Custom menu is shown in Figure 7-24.

Figure 7-24. Screen 6 of Custom Menu

## DIAL GUIDE

When this option is turned on, the camera places a small diagram in the lower right corner of the display for a few seconds that shows the current functions of the control ring and rear dial. The diagram appears when you switch the recording mode by turning the Mode dial.

For example, in Figure 7-25, the display shows that the control ring and the rear dial both control Program Shift, because the camera is in Program mode. If you move the Mode dial to change the recording mode, the display will change accordingly and appear for another few seconds. I find this display helpful, and it disappears soon after appearing, so I generally leave it turned on.

Figure 7-25. **Dial Guide in Use**

## LVF Display Style

This option controls how informational icons are displayed in the viewfinder. There are two choices, indicated by graphic icons. With the top choice, known as live viewfinder style, several of the icons, including those for Metering Mode, ISO, exposure compensation, and number of images remaining, are displayed below the live view area, so you can see more of the live view with no icons blocking the view. In addition, those icons remain on the display even when the no-information screen is selected. With the bottom choice, known as monitor style, all of the icons are placed within the live view area and that area extends farther down to accommodate them. I find the differences between these views to be minimal, but this is one way to tweak the viewfinder's operation if you want to.

## Monitor Display Style

This option is the same as the previous one, except that it applies to the LCD display, rather than the viewfinder. For this setting, I prefer using the bottom option, which places all of the icons within the live view of the image, so you have a slightly larger view of the scene. I find that the icons do not significantly block the view.

## Recording Area

This next option lets you set the camera's recording screen to display either the recording area used for still photos or the area used for motion pictures. For still pictures, that area is determined by the aspect ratio setting; for motion pictures, it is determined by the Recording Quality option on the Creative Video menu's second screen. For still images, there are four options: 3:2, 16:9, 1:1, and 4:3. For motion pictures there are only two choices: 16:9 for the HD settings and 4:3 for the VGA setting.

The reason for having this menu option available is that the ZS100 does not ordinarily show the area available for motion picture recording until you press the red motion picture button to start the recording. So, if the aspect ratio menu option is set for, say, 3:2, and the movie quality is set to HD, you will not see the actual shape of the motion picture recording screen until the recording starts, so you will not be able to compose the scene on the camera's monitor or in the viewfinder properly. But, if you set the Recording Area menu option to the Motion Picture option, then you will see the available recording area on the camera's screen before you start the recording.

The choice here depends on whether you are planning to capture still images or record motion picture sequences in your shooting session. To make the choice, just use this menu item to select the icon for the still camera or the icon for a movie camera.

## Remaining Display

This feature lets you choose whether the camera's display shows how many still images can be taken with current settings, as shown in Figure 7-26, where the display in the lower right corner of the screen shows the number of still images that can be recorded (472 in this case), or how much time is available for video recording.

Figure 7-26. **Remaining Display in Use**

Again, as with the previous menu option, your choice may depend on whether you are shooting mostly stills or videos.

Screen 7 of the Custom menu is shown in Figure 7-27.

Figure 7-27. Screen 7 of Custom Menu

## AUTO REVIEW

This option controls how long your images are displayed immediately after they are recorded by the camera. The possible settings are Off, one second, two seconds, three seconds, four seconds, five seconds, or Hold. These choices are fairly self-explanatory. After the shutter button is pressed, the image appears on the screen (or not) according to how this option is set. If you set it to Hold, the image stays on the screen until you press the shutter button halfway. Auto Review does not work when recording motion pictures.

## FUNCTION BUTTON SET

As I discussed in Chapter 5, the ZS100 has four physical function buttons labeled Fn1, Fn2, Fn3, and Fn4. It also has five virtual function buttons represented by icons on the touch screen, labeled Fn5 through Fn9. Each of those buttons, except for Fn9, has a particular function assigned to it by default. For all nine buttons, though, you can choose the function that is assigned when the camera is in recording mode. For the Fn1, Fn2, and Fn4 buttons, you also can choose a function to be assigned when the camera is in playback mode. To make those assignments, you use the Function Button Set menu option.

When you highlight this option and press the Menu/Set button or the Right button, the camera will display the screen shown in Figure 7-28, letting you choose the settings in recording mode or playback mode.

Figure 7-28. Main Options Screen for Function Button Set

For now, select recording mode, and the camera will display the special screen shown in Figure 7-29, with a graphic display of the assignable buttons.

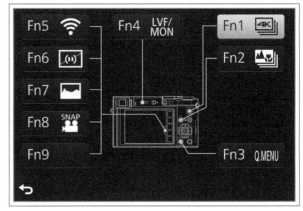

Figure 7-29. Graphic Display for Function Button Set

On that screen, turn the rear dial or press the Up and Down buttons to move the highlight to the button whose assignment you want to change, and press Menu/Set. (Or, just touch the button's icon on the touch screen.) You will then see a display like that in Figure 7-30, which highlights the current setting for that button on a sub-menu screen. Scroll through that series of 12 or 13 screens until you find the new setting you want to make, and press Menu/Set to confirm it. I discussed the possible settings in Chapter 5.

Don't forget that several of the items that can be assigned, including Photo Style, Motion Picture Setting, Quality, AFS/AFF/AFC, and Metering Mode, also can be adjusted using the Quick Menu system by pressing the Q.Menu button and then navigating through the easy-access menu that appears.

Figure 7-30. List of Possible Assignments for a Function Button

Also, although most of the items that can be assigned to the function buttons also can be reached through the menu system, there are some items that cannot be reached that way: Preview, Focus Area Set, Cursor Button Lock, and AF Mode/MF. I discussed those settings in Chapter 5.

You also can assign the Fn1, Fn2, and Fn4 buttons to carry out a function when the camera is in playback mode. To do that, go back to the main options screen for this menu item and select Setting in Play Mode, and the camera will display the screen shown in Figure 7-31.

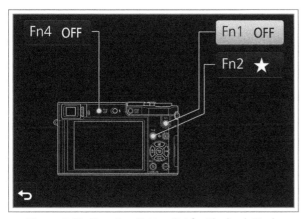

Figure 7-31. Function Button Set for Playback Mode

As discussed in Chapter 5, there are very few settings available for assignment during playback mode: Favorite, Print Set, Protect, Delete Single, Off, and Restore to Default.

## ZOOM LEVER

This next option lets you control how the zoom lever operates. By default, this lever zooms the lens continuously through its full range of focal lengths, which is 25mm to 250mm if no enhanced zoom

settings are in use. If you choose the second option here, the zoom lever uses step zoom, which allows the lever to zoom only to several preset zoom ranges: 25mm, 28mm, 35mm, 50mm, 70mm, 90mm, 135mm, 160mm, 200mm, and 250mm, when only the optical zoom is in use. It will not stop at any other focal length.

If you turn on other options for zooming, such as Digital Zoom, Intelligent Zoom, and Extended Optical Zoom, the step zoom function will take the focal length to further stages of 300mm, 400mm, 500mm, 600mm, 800mm, 1000mm, 1200mm, 1400mm, 1600mm, and 2000mm, depending on what settings are in effect.

As I discussed in Chapter 5, the control ring also can be assigned to operate step zoom, through the Ring/Dial Set option on screen 8 of the Custom menu (discussed later in this chapter). So, if you want to use step zoom, you can choose either the control ring or the zoom lever for that function.

My preference is to leave both the control ring and the zoom lever with their normal operation of zooming through the full range of focal lengths, rather than limiting them to the step zoom increments. However, if there are situations in which you want to have the zoom lens move in specific increments, you can use this option.

## ZOOM RESUME

If you turn on zoom resume, then, after you turn the camera off and back on, the lens will return to its last zoom position. If you leave this setting turned off, the lens will zoom out to its 25mm setting when the power is turned back on. This option is convenient if you need to use a particular focal length, such as 60mm, for a series of shots that will be interrupted by turning the camera off for periods of time.

## QUICK MENU (Q.MENU)

This option gives you the ability to customize the settings that are available from the Quick Menu. As I discussed in Chapter 5, when you press the Q.Menu button, the camera displays an easy-access menu system that lets you select various settings quickly. By default, the Quick Menu includes 11 settings: Photo Style, Flash Mode, Motion Picture Setting, Picture Setting, Quality, AFS/AFF/AFC, AF Mode, Metering Mode, Exposure Compensation, Sensitivity, and White

Balance. To keep those settings in place or restore them after custom settings have been used, just select the Preset option for this menu item. If you want to set up the Quick Menu with your own selection of settings, select the Custom option for this menu item.

Once you have selected Custom for the Quick Menu item, exit this menu system and press the Q.Menu button. On the screen that appears, use the Down button to move to and highlight the tool icon at the lower left of the display, as shown in Figure 7-32. (Or select that icon using the touch screen.)

Figure 7-32. Quick Menu with Custom Tool Icon

After you select that icon, the camera will display the Q. Menu Customize screen, as shown in Figure 7-33.

Figure 7-33. Quick Menu Customize Screen

On that screen, navigate through the icons at the top of the display until you find the icon for a setting you want to install in the Quick Menu. With that icon highlighted, press Menu/Set and the camera will prompt you to move to the "desired position." At that point, one of the icons in the bottom row will be highlighted; use the rear dial or the Left and Right buttons to move that highlight to the position where you want to locate the setting whose

icon you selected from the top rows. If there is no blank space available in the bottom row, just highlight an occupied space and press Menu/Set; the new icon will replace the existing one.

An easier way to add icons to the bottom row is simply to touch an icon with your finger and drag it to the bottom row, onto an empty spot, or drag it onto an occupied slot to replace the icon that is already there. When you have finished adding icons to the Quick Menu, press the Q.Menu button to return to the shooting screen.

The eighth and final screen of the Custom menu is shown in Figure 7-34.

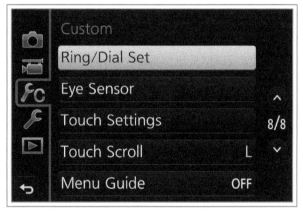

Figure 7-34. Screen 8 of Custom Menu

## RING/DIAL SET

This first option on screen 8 of the Custom menu lets you set the function or functions of the rear dial, at the top right of the camera, and the control ring, the large ring around the lens. When you select this menu option, the camera displays the screen shown in Figure 7-35. On that screen, highlight and select the icon for the control you want to customize, and the camera will display the available settings for that control.

In Chapter 5, I discussed the settings that are assigned to each control by default, as well as the settings that can be assigned instead, using this menu option. I generally use the default settings, which are very useful, but, if you want to have the control ring or rear dial control just one option, you can do that with this menu item.

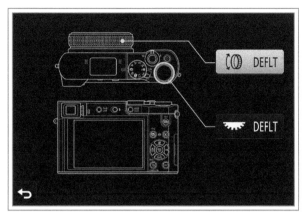

Figure 7-35. Ring/Dial Set Menu Options Screen

## EYE SENSOR

This next item on the Custom menu has two sub-options with controls for the operation of the eye sensor, the small slot at the right of the viewfinder that detects the presence of your eye (or another object). Those sub-options are Sensitivity and LVF/Monitor Switch, as shown in Figure 7-36.

You can set Sensitivity to High or Low. I have not found much difference between these settings. If you find that the eye sensor is triggering the switch from LCD to viewfinder when you don't want it to, you can try setting this option to Low to see if that helps.

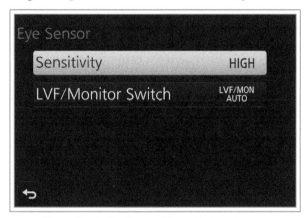

Figure 7-36. Eye Sensor Menu Options Screen

The other setting for this menu option is LVF/Monitor Switch. There are three possible choices for this item: LVF/Monitor Auto, LVF, and Monitor. With the first choice, the camera will switch automatically between using the LCD screen and using the viewfinder as your eye approaches or moves away from the eye sensor. If you choose LVF, the viewfinder will always be in use; if you choose Monitor, the LCD display will always be in use.

I find it convenient to use the LVF/Monitor Auto option, so the camera will switch to using the viewfinder whenever my head comes near to the viewfinder. However, in some cases, such as if you are doing close-up shots from a tripod, you might want to leave the monitor always in use, even though your head may come near to the camera as you adjust a setting. Or, you might want to set the viewfinder to be in effect at all times when you don't want to have the LCD display illuminate to distract those around you.

You can also switch the behavior of the eye sensor by pressing the Fn4/LVF button, assuming it remains assigned to this option. (Or, you can assign another button to this option if you want, though it makes sense to leave the Fn4 button with this duty, because it is located next to the eye sensor.)

## TOUCH SETTINGS

With the four sub-options of this menu item, you can control several aspects of the operation of the ZS100's excellent touch screen capability.

### Touch Screen

This first option can be turned either on or off. If it is on, the touch screen works as expected. If it is off, none of the touch screen operations are active, and the touch screen icons do not appear at all. The next three sub-options on this menu will be dimmed and unavailable in that case.

If you prefer the classic operation of a camera that uses only traditional buttons and dials, you can leave this setting turned off and not have to worry about using the touch screen options. I find it useful to turn the touch screen off when I am using the viewfinder on a sunny day, because my nose may bump into the screen and activate a focus frame or otherwise cause distraction. However, the touch screen adds a great deal of convenience to using the camera, and in most situations I leave it turned on.

### Touch Tab

In Chapter 5, I discussed the operation of the touch tab, a set of touch controls at the right edge of the shooting screen. When you touch the small left-facing arrow, the tab opens up to reveal controls for touch zoom, touch shutter, touch autoexposure, and touch peaking (available when manual focus is in use). If you want to use the camera's other touch capabilities but not the particular functions available through the touch tab, you can turn this option off.

### Touch AF

This sub-option enables or disables the use of the Touch AF and Touch AE functions. There are three possible settings for this item: AF, AF+AE, or Off, as shown in Figure 7-37. If you choose Off, then touching the screen does not have any effect on autofocus or autoexposure.

**Figure 7-37. Touch AF Menu Options Screen**

If you choose AF, you can change the location of the focusing area on the shooting screen just by touching the screen. If AF Mode on screen 2 of the Recording menu is set to Face/Eye Detection, 49-Area, 1-Area, or Pinpoint AF, touch the focus frame that is displayed on the screen, and you can then move that frame around the screen. You can change the size of the frame by pinching or pulling the area of the frame with your fingers. When you have the frame located as you want it, press the Set icon in the lower right corner of the screen, or press the Menu/Set button.

If the 49-Area option for AF Mode is in use, touching the screen brings up the screen for adjusting the area of the focus zones. With the 1-Area option, touching the focus frame makes it movable and resizable. The same is true for the Pinpoint AF option.

If AF Mode is set to Tracking, touch a subject on the screen to start tracking that subject.

For Touch AF to operate properly, the Touch Shutter option must be turned off. Otherwise, the camera would take a picture when you touched the screen. To turn off the current AF operation, touch the AF Off icon on the left side of the screen.

The second choice of setting for Touch AF is AF+AE. If you choose this option, the camera uses the same focus frame as with the 1-Area AF Mode setting, regardless of the AF Mode setting that is in effect. You can change the location and size of the focus frame by moving it with your finger and resize it by pinching and pulling the screen. In addition, the camera places a small, blue cross in the center of the frame and optimizes exposure for that area.

### Touch Pad AF

The last sub-option for the Touch Settings menu item is Touch Pad AF. This option is for use only when you are using the viewfinder. As you look at the scene through the viewfinder, you can move the autofocus frame around the display with your finger.

There are three sub-options: Exact, Offset, and Off. If you choose Off, this option is not activated at all. With Exact, you press on the screen in the position where you want the focus frame to be located on the viewfinder display. If you choose Offset, you can cause the focus frame to move just by moving your finger a certain distance in the desired direction, without pressing at the exact location of the frame in the viewfinder. I prefer the Exact option, because I can just press the screen where I want the focus frame to be located.

This option can be quite useful if you are taking pictures on a sunny day and need to move the focus frame around on the viewfinder display. However, if you don't need to move the focus frame often, it can be distracting, because your nose can touch the screen and put a confusing focus frame display in the viewfinder.

## TOUCH SCROLL

This next option on the last screen of the Custom menu lets you set the speed for scrolling of the display when you are viewing images and videos using the touch screen in playback mode. Choose High or Low for the speed with which images scroll when you drag them with your finger.

## MENU GUIDE

This final option on the Custom menu determines what screen is displayed when you turn the Mode dial to select Scene mode or Creative Control mode. If Menu Guide is turned on, then, when you turn the dial to the SCN or artist's palette position, the camera displays the selection screen for that mode. For example, if you turn the Mode dial to the Creative Control position with this option turned on, the camera will display a screen like that shown in Figure 7-38, where you can immediately select a setting for this mode. For Scene mode, the camera displays the selection screen for choosing one of the numerous scene settings.

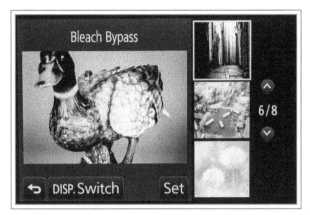

Figure 7-38. Creative Control Mode Screen with Menu Guide On

If this menu option is turned off, then, when the Mode dial is turned to one of those two settings, the camera displays the recording screen, so you will be ready to start shooting an image or video without pausing to select a scene type or filter effect first.

What setting you choose for this option depends on whether you are likely to want to change the setting for either of these modes when you first select it. It is easy to change the setting from the recording screen; you can just touch the setting's icon in the upper left corner of the screen to bring up the selection screen, so I tend to leave Menu Guide turned off.

## The Setup Menu

The Setup menu, designated by the solitary wrench icon, has five screens of options for adjusting settings having to do with general camera functions. Its first screen is shown in Figure 7-39.

Figure 7-39. Screen 1 of Setup Menu

### ONLINE MANUAL

This first option on the Setup menu provides information about where to download the online user's guide for this camera from Panasonic. The item has two sub-options, URL Display and QR Code Display, as shown in Figure 7-40.

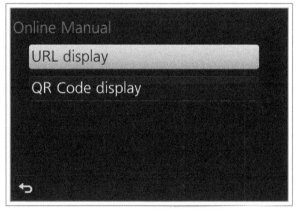

Figure 7-40. Online Manual Menu Options Screen

With the URL Display option, you can use a computer to go to the URL that is provided in this item and download the manual from that URL. With the QR Code Display option, you can display the QR code. When that code is displayed, you can aim the camera of a smartphone at the code, and, using a QR reading app on the phone, download the manual to the phone (or tablet).

### CLOCK SET

When you use your ZS100 camera for the first time, it should prompt you to set the clock. If it does not do so, or if you later need to adjust the date and time, use this menu option. When you select it and press the Right button or Menu/Set, the camera will display a screen like that shown in Figure 7-41.

Figure 7-41. Date and Time Settings Screen

On that screen, navigate through the blocks for time and date using the rear dial, the Left and Right buttons, or the touch screen, and adjust the settings with the Up and Down buttons or icons. You can then highlight the Style block to select the order for month, day, and year and whether to use 24-hour format for the time. When everything is set properly, navigate to the Set block in the lower right corner of the display and select it to confirm the settings. (The Set block appears only if some change has been made.)

## WORLD TIME

This is a handy function when you're traveling to another time zone. Highlight and select World Time to move to the next screen, which gives you the options of choosing Destination and Home. First, select Home and use the Left and Right buttons, the rear dial, or the touch arrows to scroll through the world map as shown in Figure 7-42, and use the Menu/Set button or touch the Set icon to set your Home area.

Figure 7-42. World Map for World Time Menu Option

Then, on the World Time screen, highlight Destination, and again scroll through the world map to select the time zone you will be traveling to. The map will show

you the time in both locations. Press Menu/Set or touch the Set icon to select this zone for the camera's internal clock. Then, any images taken will reflect the correct time in the new time zone. When you return from your trip, go back to the World Time item and select Home to cancel the changed time zone setting.

On both the Home and Destination screens, you can press the Up button or touch the sun and clock icon in the lower right corner to turn Daylight Saving Time on or off for that time zone.

## TRAVEL DATE

This menu item has two sub-options for entering information when you take a trip, so the camera can record that information with your images. First, Travel Setup lets you set a range of dates for the trip, so the camera can record which day of the trip each image was taken. When you return from the trip, if you use the Text Stamp function to "stamp" the recorded data on the images, the images will show they were taken on Day 1, Day 2, etc., of the trip. In addition, the camera will remind you of how many days remain before your trip, by displaying notations such as - 3 Days, etc., until the date of the trip arrives. The date entries for Travel Setup are self-explanatory; just follow the arrows and the camera's prompts.

After you set departure and return dates, you also can set the location, which will display along with the day number. To do that, after setting up the dates, select Location from the Travel Date menu item, enter the name of the location using the text-entry tools, and select Set from that screen, as shown in Figure 7-43.

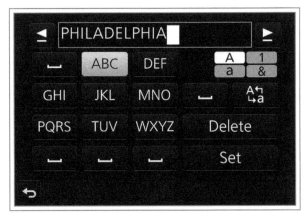

Figure 7-43. Travel Date Text Entry Screen

## Wi-Fi

This option is used to set up a Wi-Fi connection with the ZS100. I will discuss the Wi-Fi operations of the camera in Chapter 9.

Screen 2 of the Setup menu is shown in Figure 7-44.

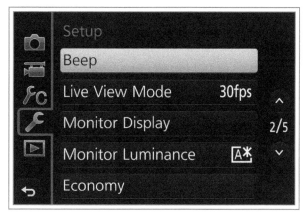

Figure 7-44. Screen 2 of Setup Menu

## Beep

This first option on screen 2 of the Setup menu lets you adjust several sound items, as shown in Figure 7-45. First is the volume of the beeps the camera makes when you press a button, such as when half-pressing the shutter button to evaluate focus. You can set the beeps to off, normal, or loud. It's useful to be able to turn the beeps off if you're going to be in an environment where such noises are not welcome.

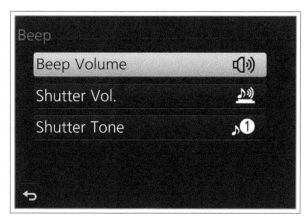

Figure 7-45. Beep Menu Options Screen

Second is the volume of the shutter operation sound. Again, it's good to be able to mute the shutter sound. Finally, you can choose from three shutter sounds. If you want to silence all sounds quickly while also disabling the flash and the AF assist lamp, use the Silent Mode option on screen 1 of the Custom menu.

## Live View Mode

This option lets you choose either 30 fps (the default) or 60 fps for the operation of the camera's LCD display screen. The setting of 30 frames per second emphasizes quality, but the display may not always refresh quickly enough to keep up with a fast-moving subject. In addition, with some settings, such as the Rough Monochrome or Silky Monochrome settings, the display slows down as the camera processes the effect. If you choose the 60 fps setting, the display will be better able to show any action smoothly, or to maintain a smooth appearance as you pan across the scene. The quality of the display may suffer slightly, but not badly. So, if you find the display stuttering or smearing, you may want to try the 60 fps option.

This setting does not affect the viewfinder, which always uses the 60 fps setting.

## Monitor Display/Viewfinder

This menu option is unusual because its name changes depending on whether you are viewing the menu on the LCD monitor or in the viewfinder. If you are viewing it on the monitor, it is called Monitor Display; if you are using the viewfinder, it is called Viewfinder. It operates the same way in either case. However, if you make adjustments to this item while using the monitor, those adjustments will affect only the monitor. You can make separate adjustments while using the viewfinder, and those adjustments will affect only the viewfinder.

Figure 7-46. Monitor Display Adjustment Screen

As shown in Figure 7-46, which shows the version for adjusting the monitor, this option has five linear scales for making adjustments. Use the Up and Down buttons or the touch screen icons to select a scale, and then use the Left and Right buttons, the rear dial, or the touch screen to adjust the settings on the scale for each item. The normal settings are in the middle of the scale; move the yellow blocks to the left of the scale to decrease a setting, or to the right to increase the value.

Starting from the top, the scales control brightness, contrast, saturation, red tint, and blue tint. When you have made your adjustments on each scale, you have to press the Menu/Set button to make them take effect.

I have never found a need to adjust the settings for either the LCD display or the viewfinder, but if you find the color, contrast, or brightness of either display is not to your liking, you can use these adjustments as you wish.

## MONITOR LUMINANCE

This setting affects the brightness of the LCD display, but not the viewfinder, though you can adjust it while using the viewfinder. This setting is different from the brightness setting of the previous menu option in that it provides overall, on-or-off adjustments, rather than a sliding scale. As shown in Figure 7-47, this menu item has four settings, each accompanied by an asterisk: A*, 1*, 2*, and 3*.

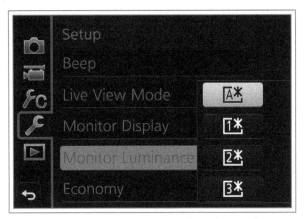

Figure 7-47. Monitor Luminance Menu Options Screen

With the A* (Auto) setting, the brightness will adjust according to ambient lighting conditions. With the 1* setting, the screen becomes extra-bright to compensate for sunlight or other conditions that make it hard to see the screen. It reverts to normal after 30 seconds, but you can press any control button to restore the brightness. The 2* setting provides standard illumination, and the 3* setting sets the display to a dimmer level than normal.

Using the A* or the 1* setting decreases battery life. If you find it hard to see the screen in bright sunlight and

don't want to use the viewfinder, you might want to try the 1* setting to see if the added brightness gives you enough visibility to compose your shots or view your recorded images clearly.

I use the A* setting myself, and always keep an extra battery handy.

## ECONOMY

The next option on the Setup menu, Economy, has two sub-options, Sleep Mode and Auto LVF/Monitor Off

### Sleep Mode

The Sleep Mode option puts the camera into a dormant state after a specified period when you have not used any of the camera's controls. The period can be set to one, two, five, or ten minutes, or the option can be turned off, in which case the camera never turns off automatically (unless it runs out of battery power). To cancel Sleep Mode, press the shutter button halfway and the camera will come back to life. Sleep Mode does not turn off the camera during a slide show or when an AC adapter is connected, or during the recording or playback of a motion picture, along with a few other situations.

### Auto LVF/Monitor Off

The Auto LVF/Monitor setting controls how soon the monitor turns off when no controls have been used for a time. The possible choices are five minutes, two minutes, or one minute. After the monitor goes blank, you can press any control button or touch the screen to restore the display. As with the Sleep Mode setting, this setting does not operate during slide shows, during a Time Lapse Shot session, and in a few other situations.

Screen 3 of the Setup menu is shown in Figure 7-48.

Figure 7-48. Screen 3 of Setup Menu

## USB MODE

If you are going to connect the camera directly to a computer or printer, you need to go to this menu item and select the appropriate setting from the choices shown in Figure 7-49: Select on Connection, PictBridge (PTP) (for connecting to a printer), or PC. PTP stands for Picture Transfer Protocol, a standard used for this type of connection.

Figure 7-49. USB Mode Menu Options Screen

If you choose Select on Connection, you don't select the setting until after you have plugged the USB cable into the device to which you are connecting the camera. The ZS100 connects to a computer using the USB 2.0 connection standard, assuming your computer has a USB port of that speed. (If not, the camera will still connect at the slower speed of the computer's older USB port.)

## TV CONNECTION

This menu item has three sub-options: HDMI Mode (Play), HDMI Info Display (Rec), and Viera Link. The HDMI Mode option sets the output resolution for the images that are sent to an HDTV when the camera is connected to the TV with a micro-HDMI cable in playback mode. The available choices are Auto, 4K, 1080p, 1080i, 720p, and 480p. Ordinarily, if you select Auto the images should appear properly on the HDTV. If they do not, you can try one of the other settings to see if the display improves.

The HDMI Info Display (Rec) option determines whether or not the camera outputs setting icons and other technical information when it is connected to an HDTV or other device, such as a video recorder or monitor, by a micro-HDMI cable in recording mode. If this option is set to On, then the signal that goes

through the cable includes all of the information that appears on the camera's screen. If it is set to Off, then the signal going through the cable includes only the image or video (and audio, if applicable).

This option is of use when you are using the ZS100 to capture images while the camera is connected to a monitor. With this setting turned off, the signal sent to the monitor will include only the actual scenes viewed by the camera, rather than the setting icons, focus frames and other items that would not be wanted in the final images. However, this option's usefulness is limited because the ZS100 camera cannot output any signal through the HDMI port when it is recording video. So, although the camera can output a "clean" HDMI signal, that signal cannot originate with a video recording, only with recording of still images.

As a workaround for this issue, you can output a clean HDMI signal while the camera is in standby mode, when you have not pressed the motion picture button to start video recording. In that mode, you can connect the camera to an external video recorder using a micro-HDMI cable, and the recorder can record the scene that is being viewed by the camera in standby mode. I have done this successfully with an Atomos Shogun video recorder. With the HDMI Info Display option turned off, the recorder captured the scene viewed by the camera, with no icons or other extraneous information. The resulting video file was of excellent quality and could be readily imported into software for editing. However, it is expensive and cumbersome to use an external recorder, so this option is not one you necessarily would use often.

The Viera Link option is for use when you are connecting the ZS100 to a Panasonic Viera HDTV using a micro-HDMI cable. If you leave this option turned off, then the operations of the camera are controlled by the camera's own controls. If you turn it on, then the Viera TV's remote control can also control the operations of the camera, so you can play slide shows or review individual images and movies.

### M/FT

This option lets you choose whether distance is displayed using meters or feet as the unit of measure on the zoom scale.

## Menu Resume

This menu item can be set either on or off. When it is turned on, whenever you enter the menu system, the camera displays the last menu item you had selected previously. When this option is turned off, the camera always starts back at the top of the first screen of the Recording menu. If there is a particular menu item you need to adjust often, this option can be of considerable use, because you can just press the Menu/Set button and the item will appear, ready for you to make your setting. For example, if you need to change the Metering Mode setting frequently, you can turn on Menu Resume. Then, whenever you need to get back to the Metering Mode setting, just press Menu/Set, and the item will be there at your fingertips. (Of course, you also could set a function button to bring up this option, or you could use the Quick Menu, but this is one other approach to consider.)

## Menu Background

This option lets you choose the background color for the menu screens. If you don't like the default option of dark gray, you can choose one of the other selections. You might find the menus are more readable with one of the lighter colors, but I have found no reason to use this setting.

Screen 4 of the Setup menu is shown in Figure 7-50.

Figure 7-50. Screen 4 of Setup Menu

## Menu Information

This option lets you turn on or off the display of information at the top of each menu screen, which provides a line of informative text explaining the function of whichever menu item is currently highlighted. For example, Figure 7-51 shows the menu

screen with this feature in use when the Burst Rate option is highlighted on screen 2 of the Recording menu.

Figure 7-51. Menu Information Display for Burst Rate Option

Most of the entries are too long to fit on one line, and they scroll across the display. There are entries for all of the main menu items and for many of the sub-options as well. I find this feature to be very helpful and it is not obtrusive, so I always leave it turned on.

## Language

This option gives you the choice of language for the display of commands and information on the LCD screen. The language selection screen for my U.S. version of the camera is shown in Figure 7-52.

Figure 7-52. Language Selection Screen

Presumably, models sold elsewhere offer different choices. If your camera happens to be set to a language that you don't read, you can find the language option by going into the Setup menu (look for the wrench icon), and then scrolling to this option, which is marked by an icon showing a man's head with a word balloon.

## VERSION DISPLAY

This item has no settings; when you select it, it displays the version of the camera's firmware that is currently installed. As I write this, my ZS100 has version 1.0 of the firmware installed, as shown in Figure 7-53.

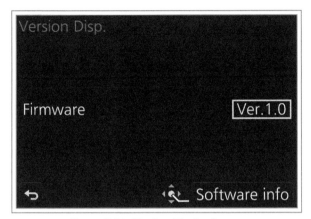

Figure 7-53. **Version Display Screen**

Firmware is somewhat like both software and hardware; it is the programming electronically recorded into the camera, either at the factory or through your computer if you upgrade the firmware with an update provided by Panasonic. A new version of the firmware can fix bugs and can even provide new features, so it's well worthwhile checking the Panasonic website periodically for updates. Instructions for installing an update are provided on the website. The process usually involves downloading a file to your computer, saving that file to an SD card formatted for the camera, then placing that card in the camera so the firmware can be installed.

## EXPOSURE COMPENSATION RESET

This option controls whether or not an exposure compensation value that has been set will be retained in memory when the camera is turned off or the recording mode is changed. By default, this option is turned off, and any positive or negative brightness value is not reset to zero. In other words, the value is retained in memory for the next time the camera is turned on, or the current recording mode is selected again.

If you set this option to On, then the exposure compensation value is reset to zero when the camera is powered off or the recording mode changes.

I generally leave this option set to On, because I am unlikely to want to use the same amount of exposure compensation the next time I use the camera, and I

might forget to reset it to zero on my own. However, if you have a practice of usually shooting with a certain amount of exposure compensation, you might want to leave this option off, so the value will be retained in memory from one shooting session to the next.

## SELF TIMER AUTO OFF

This next option controls whether the self-timer remains set after you turn the camera off and back on. If this option is turned on, then, when the camera turns off the self-timer will be deactivated and will not be in effect when the camera is turned on the next time. If this option is turned off, then the self-timer will remain in effect even after the camera has been powered off.

How you use this feature depends on your particular needs. If you often use the self-timer, it can be convenient to leave it activated so it will be ready the next time you turn on the camera. Or, if you use it rarely, you can turn this option on so the self-timer will not be in effect when you don't want it.

The fifth and final screen of the Setup menu is shown in Figure 7-54.

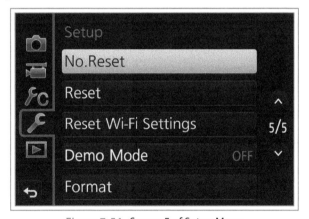

Figure 7-54. **Screen 5 of Setup Menu**

## NUMBER RESET

This function lets you reset the folder and image number for the next image to be recorded in the camera. If you don't use this option, the numbers of your images will keep increasing until they reach 999, even if you change to a different memory card. If you want each new card to start with images numbered from 1 up, use the Number Reset function each time you start a new card, or a new project for which you would like to have freshly numbered images. I prefer not to reset the numbers, because I find it easier to keep track of my images if the numbers keep getting larger; I would find it confusing to have images with duplicate numbers on my various SD cards.

## RESET

This menu option resets all Recording menu settings to their original states, except for Face Recognition and Profile Setup settings, which can be reset separately using this option. It also resets all Setup and Custom menu settings to their original states. This is a convenient way to get the camera back to its default mode, so you can start with fresh settings before you experiment with new ones. The camera prompts you several times, asking if you want to reset all Recording menu settings, then all Face Recognition and Profile Setup settings, and then all Setup/Custom menu parameters. Folder numbers and date and time settings are not reset by this option.

## RESET WI-FI SETTINGS

This option resets all Wi-Fi settings for the camera. You might want to use this option if you are selling your camera, to avoid giving away information about your wireless networks. You also might want to use this option if you are having trouble getting the Wi-Fi settings configured and you want to make a fresh start.

## DEMO MODE

If you choose this option, the camera takes a while to carry out an internal process and then places a demonstration image on the screen, with several different areas of possible focus. You can then touch the screen to see how the Post Focus option works. You also can touch the Peak icon for a demonstration of focus peaking. To cancel this demonstration, press the shutter button halfway.

## FORMAT

This last item on the Setup menu is one of the more important menu options. Choose this process only when you want or need to completely wipe all of the data from a memory card. When you select the Format option, the camera will ask you if you want to delete all of the data on the card, as shown in Figure 7-55.

**Figure 7-55. Format Confirmation Screen**

If you reply by selecting Yes, the camera will proceed to erase all images and videos, including any that have been locked using the Protect option on the Playback menu. It's a good idea to use this command with any new memory card you place in the camera for the first time so the card will be properly formatted to store new images and videos.

# Chapter 8: Motion Pictures

Until fairly recently, the video recording features of compact cameras seemed to be included almost as afterthoughts, so the user would have some ability to record video clips but without many advanced features. Over the past few years, though, camera makers, particularly Panasonic, have increased the sophistication of the video functions of small cameras to a remarkable level. The ZS100 is not ready to take the place of a dedicated video camera for professional productions, because it lacks features such as jacks for external microphones and clean HDMI output while recording video. But in terms of pure video recording capability, it has great abilities. I will discuss how to take advantage of those features in this chapter.

## Basics of ZS100 Videography

One aspect of motion picture recording with the ZS100 that can be somewhat confusing is how to select the shooting mode. For still photography with this camera, when you choose a shooting mode by turning the Mode dial on top of the camera, that is the mode that you will shoot your pictures in. That is not quite how it works with movie recording. In the motion picture arena, where you set the Mode dial has some effect on your shooting, but not as direct an effect as for still photos.

Figure 8-1. **Mode Dial - Creative Video**

If you look at the Mode dial, as shown in Figure 8-1, you will see icons for the various shooting modes for still photography: Intelligent Auto, Program, Aperture Priority, Shutter Priority, Manual, Custom, Panorama, Scene, and Creative Control. There is also one entry on the dial for movies, represented by the letter M with a movie camera icon: Creative Video mode, which is

shown as selected in this illustration. However, because of the red motion picture button, you do not have to set the Mode dial to Creative Video mode to record a movie (though you certainly can, as I'll discuss shortly). In fact, you can set the Mode dial to any of its settings except Panorama and still record a movie. (For the C setting, it depends on what shooting mode was saved to the Custom mode slot.) But the results may not be what you might expect based on the name of the shooting mode.

For example, when the Mode dial is set to M for Manual exposure mode, if you press the red button you will not be shooting a movie in Manual exposure mode. In fact, you'll be shooting a movie with the camera adjusting the exposure automatically by setting the aperture and shutter speed. This is the same result you'll get with any of the four PASM shooting modes on the Mode dial (Program, Aperture Priority, Shutter Priority, and Manual).

Here is where the situation gets slightly complicated. As I just noted, when you set the Mode dial to some of the major still-shooting modes, such as A, S, or M, the camera does not follow that mode's behavior for setting exposure when you press the red motion picture button. But the camera does use some (but not all) of the other settings that have been made in that shooting mode. For example, if you have the camera set to Aperture Priority mode on the Mode dial, when you press the red button to make a movie, the camera does not let you set the aperture; instead, it chooses both aperture and shutter speed. However, the camera does use some of the settings that have been chosen through the Recording menu while the camera was in Aperture Priority mode, such as white balance, metering mode, and AF Mode. Of course, several options from the Recording menu make no sense when recording movies, and therefore have no effect when you press the red button, including Flash Mode, Auto Bracket, and Burst Rate.

You also can set the Mode dial to Intelligent Auto mode, and the camera will take over even more of the settings for your movies, or you can set it to Scene mode and for movies it will use the basic settings for the type of scene you select, in many cases. For certain settings, though, the camera will use different scene types, as follows: For the Clear in Backlight scene type, the camera will use the Portrait type. For Clear Nightscape, Artistic Nightscape, Handheld Night Shot, and Clear Night Portrait, the camera will use what Panasonic calls the "Low Light mode."

If you want to have more control over the camera's exposure settings while shooting a movie, that's the role of the movie-oriented setting on the Mode dial, Creative Video.

After you turn the Mode dial to that position, go into the menu system and select the top icon in the column at the left, which looks like a movie camera and stands for Creative Video mode, as shown in Figure 8-2.

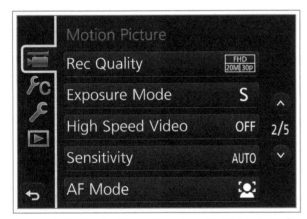

Figure 8-2. Creative Video Menu Icon Highlighted at Left

Then navigate to the Exposure Mode item on screen 2 of this menu and select it. The screen will display a menu of four exposure modes: P, A, S, and M, for Program, Aperture Priority, Shutter Priority, and Manual Exposure, as shown in Figure 8-3. (You also can get to a screen for selecting an exposure mode by touching the icon in the upper left corner of the display that represents the currently selected mode.)

You have to select one of those modes, which will then be in effect when you press the red button to record a movie. These modes work in ways similar to their still-photography counterparts, but they are distinctly separate, video-oriented shooting modes.

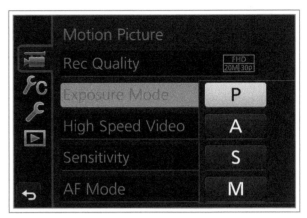

Figure 8-3. Exposure Mode Menu Options Screen

If you select Program, the camera chooses shutter speed and aperture, just as it does when the camera is set to one of the basic still-shooting modes on the Mode dial (P, A, S, or M).

If you choose Aperture Priority, you use the rear dial to select the aperture, and the camera will adjust its shutter speed for the correct exposure, if possible. The ZS100 has the same range of apertures available for setting in Creative Video mode as in Aperture Priority and Manual exposure mode: f/2.8 to f/8.0 when the lens is zoomed back to its full wide-angle position, and f/5.9 to f/8.0 when the lens is zoomed in fully.

If you choose Shutter Priority, you set the shutter speed and the camera sets the aperture. Because of the nature of video footage, which is normally recorded (in the United States) at 24 or 30 frames per second, the slowest shutter speed you can normally choose is 1/25 second (but see the note below under Manual mode, for an exception). You can choose from a wide range of faster shutter speeds, though. In fact, for motion pictures in Creative Video mode, the camera has a special range of shutter speeds for video recording: 1/25 second to 1/16000 second when recording with a 24 fps format, and 1/30 second to 1/16000 second when recording with a 30 fps or 60 fps format.

If you choose Manual Exposure, you set both shutter speed and aperture, in the same way as for still photography. Of course, as with shooting stills, the camera will not make any changes until you change one or both of the values, so, if the lighting changes, the exposure may be incorrect. There is one more benefit in terms of creative options if you shoot your video in this Manual mode: If you also have the focus mode set to manual focus, you can set the shutter speed as slow as 1/2 second. This shutter speed setting results in a video frame rate of two frames per second, considerably slower than the normal (U.S.) frame rate of 30 frames per second. It lets you record usable footage in conditions of very low light and can result in interesting effects, such as ghost-like streaks on the video frames if you move the camera. You would not want to use this slow shutter speed for taking video of a sporting event, but if you're making a science-fiction or horror movie, this feature could present some promising possibilities.

Note that you can change either shutter speed or aperture, or both, during your shot. So, for example, if you're shooting a movie in Creative Video mode using the Shutter Priority or Manual Exposure setting, you can gradually increase the shutter speed to a faster and faster value to make the picture fade gradually to black. One problem is that the motions of the rear dial may be heard on the audio track. But you can correct that problem in post-production by replacing or editing the audio track using video editing software such as Adobe Premiere Elements, if you are so inclined.

With the Manual Exposure mode for video recording, you can adjust the ISO setting, as with the other advanced modes. However, you cannot set ISO to Auto ISO when recording movies with Manual Exposure mode; ISO must be set to a numerical value.

With the Program, Aperture Priority, and Shutter Priority settings for Exposure Mode in Creative Video mode, you can adjust exposure compensation, just as with still photography, by pressing the Up button and then adjusting the on-screen scale. Also, when the camera is set to Creative Video mode, you can use the shutter button to start and stop video recording. In all other modes, pressing the shutter button will take a still picture, but in this one situation, you can use either the red motion picture button or the shutter button to control movie-making. This means, of course, that you cannot take still pictures with the camera in this mode.

## High Speed Video Recording

Another option for video recording in Creative Video mode is high speed video, which is selected from screen 2 of the Motion Picture menu, as shown in Figure 8-4. This feature is a specialized setting for shooting movies at a higher speed than normal, so the action will appear to be in slow motion when the footage is played at

normal speed. To record using this option, you need to use a memory card rated in UHS Speed Class 3.

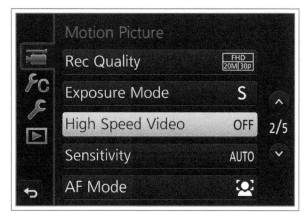

Figure 8-4. High Speed Video Highlighted on Menu

Once you have selected the High Speed Video option, there are very few other settings you can make for the motion pictures. They will be recorded at 120 frames per second, which is four times the normal speed for video recording (in the United States). Therefore, when the video is played back at the normal rate of 30 frames per second, the action will appear to be slowed down to one-fourth of the normal speed. You can use this option to analyze golf swings or other quick actions, or just to produce a dream-like aura for your scenes.

All high speed video is recorded using the MP4 format with full HD quality but with no sound. The AF Mode setting is fixed at 1-Area. You can choose from the complete range of options for the Photo Style setting, so you can, for example, record a slow-motion sequence in black and white. You cannot change the focus, zoom, exposure, or white balance settings once the recording has started. The maximum recording length is 7 minutes 29 seconds, which will play back at normal speed for roughly 30 minutes.

## Making Other Settings When Recording Movies

You likely will get excellent results if you use the camera's default settings and shoot your video using Intelligent Auto mode and following the guidelines for exposure and focus discussed above. But there are numerous other settings you can make using the camera's physical controls and the menu system. I will discuss those settings next, so you can take advantage of the flexibility they provide for motion picture recording with the ZS100.

## THE CREATIVE VIDEO MENU

First, I will discuss the one menu system I have not discussed in detail—the Creative Video menu, designated by the movie camera icon, as shown earlier in Figure 8-2. Before I discuss the individual items on the menu, there are a couple of general points to mention. First, the menu has five screens in most recording modes, but only one screen with four items when the camera is in the basic Intelligent Auto mode. In that mode, the only Motion Picture menu settings you can adjust are Snap Movie, Recording Format, Recording Quality, and AFS/AFF/AFC.

Second, when the full Creative Video menu is available, 11 of the items on that menu also appear as items on the Recording menu: Photo Style, Filter Settings, Sensitivity, AF Mode, AFS/AFF/AFC, Metering Mode, Highlight Shadow, i.Dynamic, i.Resolution, i.Zoom, and Digital Zoom. These settings are included on the Creative Video menu for convenience in setting them. You can adjust any of these 11 settings using either menu system, and the adjustment will take effect for both menus at the same time. For example, if you set Photo Style to Monochrome on the Recording menu, you will see that the Photo Style setting on the Creative Video menu has also changed to Monochrome. Or, if you turn on Digital Zoom on the Creative Video menu, you will see that Digital Zoom has been activated on the Recording menu as well.

Following is the list of all items that can appear on the Creative Video menu, whose first screen is shown in Figure 8-5. I will not include detailed information here for the settings that also appear on the Recording menu; for more information about them, see Chapter 4.

Figure 8-5. Screen 1 of Creative Video Menu

### Photo Style

This setting lets you choose the "look" of your footage. It works the same as it does for still photos. The choices are Standard, Vivid, Natural, Monochrome, Scenery, Portrait, and Custom. For more details, see Chapter 4.

### Filter Settings

This second menu item lets you select one of the numerous filter effects for your video. Several of the settings are not available: Rough Monochrome, Silky Monochrome, Soft Focus, Star Filter, and Sunshine. Toy Effect and Toy Pop are not available when 4K Live Cropping is active, and Miniature Effect is not available when 4K Live Cropping or 4K recording is active. None of the effects are available when High Speed Video is in use.

### 4K Live Cropping

This novel feature takes advantage of the ZS100's ability to shoot 4K video to let you create full HD video footage that is more stable and quiet than might otherwise be possible. It is designed to address two problems with normal video shooting. First, if you pan the camera (move it from side to side) across a scene, unless you have a tripod with a fluid pan head or some sort of mechanical stabilizing system, the footage is likely to be somewhat jerky, moving unevenly from side to side and possibly jerking up and down as well. Second, if you zoom the lens in on a subject, there may be some jerkiness and some sound from the zoom mechanism.

With the 4K Live Cropping feature, you shoot such scenes in the ultra-HD 4K format, and, because of the extra resolution in 4K footage, the camera is able to crop the full video frames down to create an in-camera panning or zooming effect. For example, if you shoot a 4K scene showing a garden wall that is fairly distant, the camera can crop the video frames down to show the same wall closer up, in full HD instead of 4K, and artificially create a panning effect across that wall. Similarly, if you shoot a building in the distance, the camera can convert the 4K footage to a closer, HD view of the building and create a zooming effect in the camera.

Figure 8-6 shows how a view of items on shelves looked when shot in 4K, and Figure 8-7 shows how that scene looked after it was cropped using Live Cropping, so the camera could pan across it.

Figure 8-6. Live Cropping Example: Before

Figure 8-7. Live Cropping Example: After

These are the steps to take to use this feature.

1. Turn on the camera and set the Mode dial to the Creative Video position.

2. Select 4K Live Cropping from screen 1 of the Creative Video menu.

3. On the next menu screen, choose 20 seconds or 40 seconds. That is the duration the camera will use for the panning or zooming motion it creates.

4. The camera will display a screen like that in Figure 8-8, with a yellow frame with arrows at the sides.

5. Using the touch screen or the rear dial and direction buttons, move the screen where you want it to start and resize it as you wish. If there is a feature you want the camera to pan across, for example, set the frame over the starting area for the panning motion. Press the Menu/Set button or touch the Set icon to lock the frame in place. This is the starting frame.

Figure 8-8. Live Cropping Setup Screen

6. The camera will then display the ending frame. Use the same process to size and locate the frame over the ending area for the panning or zooming action. If you want the camera to create a panning action, keep both frames the same size. If you want a zooming-in effect, make the ending frame smaller than the starting frame; for a zooming-out effect, make the ending frame larger than the starting frame. Use Menu/Set or the Set icon to lock it in place.

7. If you need to go back and change the locations of the frames, press the Fn1 to make the adjustment screens active again.

8. When the start and end frames are set as you want them, press the motion picture button and release it, to start the recording. Hold the camera as steady as possible, or have it on a tripod. After the set time period (20 or 40 seconds), the recording will end.

The result should be a smooth, professional-looking zoom or pan sequence, with no sounds from the zooming mechanism. This feature is worth experimenting with.

## Snap Movie

This feature lets you set up the camera to take a "snap movie," which is Panasonic's term for a video version of a snapshot. The resulting video is very short—just two, four, six, or eight seconds in duration, recorded using the FHD/20M/30p setting for MP4. You can specify whether to add a pull-focus effect (sudden changing of focus from one object to another) or a fade-in and/or fade-out effect, to add extra visual interest. Here are the steps to follow.

1. Turn on the camera in any recording mode other than Panorama.

2. Select Snap Movie from the first screen of the Motion Picture menu.

3. Select Set from the sub-options, and set the recording time to two, four, six, or eight seconds, turn Pull Focus on or off, and leave Fade turned off, or select from white-in, white-out, black-in, black-out, color-in, or color-out. You have to scroll through two screens to see all of the Fade options. The white and black options fade to or from a white or black screen. The color Fade options involve transitions between color and monochrome.

4. Go back to the main options screen and select On for Snap Movie, then press the Q.Menu button to go to the shooting screen.

5. If you turned on Pull Focus, touch your finger on the screen over the object that should start out in focus, then drag your finger to the second object, which should have the focus "pulled" to it. (To use physical buttons for this setting, you have to assign AF Mode to a function button and press that button at each position for the pull focus frames.)

6. Press and release the motion picture button and hold the camera as still as possible, keeping the pull focus objects in their proper locations, if Pull Focus is turned on.

The result should be a brief video snapshot, optionally including a fade-in or fade-out effect, and possibly a pull focus action as well. The camera records sound, though it fades in or out if a fade option is selected. You might find it worthwhile to use this option with no effects as a way to record a brief view of a scenic vista or an historic site, for example. If you record multiple snap movies, you can send them to your smartphone via Wi-Fi, as discussed in Chapter 9, and then combine them using the Panasonic Image App.

## Recording Format

With this setting, you choose the video format for any movies you make—AVCHD or MP4. Both options have advantages and disadvantages, and with either one, you have to also select Recording Quality, the next option on the menu. One major consideration is whether you want to shoot video using 4K quality, an advanced option that provides the highest possible resolution.

If you do want to shoot in 4K, you have to choose MP4 for Recording Format. If you don't plan to use 4K,

AVCHD gives the best results for HD (high definition) footage. If you want to record video just to make a general record of a trip or to make an inventory of household goods, MP4 lets you create files that are easier to manipulate with a computer than AVCHD files.

AVCHD stands for Advanced Video Coding High Definition. This format, developed jointly by Sony and Panasonic, has become increasingly common in advanced digital cameras in recent years. It provides excellent quality, and movies recorded in this format on the ZS100 can be used to create Blu-ray discs.

However, AVCHD files can be complicated to edit on a computer. In fact, just finding the AVCHD video files on a memory card can be a challenge. When you take a memory card from the ZS100 camera and insert it into a memory card reader for viewing on your computer, you can find the still-image files and .mp4 video files within the folder labeled DCIM and then within sub-folders with names such as 100MSDCF. The AVCHD files, however, are not within that folder; they are within a different folder named PRIVATE. Inside that folder you will find another one called AVCHD, and within that one another one called BDMV. Open that folder and you will see more files or folders, including a folder called STREAM, which contains files with the extension .mts. Those .mts files are the actual AVCHD files that can be edited with compatible software packages, such as Adobe Premiere Pro. (You don't have to worry about finding the file names if you connect your camera to the computer using the USB cable, only if you use a memory card reader, as I do.)

The next menu options are on screen 2 of the Creative Video menu, shown in Figure 8-9.

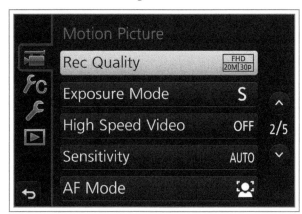

**Figure 8-9.** Screen 2 of Creative Video Menu

## Recording Quality

The choices for this next menu option depend on what you select for Recording Format, above. If you choose AVCHD, the choices for Recording Quality are FHD/28M/60p, FHD/17M/60i, FHD/24M/30p, and FHD/24M/24p. All of these provide Full HD (FHD) video with a resolution of 1920 x 1080 pixels. The 28M, 17M, and 24M figures state the maximum bit rate for each format, meaning the maximum number of megabits of information recorded per second. For example, the highest-quality format records up to about 28 million bits of information per second. The higher the bit rate, the more information is available to provide a clear image.

The last three characters of each format state the frames or fields per second that are recorded, along with the letter "p" or "i" standing for progressive or interlaced. With progressive formats, the camera records full frames of information; with interlaced formats, the camera records fields, or half-frames, and then interlaces them to form full video frames. In the United States the normal rate for recording and playing back video is 30 frames per second (fps). So, the FHD/24M/30p format yields full HD video with the normal frame rate, recording 30 full frames each second. The FHD/17M/60i option yields the same frame rate by recording 60 fields and interlacing them to form 30 full frames.

The FHD/24M/24p option is provided for those users who like to use a 24 fps video format. That frame rate is the one traditionally used by film-based movie cameras, and some people believe that using this standard provides a more "cinematic" appearance than the 30 fps option.

Finally, with the FHD/28M/60p setting, the ZS100 records 60 full frames per second, which yields higher quality than the alternative, which is "interlaced" video. The 60 frames are later translated into 30 frames for playback at the standard rate of 30 fps. However, if you want to, and your video editing software has this capability, you can play 60p footage in slow motion at one-half the normal speed and still maintain full HD quality. This possibility exists because, as noted above, the 60p footage is recorded with twice the number of full frames as 60i footage, so the quality of the video does not suffer if it is played back at one-half speed. (With other video formats, playback at half speed will appear choppy or jerky, because not enough frames were recorded to play smoothly at that speed.) So, if you think you may want to slow down your footage significantly with a computer for playback, you should choose the 60p setting.

If you choose MP4 for the Recording Mode, the Quality choices are the following, in descending order of quality: 4K/100M/30p; 4K/100M/24p; FHD/28M/60p; FHD/20M/30p; HD/10M/30p; and VGA/4M/30p.

The two available 4K options are special cases. The ability to shoot 4K video is one of the distinguishing features of the ZS100 camera. The standard known as 4K, sometimes known as UHD for ultra HD, is a relatively recent option for HDTVs. The 4K stands for 4,000, meaning each frame has a horizontal resolution of about 4,000 pixels. A standard HDTV has a horizontal resolution of 1920 pixels and a vertical resolution of 1080 pixels. The 4K format of the ZS100 has a horizontal resolution of 3840 and a vertical resolution of 2160. The overall resolution of this 4K image is about 8 megapixels, while the resolution of full HDTV is about 2 megapixels, so a 4K picture has 4 times the resolution of full HDTV.

Of course, to get the full benefit of 4K video footage, you need to view it on a 4K-capable TV set or monitor. However, if your editing software permits, you can shoot using the 4K format and then convert it to the more standard 1080 format for ordinary HDTV sets. With that approach, your video footage will contain considerably more detail than if you just recorded it using one of the 1080 formats.

There is one caveat about recording with the 4K quality setting: As noted earlier in this chapter, to record with this format you have to use a memory card of the fastest speed class, which is UHS Speed Class 3.

If you are not planning to record using the 4K setting, the other MP4 formats give you excellent options. You can record in full HD with a 28 megabit-per-second bit rate, giving you excellent quality. You can choose 60p for highest quality and the ability to produce slow-motion footage at one-half speed, or the more standard 30p option. If you would like to work with smaller files that still produce excellent quality, you can choose to record with the HD/10M/30p option, which records using HD rather than FHD, meaning the image size is 1280 x 720 pixels, rather than 1920 x 1080.

Finally, if you need the smallest possible files at a much lower quality, you can record with the VGA option (640 X 480 pixels, 4:3 aspect ratio). VGA is a low-resolution format that is suitable if you need to make an inventory of possessions or some other non-critical video recording. It also can be useful if you need a video recording with a small file size that can be sent by e-mail.

### Exposure Mode

I discussed this option earlier. It is available for selection only when the Mode dial is at the Creative Video position. It provides choices of Program, Aperture Priority, Shutter Priority, or Manual Exposure for the mode for recording motion pictures. With the Aperture Priority, Shutter Priority, and Manual Exposure modes, you can control aperture and/or shutter speed. With the Manual and Shutter Priority settings, you can select a shutter speed as fast as 1/16000 second and as slow as 1/25 second, depending on the recording format. With the Manual Exposure setting, you can select a shutter speed as slow as 1/2 second when manual focus is in effect.

### High Speed Video

As discussed earlier in this chapter, this setting lets you record movies at 120 fps so they can be played back at one-fourth the normal speed for slow-motion footage. It is available only in Creative Video mode.

### Sensitivity

This menu option also is available for selection only when the Mode dial is set to the Creative Video position. Ordinarily, ISO sensitivity cannot be set to anything other than Auto ISO when recording motion pictures. However, in Motion Picture mode, you can use this option to set ISO to Auto ISO, or to specific values of 125, 200, 400, 800, 1600, 3200, or 6400. If Auto ISO is in effect during movie recording, the ISO Limit Set option on screen 6 of the Recording menu has no effect. Auto ISO is not available for video recording when Exposure Mode is set to Manual Exposure.

### AF Mode

The AF Mode option operates as it does for still images. You can select a method of autofocus operation and place the frame or zones, as discussed in Chapter 4. However, the Pinpoint setting is not available for video.

Figure 8-10 shows Screen 3 of the Creative Video menu.

Figure 8-10.  Screen 3 of Creative Video Menu

### AFS/AFF/AFC

This next menu option, as discussed earlier, mirrors the same setting on the Recording menu. It does not matter which one of these choices you select for purposes of autofocus for video recording, so you should select the option that you will want to use for recording still images. The camera's autofocus behavior for video recording is controlled by the Continuous AF menu option, discussed below. If you have Continuous AF turned off, the camera will not focus on its own during video recording; you have to press the shutter button halfway to cause the camera to use its autofocus mechanism. If you have Continuous AF turned on, the camera focuses continuously during video recording. (Of course, the focus mode has to be set to AF, AF Macro, or Macro Zoom for the camera to use autofocus at all.)

### Continuous AF

As discussed above, this setting controls how the ZS100 uses its autofocus during video recording, assuming you have the focus mode set to an autofocus setting. If the Continuous AF option is turned on, the camera will adjust its focus continuously as the distance to the subject changes. If it is turned off, the camera will use its autofocus only when you press the shutter button halfway.

### Level Shot

This option is designed to correct a tilt away from the horizontal in a video sequence. When this function is turned on, if the camera detects that the camera is tilted to one side or the other, it will correct the tilt to make the video frame appear horizontal, to the extent possible. The camera uses electronic processing to crop the frame slightly to accomplish this leveling, so some pixels are lost at the edges of the frame.

I have found this function to be quite capable of straightening a video frame, within some limits. Figures 8-11 and 8-12 illustrate how well the camera leveled a scene shot with a considerable tilt.

Figure 8-11. Level Shot Example: Without Correction

Figure 8-12. Level Shot Example: With Correction

For these images, I recorded two brief videos of the same scene with the ZS100 on a tripod, in both cases with the camera tilted to one side, but with Level Shot turned on for one version.

Figure 8-11 is a still frame saved from the video with Level Shot turned off, showing the degree of tilt. Figure 8-12 is a frame from the video with Level Shot turned on, in which the camera electronically corrected the tilt so the scene looks level. Of course, there may be times when it is appropriate for the scene to be tilted. In that case, be sure to leave this option turned off. This feature does not affect still images, only video. It also cannot be used with 4K video or VGA video.

## Metering Mode

This menu option gives you access to the same three metering methods found on the Recording menu: Multiple, Center-weighted, and Spot. As with several other Motion Picture menu options, this one mirrors the item on the Recording menu; if either one is changed, the corresponding entry on the other menu is

changed to the same setting. If AF Mode is set to an option with a movable focus frame, such as 1-Area, and Spot metering is also active, you can move the focus frame and Spot metering cross around the frame during video recording, just as with still shooting.

## Highlight Shadow

This option, also, is identical to the corresponding one on the Recording menu.

Screen 4 of the Creative Video menu is shown in Figure 8-13.

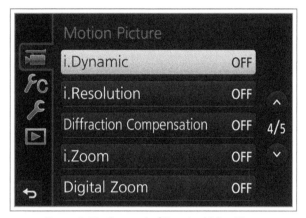

Figure 8-13. Screen 4 of Creative Video Menu

## Intelligent Dynamic

This setting works the same as the similar setting on the Recording menu and mirrors its setting.

## Intelligent Resolution

This setting also works the same as its still-photo counterpart, except that the Extended setting will be changed to Low when recording movies.

## Diffraction Compensation

This setting operates the same way as the option on the Recording menu.

## Intelligent Zoom

This setting is another one that is no different from the version on the Recording menu.

## Digital Zoom

This is another setting that's the same as that on the Recording menu.

Screen 5 of the Creative Video menu is shown in Figure 8-14.

Figure 8-14. Screen 5 of Creative Video Menu

Figure 8-16. Set of Icons for Silent Operation

### Flicker Decrease

This option, is not available when the Mode dial is set to the Creative Video position; it is available only in the PASM shooting modes. It provides a way to set the shutter speed used for video recording to reduce the flickering effect that can occur in some cases. You can leave the option turned off, or select 1/50, 1/60, 1/100, or 1/120 second.

### Silent Operation

This menu option is available only when the Mode dial is at the Creative Video position. When it is turned on, the camera gives you a special set of touch screen icons that you can use to control settings during motion picture recording, to avoid using physical controls that might make sounds that are recorded with the video.

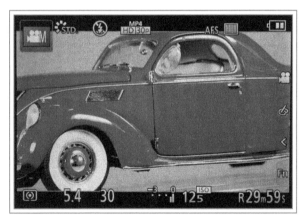

Figure 8-15. Touch Icon to Turn on Silent Operation

To use this feature, once a video recording is in progress, touch the movie camera icon at the top of the line of touch icons on the right side of the screen, as shown in Figure 8-15. The camera will open up a tab with a set of video-related icons, as shown in Figure 8-16.

Touch one of those icons to control the setting it represents. From the top, they stand for zoom, aperture, shutter speed, exposure compensation, and ISO. Of course, aperture and shutter speed are adjustable during video recording only if Exposure Mode is set to a mode that permits that adjustment, such as Aperture Priority or Shutter Priority. To control the setting, use the touch slider control that appears beneath the active tab.

If you want to change to another setting, touch the top icon to open up the line of control icons again, and touch another one.

### Wind Noise Canceller

This setting on the Creative Video menu can be left turned off or set to Standard or High. If it is turned on at Standard, the camera attempts to reduce the noise from wind while recording a video sequence. With the High setting, the reduction of noise is stronger, and is more likely to remove some sounds other than wind noise. Either level of this processing may have an adverse effect on the quality of the audio. If you are recording casual scenes from a vacation, I recommend turning this option on when recording in a windy area. If you will be using video-editing software, though, you may want to turn this setting off, because, at either level, it can reduce some wanted sounds, and you can adjust the sound track later with your software to minimize the unwanted sounds.

### Zoom Mic

This last option on the Creative Video menu can be turned either on or off. If it is turned on, the camera's built-in microphone concentrates on recording more distant sounds as the lens zooms in. I have not found this option to make much difference, and I generally leave it turned off.

## Recording Still Images During Video Recording

Whenever the ZS100 is recording a video sequence, you can press the shutter button to capture a still image. This function is available in all shooting modes in which movies can be recorded, except for Creative Video mode. In that mode, pressing the shutter button starts or stops a video recording. You can capture up to 30 still images during a video sequence. You can use the touch shutter function to take the pictures.

There are a couple of limitations on recording still images during video recording. First, all images will be JPEG images in the 16:9 aspect ratio, with a Picture Size of S (2 megapixels). Second, you cannot record still images while recording MP4 video with 4K or VGA quality. If you want to record still images that take advantage of the camera's 4K capability, you can use the 4K Photo option, discussed in Chapter 4.

## Using External Audio Recorder

Although the Lumix ZS100 has excellent features for recording video, Panasonic did not include a jack for accepting an external microphone, which makes it challenging to record high-quality audio with this camera. The stereo microphone built into the ZS100 records good-quality sound, but, with the superior video quality available with this camera, you may want to record audio using higher-quality microphones.

Fortunately, it is not difficult to do this with the ZS100, using current technology and software. The best solution I have found is to use a separate digital audio recorder and then synchronize the sound from the recorder with the video from the camera.

This system, often called double-system or dual-system sound recording, would have seemed more complex than I wanted to handle a few years ago. It probably would have involved using a clapper board to mark the first point of synchronization and a laborious process to synchronize the audio and video tracks using time code.

Now, though, if you use good equipment and software, it can be easy to use this type of system. I'll outline the steps I used; you may find equivalent techniques that work as well.

Get a good digital recorder like the Zoom H1, the Zoom H6, the Shure VP83F, the Tascam DR-40, or the Tascam DR-100mkII, which is discussed in Appendix A.

Set the external recorder to record high-quality audio in a .wav file and place it, or one or more microphones connected to it, in a location to receive the sound clearly.

Start the audio recorder, then start the camera recording video and audio.

When the recording is done, load the video file and its attached sound track, along with the separate audio file from the external recorder, into a video-editing program such as Adobe Premiere Pro CC, Final Cut Pro, or others. You also can use Plural Eyes, a program from redgiant.com that synchronizes audio and video. The software will compare the waveforms from the camera's sound track and the external audio track to move them into sync. With Premiere Pro CC, which I use, the procedure is to select the video track and the 2 audio tracks, right-click on them, and select Synchronize-Audio-Mix Down. The software will move the external audio track into sync with the video track.

Once the external audio track has been synchronized with the video track, you can delete the audio track recorded by the camera.

Of course, this system introduces more complexity and expense into your video-recording process. But, if you want the highest quality audio for your movies, it is worth exploring this method.

## Physical Controls

Next, I will discuss options for using the camera's physical control buttons, switches and dials in connection with video recording. The situation is complicated because each of the four physical function buttons can be assigned to any one of about 50 options. Table 8-1 lists all of the physical controls and shows whether their settings will have an effect during video recording, as well as whether the control can be activated during video recording. For the function buttons, the table lists all of the possible assignments.

Table 8-1.    **Use of Camera Controls Before and During Motion Picture Recording**

| Control or Function | Effective if Used Before Video Recording | Effective if Used During Video Recording |
|---|---|---|
| **Physical Controls** | | |
| Control ring | Yes (depends on setting) | Yes (depends on setting) |
| Rear dial | Yes (depends on setting | Yes (depends on setting) |
| Zoom lever | Yes | Yes |
| Q.Menu button (default setting) | Yes | No |
| White Balance button | Yes | No |
| Drive Mode button | No | No |
| Display button | Yes | Yes |
| Menu/Set button (access to menus) | Yes | No |
| Exposure comp. button | Yes | Yes (up to 3 EV only) |
| Focus Mode button | Yes | No |
| AF/AE Lock button | Yes | Yes |
| **Functions Assigned to Function Buttons** | | |
| 4K Photo Mode | No | No |
| Wi-Fi | No | No |
| Q.Menu | Yes | No |
| LVF/Monitor Switch | Yes | Yes |
| AF/AE Lock | Yes | Yes |
| AF-On | Yes | Yes |
| Preview | No | No |
| One Push AE | Yes | No |
| Touch AE | Yes | Yes |
| Level Gauge | Yes | Yes |
| Focus Area Set | Yes | Yes |
| Cursor Button Lock | Yes | No |
| Photo Style | Yes | No |
| Filter Effect | Yes | No |
| Aspect Ratio | No | No |
| Picture Size | No | No |
| Quality | No | No |
| Sensitivity (ISO) | Yes | Yes |
| AF Mode | Yes | Yes |
| AFS/AFF/AFC | Yes | Yes |
| Metering Mode | Yes | No |
| Burst Rate | No | No |
| Auto Bracket | No | No |
| Self Timer | No | No |
| Highlight Shadow | Yes | No |
| i.Dynamic | Yes | No |
| i.Resolution | Yes | No |
| Post Focus | No | No |
| HDR | No | No |
| Shutter Type | No | No |
| Flash Mode | No | No |

| | | |
|---|---|---|
| Flash Adjustment | No | No |
| i.Zoom | Yes | No |
| Digital Zoom | Yes | No |
| Stabilizer | Yes | No |
| 4K Live Cropping | Yes | No |
| Snap Movie | Yes | No |
| Motion Picture Setting | Yes | No |
| Silent Mode | Yes | No |
| Peaking | Yes (if MF in effect) | Yes (if MF in effect) |
| Histogram | Yes | Yes |
| Guide Line | Yes | No |
| Zebra Pattern | Yes | Yes |
| Monochrome Live View | Yes | Yes |
| Recording Area | No | No |
| Zoom Lever | Yes | No |
| Touch Screen | Yes | No |
| Exposure Compensation | Yes | Yes |
| White Balance | Yes | No |
| Focus Mode (AF-Macro-MF) | Yes | No |
| Drive Mode | No | No |

As you can see from the above table, there are many options for controlling the camera with the physical controls before and during video recording, though there are some limitations. For example you can adjust Sensitivity (ISO) during recording using a function button assigned to that setting, but you can only set it to Auto ISO or a value from 125 through 6400. You cannot use the lowest or highest settings or the Intelligent ISO feature. The ISO Limit setting on the Recording menu does not apply for video recording. You can switch focus mode between autofocus and manual focus, but not during recording. However, you can move the autofocus area around the display during recording. You also can turn on or off the Zebra patterns, the histogram, or the peaking feature for manual focus while recording a video sequence.

You can select a picture effect that will work during recording, but you cannot select an effect during the recording. You cannot record a motion picture using the Rough Monochrome, Silky Monochrome, Soft Focus, Star Filter, or Sunshine effect. You cannot record a video at 4K quality using the Miniature setting. When you use the Miniature effect for a motion picture, the camera does not record sound, and the footage is recorded at about one-tenth the normal speed, resulting in playback that is speeded up ten times

faster than normal to help simulate the appearance of a tabletop model layout.

## Using the Touch Screen During Video Recording

The touch screen is available for use during motion picture recording, provided the appropriate options are turned on through the Touch Settings option on screen 8 of the Custom menu. If Touch Screen, Touch Tab, Touch AF, and Touch Pad AF are turned on through that menu option, you can use all of those functions while the camera is recording a motion picture. However, these actions are limited by the same restrictions set out above in Table 8-1. For example, although you can use the Touch Tab to get access to various settings, you cannot turn on or off a filter effect during motion picture recording, because that function cannot be controlled during recording.

You can, however, use the Touch Tab to adjust zoom, autoexposure, and function button actions, provided the functions in question are available for use. If AF Mode is set to an option with a movable frame, such as 1-Area, you can use the Touch AF function to move the frame around the screen and resize it during a video recording. When the Mode dial is set to a still-shooting mode, you can use the Touch Shutter function to take still pictures while recording a video.

## Recommendations for Recording Video

Now that I have covered the essentials of how to record video footage with the ZS100, here are some recommendations for how to approach that process. For everyday use, such as for video clips of a vacation trip or a birthday party, it's probably a good idea to stick with the Intelligent Auto setting and, on the Creative Video menu, set Recording Mode to MP4 and Recording Quality to FHD. The result should be excellent-quality video, well exposed, and ready to show on an HDTV or to edit in video-editing software.

If you aren't ready to deal with a whole host of manual settings, but would like to add some flashy coloring to your movie scenes, consider shooting in Program mode, and use the Filter Settings menu option to add an effect such as Impressive Art. If you would like to produce slow-motion footage, use a 60p setting for Recording Quality and slow the footage to one-half speed using your editing software. For even slower motion, use the High Speed Video setting on screen 2 of the Creative Video menu.

The possibilities for creativity with the ZS100's movie-making apparatus are, if not unlimited, at least sufficient to provide a framework for a great array of experimentation. So consider the options, and don't hesitate to press the red motion picture button when inspiration strikes.

## Motion Picture Playback and Editing

To play a motion picture in the camera, display the file you want and press the Up button to start playback, as indicated by the movie camera icon and up arrow, shown in Figure 8-17. (If the icons have disappeared, press the Display button to bring them back on the display.) You also can touch the playback triangle icon on the screen. The motion picture will start to play. The camera will briefly display at the bottom of the display a line of icons showing the playback controls: Up button for playback/pause; Right button for fast forward; Down button for stop; and Left button for fast backward.

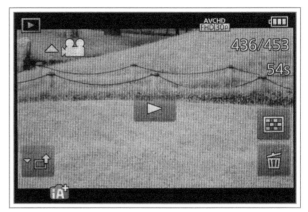

Figure 8-17. Movie Ready to Play in Camera

Either during playback or when playback is paused, you can adjust the volume using the rear dial. When playback is paused, the camera displays more icons, as shown in Figure 8-18: Left button for frame backward; Down button for stop; Up button for playback/pause; Right button for frame forward; and Menu/Set button to save a still frame from the video.

Figure 8-18. Movie Playback Icons When Paused

You cannot do much editing of a video in the camera, but you can trim its length or split it into two segments. To do that, follow the steps below.

1. Find the movie you want to divide and display it in playback mode. (You can use the Playback Mode menu option on the Playback menu to find all videos.)

2. Press the Menu/Set button and select Video Divide from screen 2 of the Playback menu.

3. Press the Menu/Set button or touch the Set icon to start playing the video in the camera.

4. Press the Up button to pause the video at the approximate place where you want to divide it.

5. Use the Right and Left buttons to locate the splitting point more precisely.

6. When you are satisfied with the position, press the Down button to divide the video into two sections, as indicated by the scissors icon in the group of icons at the bottom of the display, as shown in Figure 8-19.

Figure 8-19. Scissors Icon on Screen for Video Divide

The camera will display a message asking you to confirm the operation. If you confirm it, the camera will divide the video into two parts. You will then have two separate video files; the original will no longer exist. You can delete either segment if you want, or keep them both.

You also can save a still image from a video file. To do that, follow the steps below.

1. Find the video that contains the image you want and start playing it in the camera.

2. At the approximate place where the image is located, press the Up button to pause the video.

3. Use the Right and Left buttons to find the location of the desired image.

4. Press the Menu/Set button or the corresponding touch screen icon, and the camera will display a message asking if you want to save this image, as shown in Figure 8-20.

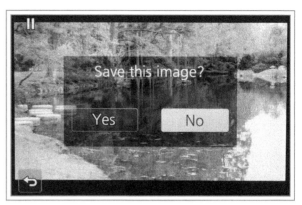

Figure 8-20. Confirmation Message to Save Still Image

5. If you confirm the operation, the camera will save the image in Standard quality with an aspect ratio of 16:9. The image's size will be 8 MP if the video was recorded with 4K quality, or 2 MP for other quality settings. You cannot save an image from an MP4 video recorded with VGA quality.

## Editing with a Computer

You can edit video files from the ZS100 camera using most standard editing software that has been updated to handle recent video formats. For example, I have found it easy to import all formats of video from the ZS100 into the iMovie software on my Macintosh. One way to do that is to copy the video files from your camera's memory card to your computer. The MP4 files are easy to find on the card; they are in the same folders as the still images. For example, an SD card I am using now has .rw2 (Raw), .jpg (JPEG), and .mp4 files in a folder whose path is LUMIX:DCIM:101_PANA.

The AVCHD video files are harder to locate. The actual video files that you can import into your editing software have the extension .mts. They are located in a folder with the path LUMIX:PRIVATE: AVCHD:BDMV:STREAM. On my Macintosh, you cannot see the contents of the AVCHD and BDMV folders directly; you have to right-click on those folder names in the Finder and select the menu command, Show Package Contents. Once you do that, you can find all of the .mts files and import them into iMovie or any other modern video editing software, which can edit them readily.

On a computer running Microsoft Windows version 8.1, I was able to find the .mts files just by using Windows Explorer with no special steps. I then imported them readily into Windows Movie Maker software, where they played with no problems.

I also had no major problems using the videos I recorded using the 4K quality setting. Because those files use the .mp4 format, they can be imported like ordinary MP4 files. Of course, they contain a great deal more data than ordinary files, so they may play in a slow and choppy manner in software such as Movie Maker or iMovie, but they can be imported and edited. Using more sophisticated software, such as Adobe Premiere Pro CC, I had no problem importing, playing and editing the 4K video files on my Macintosh.

# CHAPTER 9: WI-FI AND OTHER TOPICS

## Using Wi-Fi Features

The Panasonic ZS100 camera has a good set of features for using Wi-Fi (wireless) networks to transfer images and videos to computers and other devices or to control the camera remotely from a smartphone or tablet. You also can upload images directly from the camera, smartphone, or tablet to social networks. There are several approaches to making wireless connections, and I will not discuss all of the possibilities in this book. The Panasonic user's guide provides general guidance for making the connections. I will discuss the steps that worked for me to accomplish various Wi-Fi-related activities.

### CONNECTING TO A SMARTPHONE OR TABLET

There are two ways you can set up the camera to connect wirelessly with your smartphone or tablet: You can either use the Wi-Fi menu item on screen 1 of the Setup menu or you can press a function button that is assigned the Wi-Fi function. By default, the virtual Fn5 button (touch screen icon) is assigned to Wi-Fi, but you can assign another button if you want.

I will discuss the steps for using the Fn5 button to make this connection with an iPhone. For later connections, you will not need to follow all of these steps, as noted in Step 3, below. The steps are similar for an Android device, except that the screen may appear different, and, for example, you use Google Play instead of the App Store to download the Image App.

The steps included here assume that you have set the Wi-Fi Password menu option to Off, under the Wi-Fi Setup option under the Wi-Fi item on screen 1 of the Setup menu. If you turn the Wi-Fi Password option on, you will have to enter a password or read a QR code on the camera's screen in order to establish a Wi-Fi connection. In most situations, I find it much easier to leave the password option turned off.

1. Go to the App Store for iOS devices, and install the Panasonic Image App, whose icon is indicated by the arrow in Figure 9-1.

Figure 9-1. Panasonic Image App Icon on iPhone

2. Touch the Fn icon at the bottom of the line of icons at the right side of the camera's display screen. Then touch the Fn5 icon, with a Wi-Fi icon beneath it, at the top of the line of icons, as shown in Figure 9-2. The Wi-Fi connection lamp to the left of the Playback button on the back of the camera should turn solid red.

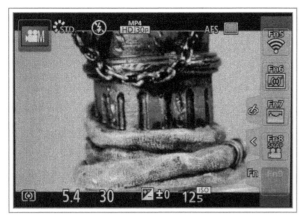

Figure 9-2. Fn5 Virtual Function Button on Display

3. The camera will display the screen shown in Figure 9-3, giving the SSID (identification data) of the camera's Wi-Fi network, and telling you to use the Wi-Fi settings on your phone to connect to that network. You can follow that prompt and connect immediately by selecting the camera's Wi-Fi network ID in your phone's Settings app.

Figure 9-3. Camera's Screen When Connecting to iPhone

-or-

As noted on the camera's screen, you can press the Display button (or touch the on-screen icon) to go to the screen shown in Figure 9-4, which gives you the option of starting a new connection or choosing one from history or favorites. If you just want to connect to your phone, it may be simplest just to go ahead and use the Wi-Fi Settings app on your phone to connect to the camera's Wi-Fi network.

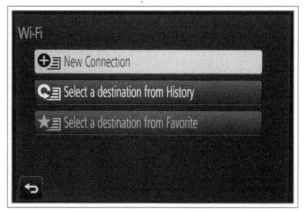

Figure 9-4. Camera's Display After Pressing Display Button

4. For now, choose New Connection, and the camera will display a screen like that in Figure 9-5, with several options. For now, select Remote Shooting & View.

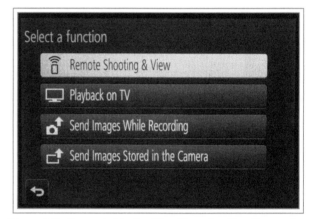

Figure 9-5. Camera's Display After Choosing New Connection

5. The camera will display a screen like that in Figure 9-3, advising you to connect your smartphone to the Wi-Fi network listed on the screen.

6. On the iPhone, select the Settings app, then Wi-Fi, and select the SSID (network ID) sent by the camera. That ID should be ZS100, followed by several other characters, such as ZS100-B6006B.

7. Once you do, the camera will display a screen advising you to launch the Image App on the phone. Touch the app's icon on the phone to launch it.

Figure 9-6. Main Screen of Panasonic Image App

Figure 9-7. Remote Operation Screen on iPhone

8. When the Image App starts with a Wi-Fi connection established, you should initially see on the phone a screen like that in Figure 9-6, with various options for remote operation, image transfer, geotagging, and others.

## CONTROLLING THE CAMERA WITH A SMARTPHONE OR TABLET

Once you have established a connection between the camera and the phone using the steps above, you are ready to control the camera using the Image App. Select the Remote Operation icon at the upper left of the phone's screen, as shown in Figure 9-6, and you will see a display on the phone like that in Figure 9-7. You can touch the icons on this screen to zoom the lens in and out; change the mix of icons on the display with the DISP. icon; and get access to various other settings, including Photo Style, Filter Select, Aspect Ratio, Picture Size, Quality, Focus Mode, Stop Motion Animation, and others by pressing the Q. Menu icon.

To take a picture, press the camera icon at the center bottom. To record a video, press the red button in the lower right corner. If you press the down-pointing arrow below the battery status icon, as seen in Figure 9-7, you will get access to additional settings, as shown in Figure 9-8.

Figure 9-8. More Settings Screen in Image App

The touch focus icon causes the camera to focus where you touch the screen; the touch exposure icon does the same for exposure. The Drive Mode icon lets you select burst shooting, exposure bracketing, 4K Photo shooting, or the self-timer, and the focus mode icon lets you choose Face/Eye Detection, Tracking, 49-Area, 1-Area, and other options.

The WB and ISO icons let you set white balance and ISO. If the camera is in a recording mode that lets you change the aperture or shutter speed (or both), there will be an F icon (for aperture) and/or an SS icon (for shutter speed), for making those settings. In Program mode, there will be a Program Shift icon. To change the recording mode, turn the Mode dial on the camera.

You also can use a novel feature called Jump Snap, represented by the icon at the bottom of the app's screen that looks like a jumping person, as seen to the left of the red video recording icon in Figures 9-7 and 9-8. If you select that icon, you will see the screen in Figure 9-9, with settings for this option.

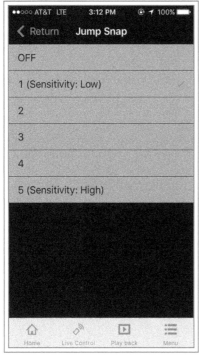

Figure 9-9. Jump Snap Settings Screen

You can leave it turned off, or set the sensitivity to low or high. If it is turned on, you use it by aiming the camera at a person who is holding the phone while the app is active. The camera will sense when the person jumps, and will snap a still picture at the highest point of the jump. The result should be an image like that in Figure 9-10, reminiscent of the famous jumping photographs taken by Philippe Halsman.

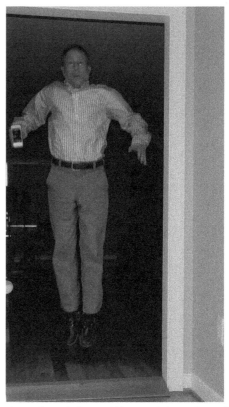

Figure 9-10. Sample Image Taken with Jump Snap Option

## SENDING IMAGES AND VIDEOS TO A SMARTPHONE OR TABLET

Once the ZS100 is connected to your smartphone or tablet, instead of controlling the camera from your device, you can choose the option at the upper right of the Panasonic Image App, Transfer Image. When you select that icon, the phone will display a screen with choices of Transfer Selection or Batch Transfer. If you choose Transfer Selection, the phone app will display a screen like that in Figure 9-11, with thumbnail images for the images and videos on the camera's memory card.

You can scroll through these images by flicking up and down the screen. It may take quite a while for all of the images and videos to load.

The thumbnails that have a movie camera icon in the lower left corner represent motion picture files. Other thumbnails may have an icon showing a camera and a phone with a line through the circle around them; that icon means that image or video cannot be transferred to the phone. In Figure 9-11, there are several thumbnails with that icon; those thumbnails represent Raw images or AVCHD or 4K videos, which cannot be transferred to a phone or tablet.

Figure 9-11. Selection Screen for Transferring Images

If you want to transfer one of the images or videos to your phone, first, tap on it to enlarge it on the display, as shown in Figure 9-12. If it is a video that can be played on the phone, you can press the Play icon on the phone's display to play it.

Figure 9-12. Individual Item Selected for Transfer

If you select the icon at the lower left, showing an arrow going to a phone, the phone will display a message

saying it is copying the file. You will then have a copy of that image or video in the standard area for photos or videos on the phone.

On the main playback screen in the Image App, you can tap the camera icon in the upper left corner to switch between viewing the images and videos from the camera or those stored on the phone or tablet. Also on that screen, if you press the Select icon in the upper right corner, you can mark images and videos with green check marks by tapping them; once you have selected them, you can select the download icon (arrow going to phone) at the bottom of the screen to download them to the phone or tablet.

From any screen that displays the sharing icon (two arrows going up out of a circle, as seen in Figure 9-12), you can tap that icon to bring up a menu that will let you upload an image or a group of selected images or videos to a social media site, including Facebook, Twitter, and others, as shown in Figure 9-13. In order to complete that upload, you need to sign up for an account with Panasonic's Lumix Club. I will discuss that process in the next section of this chapter.

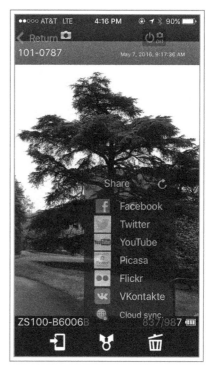

Figure 9-13. List of Social Networks for Sharing Images

Back on the home screen of the Image App, you also can select Geotagging, Snap Movie, or Photo Collage. I discussed Geotagging in Chapter 6. Basically, that function lets you transmit geolocation data from your smartphone to the camera by creating a synchronized log on the phone and later uploading the data from that log to the camera.

If you choose the Snap Movie option, the app will ask if you want to copy any videos on the camera that were shot using Snap Movie mode. As I discussed in Chapter 8, Snap Movie is a function that lets you record very brief movies, lasting no more than eight seconds each, that may have some fade-in, fade-out, and pull focus effects added. If you say yes, the app will import those videos to the phone and then ask if you want to combine the videos and save them into a single snap movie. If you say yes, it will proceed to create that composite movie and save it to the phone. You also can share the imported snap movies on social networks using the sharing icon.

The Photo Collage function lets you choose several images to be combined on the phone or tablet in a collage within a frame. You can choose the shape of the frame and then select images from the phone's display to be arranged within that frame. Figure 9-14 is an example of the result of this operation.

Figure 9-14. Photo Collage Example

If you select Menu, the final icon at the lower right of the Image App's main screen, you will see the screen shown in Figure 9-15, with options for the connection destination, Live Control settings, and other items. With the Playback Settings option, you can set the size for images copied from the camera or uploaded to websites.

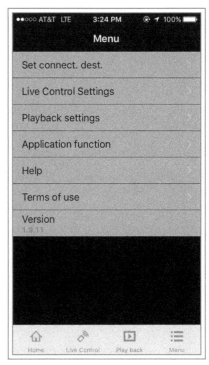

Figure 9-15. Menu Options in Panasonic Image App

## UPLOADING IMAGES BY WI-FI TO SOCIAL NETWORKS

As I mentioned briefly in the previous section, when your smartphone or tablet is connected to the ZS100 camera over a Wi-Fi network, you can tap on the Share icon to upload an image directly from the phone or tablet to a social network such as Facebook. You also can upload images in this way directly from the camera. There are some preliminary steps you have to take to make these uploads. Following are the basic steps to get this done.

1. On the camera, go to screen 1 of the Setup menu, choose Wi-Fi, then, on the next screen, Wi-Fi Setup, then Lumix Club, then Set/Add Account, then New Account.

2. If you have not previously set up an account, the camera will prompt you to connect to a Wi-Fi network using WPS Push or by entering the network ID and password. If you can use WPS push, do so; you just need to select WPS Push on the camera, then press the WPS button on the Wi-Fi router within two minutes, and the connection will be established.

3. The camera will ask you to agree to the terms for the Lumix Club account and will display a login ID

assigned to your camera, consisting of 12 numerical digits. The camera also will display a screen where you create and enter a password for the account. It must have from 8 to 16 characters and contain both letters and numbers.

4. Once the camera has accepted the login ID and password, use a computer or other device to go to the following web address: http://lumixclub.panasonic.net/eng/c/, and log in using the 12-digit user ID and password from Step 3. You will then be prompted to enter your e-mail address and a security question, so you can reset your password later if necessary.

5. After you have logged in at the Lumix Club website, you will receive an e-mail message from Panasonic to confirm the registration. After you confirm it, you will be able to log in to the page where you can link your Lumix Club account to any or all of the following social networks (as of this writing): Facebook, Twitter, YouTube, Picasa, Flickr, Ustream, and VKontakte. You also can link your account to Google Drive for storage of images in the cloud.

6. Once you have linked your Lumix Club account to one or more social networks, you can upload to those networks at any time. To do that on the camera, from playback mode, press the Down button and the camera will ask if you want to upload the current image by Wi-Fi. If you say yes, the camera will establish a Wi-Fi connection if possible, or prompt you to establish one. It will then display a screen like that in Figure 9-16, where you can highlight the service to send the image to.

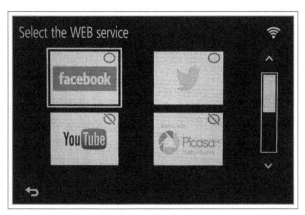

Figure 9-16. Camera Screen for Sending Images to Social Networks

7. Select the icon you want and press Menu/Set; the camera will display a screen with the estimated time to upload the image; with my tests, it took anywhere from about 20 seconds to two minutes, depending on the image. The image will then appear on the appropriate web page for Facebook or another service.

8. You also can upload an image from your smartphone or tablet, when you see the Share icon, as shown earlier in Figure 9-12, using a similar procedure.

## CONNECTING TO A COMPUTER TO TRANSFER IMAGES WIRELESSLY

The ZS100 camera also comes with the ability to transmit your images wirelessly from the camera to a computer on your local network. I found this feature worked well with the preferred configuration of using Panasonic's PHOTOfunSTUDIO software on a Windows-based PC, but I could not get it to work at all with my Macintosh. Following are the steps I used to get it working.

1. Install and run the PHOTOfunSTUDIO software on a Windows PC, as discussed in Chapter 1. (The program is not compatible with Macintosh.) Make sure the PC is connected to your local network via Wi-Fi.

2. The program should prompt you to create a folder for receiving images from the camera. If it does not, go to Tools-Settings-General-Registration Folder and create the folder, using the Auto-create option, or create it manually. When I used Auto-create, the program created the folder C:\Users\Public\Pictures\LumixShare.

3. On the ZS100, go to screen 1 of the Setup Menu, choose Wi-Fi, then Wi-Fi Function, then New Connection, then Send Images While Recording.

4. Follow the prompts on the camera's display to select the network, then the PC on the network. If prompted for a user name and password, enter the user name and password for logging onto the PC you are sending images to. Then select the folder, such as LumixShare, and follow the prompts.

5. When you take pictures with the camera, the new images will soon appear in the LumixShare folder, or other folder you have designated.

6. If you want to transfer existing images or videos from the camera to the PC instead of new ones as they are taken, in Step 3 select that option from the menu. Then, when you establish the connection, the camera will give the option of sending a single image or selecting multiple images to send. Make your choice, and the camera will start sending one or more images to the designated folder on the PC as shown in Figure 9-17.

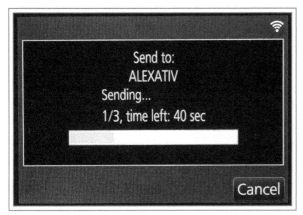

Figure 9-17. Camera Screen When Sending Images to PC

7. Once you have established a connection as described above, you can choose Select a Destination from History, and go immediately to one of the connections listed by the camera. As you can see in Figure 9-18, each previous destination has an icon and a name to indicate whether that connection is for sending images to a PC or for connecting to a phone or other device. Select a destination to a PC, and the camera will be set up for the transfer of new or old images and videos.

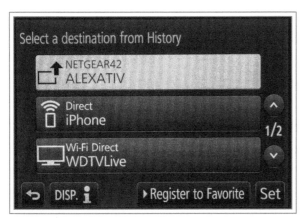

Figure 9-18. Camera Screen to Select Previous Destination

## SENDING IMAGES TO OTHER DEVICES

You also can send images directly from the camera to other devices using the Wi-Fi menu. To do this, go to screen 1 of the Setup menu, select Wi-Fi, then Wi-Fi Function, then New Connection, then Send Images Stored in the Camera. On the next screen, you can select from Smartphone, PC, Cloud Sync. Service, Web Service, AV Device, or Printer. Follow the prompts in the menu system to connect to the device you select. You also can send images from the camera to other devices while recording, though not to a printer. To do that, choose Send Images While Recording instead of Send Images Stored in the Camera.

## VIEWING IMAGES WIRELESSLY ON TV

Another option for using the Wi-Fi features of the ZS100 is to view your still images on a TV set that is compatible with the DLNA standard for sharing media files. (DLNA stands for Digital Living Network Alliance; see dlna.org for more information.) I will describe the setup I used to get my ZS100 to display images wirelessly on a TV set. This sort of setup can be complicated, and you have to use devices that work together with your network. I don't recommend trying this option unless you have some experience using a DLNA server or don't mind digging into technical details with media devices and computers.

In my case, I used a device called WD TV Live, made by Western Digital, and connected it by HDMI cable to an HDTV. Then, on the camera, I went to screen 1 of the Setup menu and selected Wi-Fi, then Wi-Fi Function, then New Connection, then Playback on TV, then Direct, then Wi-Fi Direct. The camera then found the WD TV Live device, as shown in Figure 9-19.

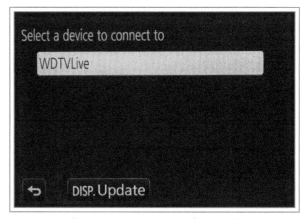

Figure 9-19. Camera Screen Upon Finding WD TV Live Device

I pressed the Menu/Set button, and the camera announced that it was connected. I could then play back images stored on the camera's memory card, and they appeared on the TV screen. Also, when I took a new picture with the camera, it almost immediately appeared on the TV screen. When I turned off the Auto Review option on screen 7 of the Custom menu, though, a new image would not appear on the TV screen. You have to have Auto Review turned on, though not for a long time period; as long as it is turned on, a new image will remain on the TV screen.

When I tried to play back a video through the TV, the TV displayed only the first frame of the video and did not produce the sound.

## Macro (Closeup) Shooting

Macro photography is the art or science of taking photographs when the subject is shown at actual size (1:1 ratio between size of subject and size of image) or slightly magnified (greater than 1:1 ratio). So if you photograph a flower using macro techniques, the image of the flower on the camera's sensor will be about the same size as the actual flower. You can get wonderful detail in your images using macro photography, and you may discover things about the subject that you had not noticed before taking the photograph. For example, I used the ZS100 to take a photograph of a plant at a botanical garden. I handheld the camera at about the minimum focusing distance of 5 cm or 2 inches, with the lens at its 25mm setting. The result, shown in Figure 9-20, provides a detailed view of the subject. The background is blurred, which is helpful to reduce distractions.

Figure 9-20. Sample Macro Image

To shoot macro images with the ZS100, you have only one basic setting to change: Press the Left button, marked with a flower and MF, to bring up the focus mode menu, and select Macro AF, as shown in Figure 9-21.

Figure 9-21. Macro AF Highlighted on Focus Mode Menu

Using Macro AF, the camera can focus as close as 2 inches (5 cm) from the subject, when the zoom lever is pushed all the way to the wide-angle setting. With the lens zoomed in for its full optical zoom, the camera can focus as close as 2.3 feet (70 cm) in Macro mode. If the camera is not set to Macro mode, then the closest focusing point is about 1.6 foot (50 cm).

You don't have to use the Macro AF setting to take macro shots; if you use manual focus by selecting MF on the focus mode menu, you can also focus on objects very close to the lens. You do, however, lose the benefit of automatic focus, and it can be tricky finding the correct focus manually.

When using the Macro AF setting, you should use a tripod, because the depth of field is very shallow at close distances and you need to keep the camera steady to take a usable photograph. It's also a good idea to use the self-timer. If you do so, you will not be touching the camera when the shutter is activated, so the chance of camera shake is minimized. If you want to use flash, you could consider using a special unit designed for closeup photography, such as a ring flash that is designed to provide even lighting surrounding the lens. You also could use the camera's built-in flash, and place a small piece of translucent plastic or a light-colored cloth in front of the flash to diffuse it.

When doing macro photography with the ZS100, you can take advantage of the Post Focus feature to increase the likelihood of getting a sharp image. See Chapter 4 for details about that feature, with which the camera records a 4K video sequence and extracts a sharp image with focus centered on an area you choose after the fact.

One question you may have is: If the camera can focus down to 5 centimeters and out to infinity in Macro mode, why not just leave it set in Macro mode? The answer is that in Macro mode, the focusing system is set to favor short distances, and it is not as responsive in focusing on farther objects. So in Macro mode you may notice that it takes more time than usual to focus on subjects at greater distances. If you don't need the fastest possible focusing, you can just leave the camera set to AF Macro at all times, if you want the whole range of focusing distances to be available.

## Street Photography

The ZS100 is well suited for street photography—that is, for shooting candid pictures in public settings, often without being noticed by the subjects. The camera has several good features for this type of work—it is lightweight and unobtrusive in appearance, so it can be held casually or hidden in the photographer's hand. Its 25mm wide-angle lens is excellent for taking in a broad field of view, for times when you shoot from the hip without framing the image carefully on the screen. Its f/2.8 lens lets in sufficient light, and it performs well at high ISO settings, so you can use a relatively fast shutter speed to avoid motion blur. You can make the camera completely silent by turning off the beeps and shutter sounds, and by using the electronic shutter. It has superior options for shooting bursts of images, so you can capture a large group of shots to choose from.

Here are some suggested settings you can start with and modify as you see fit. To get the gritty "street" look, set Photo Style to Monochrome, but dial in -2 Noise Reduction and -1 Sharpening. Set Quality to Raw & Fine to give you a good image straight out of the camera, but preserving your post-processing options. Set aspect ratio to 3:2. Set ISO to 800 for good image quality while boosting sensitivity enough to stop action with a fast shutter speed. Turn on burst mode at the High setting so you'll get several images to choose from for each shutter press.

When you're ready to start shooting, select manual focus mode and set the focus to approximately the

distance you expect to shoot at, such as 6 feet (2 meters) on the MF scale. On screen 1 of the Custom menu, go to the AF/AE Lock item and set it to AF-On. Then, when you're ready to snap a picture, use the AF/AE Lock button to make a quick fine-tuning of the focus. For exposure, set the camera to Aperture Priority mode, with the aperture set to about f/4.5. When shooting at night, you may want to open the aperture a bit wider, and possibly boost the ISO to 1600. You will probably want to leave the lens zoomed back to its full wide-angle position, both to increase the depth of field and to take in a wide angle of view.

Figure 9-22. Street Photography Example Using Intelligent Auto Mode

In Figure 9-22, I took a different approach, using the Intelligent Auto setting when I saw a couple walking toward me in the botanical garden, and I didn't have time to choose other settings.

## Connecting Camera to HDTV with Cable

Although you can send images wirelessly to a TV set or other device from the ZS100, a simpler way to view images on a large screen is to connect the camera to an HDTV set using a micro-HDMI cable. You can find such cables readily online or at electronics stores. Just connect the small end of the cable to the HDMI port on the right side of the camera, as shown in Figure 9-23, and plug the larger end into one of the HDMI inputs on the HDTV. Then put the camera into playback mode by pressing the Playback button, and you can view your images and videos on the large screen.

Figure 9-23. HDMI Cable Connected to Camera

With the ZS100, you can also view the camera's output on an external HDTV set when the camera is in recording mode. If you do that, you can use the HDTV as a large monitor to check focus and composition for your images. However, you cannot view the camera's output on an external HDTV when the camera is recording a video; that capability is disabled. When the camera is recording a movie, it will display a message on the HDTV screen to that effect if an HDMI cable is connected.

To remove camera icons and other shooting information from the HDMI signal that is output, go to screen 3 of the Setup menu, select TV Connection, and set HDMI Info Display (Rec) to Off.

# Appendix A: Accessories

The ZS100 does not need very many accessories, partly because of its compact size and built-in lens cover. It is possible to carry it in a pocket, and it does not need a lens cap. It does not have the ability to use threaded filters, although, if you feel a strong need to use filters, you may be able to construct a home-made adapter that lets you attach filters. For instructions for a similar camera model, see the YouTube video at https://youtu.be/yDWr4iWwD48. In addition, the camera has no accessory shoe, so you cannot readily attach an external flash unit or an optical viewfinder.

However, there are several items that can be useful for getting the most out of your ZS100.

## Cases

As noted above, you do not really need to have a case for the ZS100, because it is small enough to fit in a pocket and its lens is protected by the built-in lens cover. However, I usually like to keep my camera in a case or bag that has room for extra batteries, battery charger, USB cable, and other items.

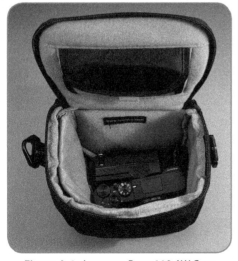

Figure A-1. Lowepro Rezo 110 AW Case

With the ZS100, I have been using the Lowepro Rezo 110 AW, shown in Figure A-1. It is compact, but has plenty of room for the camera with an extra battery and charger. It has a loop to fit over a belt.

When I need to carry more equipment, I often use a pack like the Lowepro Inverse 100 AW, shown in Figures A-2 and A-3, which has plenty of room for the camera and accessories. It also has expandable mesh pockets for holding two small water bottles, and, most important for me, it has straps for attaching a travel tripod under the bottom of the case, as shown in Figure A-3.

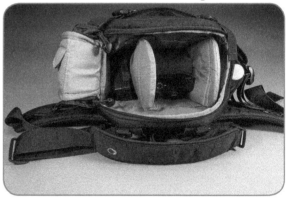

Figure A-2. Lowepro Inverse 100 AW Case

Figure A-3. Lowepro Inverse 100 AW Case with Tripod

Of course, there are many other possibilities; these are just two items that have worked well for me.

## Batteries and Chargers

I use the camera pretty heavily, and I run through batteries quickly. You can't use disposable batteries, so if you're out taking pictures and the battery dies, you're out of luck unless you have a spare battery (or an AC adapter and a place to plug it in; see below). The Panasonic battery, model number DMW-BLG10PP (in the United States), costs about $45.00 in the U.S. as I write this. You can find third-party replacement batteries from brands such as Wasabi Power, as shown in Figure A-4, for considerably less.

Figure A-4. Wasabi Power Battery for ZS100 Camera

I have used Wasabi Power batteries extensively in my ZS100 with no problems. You may note that the battery shown in Figure A-4 has a different model number than the Panasonic battery, but that is not a problem; this Wasabi Power battery works fine as a replacement for the Panasonic battery.

Figure A-5. Wasabi Power External Battery Charger

If you use a spare battery, it's useful to be able to charge it outside of the camera. To do that, you need an external charger, such as the Panasonic model no. DMW-BTC9, not shown here. You also can use a generic model, such as the Wasabi Power charger, model number LCH-BLE9, shown in Figure A-5.

For everyday use, I often find it convenient to charge the battery inside the camera, especially if I am not using the camera too intensively. I can take a few shots, and then plug in a power source to recharge the battery before I take another group of shots. If you are working near an electrical outlet, you can just plug the camera's own USB cable and charger into the outlet and charge the battery that way. If you want a more versatile charger that can also charge your smartphone and tablet at the same time, you might try a device like the Anker 40-watt desktop USB charger, shown in Figure A-6. I often use this charger to charge my ZS100, my iPhone, and my iPad at the same time, and it has no problems with that setup.

Figure A-6. Anker 40-Watt Desktop USB Charger

For more portability, you might try a device like the G-Cord 10000 mAh Boutique Mobile Power Supply, shown in Figure A-7, which will charge the camera's battery efficiently when the battery is in the camera.

Figure A-7. G-Cord 10000 mAh Boutique Mobile Power Supply

## AC Adapter

Another alternative for powering the ZS100 is the Panasonic AC adapter. (You cannot use the Anker USB charger, the G-Cord USB battery, or similar devices to power the camera; such devices can only provide power for charging the battery inside the camera.)

This accessory works well for what it does, in terms of providing a constant source of power to the camera. However, it is somewhat inconvenient to use. With the ZS100, you need to obtain not only the AC adapter, model no. DMW-AC10, but also another device called the DC Coupler, model number DMW-DCC11. That device looks like a battery, but it has a connecting port in its side. The adapter and the coupler are shown together ready to be connected to the camera in Figure A-8.

Figure A-8. Panasonic AC Adapter with ZS100

You have to insert the DC Coupler into the battery compartment of the camera, then close the battery door, open up a small flap in that door, and connect the cord from the AC adapter to the port in the DC Coupler, as shown in Figure A-9.

Figure A-9. AC Adapter Cord Going Into ZS100

This is not a very efficient (or economical) system, at least from the standpoint of the user. It is a clunky

arrangement, and you can't get access to the memory card while the AC adapter is plugged in. But, if you need constant power for a long period of time, this is the only way to get it.

Providing power to the camera is all this adapter does. It does not act as a battery charger, either for batteries outside of the camera or for batteries while they are installed in the camera. It is strictly a power source for the camera. It may be useful if you are doing extensive indoor work in a studio or laboratory setting, to eliminate the trouble of constantly charging batteries. It also could be useful for a lengthy series of time-lapse or stop-motion shots. For everyday applications and still shooting, though, the AC adapter should not be considered a high-priority purchase.

## External Flash Units

Whether to buy an external flash unit depends on how you will use the ZS100. For everyday snapshots not taken at long distances, the built-in flash unit should suffice. It works automatically with the camera's exposure controls to expose images well. It is limited by its low power, though.

If you need more flash power to take photos of groups of people in large spaces, or if you want to take advantage of the benefits of using off-camera flash, such as using multiple units and better angles for less harsh lighting, you can use optical slaves, which detect the light from the camera's small flash and fire their own flash when the camera's flash is fired.

Figure A-10. LumoPro LP180 Optical Slave Flash

One excellent unit with optical slave capability is the LumoPro LP180, shown in Figure A-10. This unit has settings that let it ignore the pre-flash fired by the camera's built-in flash unit, which can confuse the optical slave and cause it to fire prematurely. When I used the LumoPro flash with the Panasonic ZS100, I set the flash to its S1 mode, which caused it to fire the flash at the proper time for a good exposure. Figure 3-26 in Chapter 3 is an image I took using this setup.

When using a flash like this, you need to set the camera to Manual exposure mode. There are other flash units with similar capability, such as the Yongnuo YN-560 III. There also are separate optical slave units, to which you can attach any compatible flash unit.

When you use one of these flash units, it often is useful to use a softbox to diffuse the light, as shown in Figure A-11, which shows the Yongnuo flash mentioned above with a Photoflex Lite-Dome XS softbox.

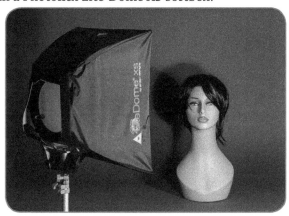

Figure A-11. Photoflex Lite-Dome XS Softbox with Flash

## External Audio Recorders

As I discussed in Chapter 8, the ZS100 camera has excellent video features but it has no provision for connecting an external microphone for high-quality audio. Although the built-in microphone records good-quality audio, you can get better results if you use an external audio recorder and synchronize the audio track from that recorder with the sound recorded by the camera.

One excellent piece of equipment for this purpose is the Tascam DR-100MkII recorder, shown in Figure A-12.

This recorder includes two sets of high-quality microphones, one set that is omnidirectional for recording lectures or classes, and another that

is directional for recording concerts or other performances. The recorder also has two XLR inputs where you can connect high-quality microphones of your choice.

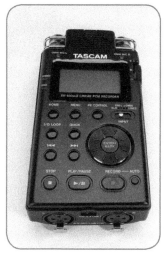

Figure A-12. Tascam DR-100MkII Audio Recorder

There are many other options that will work for this purpose, depending on your budget and needs, including the Shure VP83F, the Tascam DR-40, the Zoom H1, and the Zoom H6.

## External Video Recorder

As I discussed in Chapter 8, the ZS100 camera includes a limited capability for sending a video signal through its HDMI port to an external monitor or video recorder. When the camera is recording still images, the images can be transmitted through that port. You can prevent the camera from also transmitting its shooting information and icons by turning off the HDMI Info Display item under the TV Connection option on screen 3 of the Setup menu. However, when the camera is recording a video, the ability to transmit a signal through the HDMI port is disabled. To circumvent that limitation, you can connect the camera to an external video recorder using a micro-HDMI cable and record video while the camera is in standby mode.

One recorder that I have tested with the ZS100 is the Atomos Shogun, shown in Figure A-13. This device records high-quality video footage and has advanced features, but is quite expensive; I paid about $2,000.00 for mine. But, if you need to record high-quality video to an external device, the Shogun is an excellent piece of equipment. In the illustration shown here, the recorder is attached to the camera using a Pearstone 4.2-inch articulating arm.

Figure A-13. Atomos Shogun Video Recorder with ZS100

## Equipment for Pole Aerial Photography

As discussed in Chapter 9, you can trigger the ZS100 remotely from a smartphone or tablet using the camera's built-in Wi-Fi capability. One way to take advantage of this capability is to attach the camera to a painter's pole that is perhaps 10 feet (3 meters) long, so you can get shots over the heads of crowds, from outside second-story windows, or from higher angles than otherwise possible, for example. This procedure is sometimes referred to as pole aerial photography. You can get a device for attaching the camera securely to such a pole from a site called polepixie.com. The ZS100 is shown attached to this device in Figure A-14.

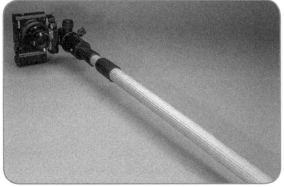

Figure A-14. ZS100 Attached to Pole for Pole Aerial Photography

## Tripods

For time exposures, multiple exposures, HDR shots, and many other types of photography, it is virtually essential to use a tripod. In addition, for macro photography and any other shots for which focus is critical, it is desirable to have a solid support when using the camera. I have not attempted to survey multiple tripods; I will just mention two models that I have found to be especially useful because of their excellent features and light weight.

Figure A-15. Manfrotto BeFree Tripod, Carbon Fiber Model

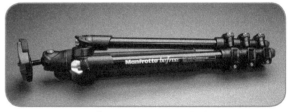

Figure A-16. Manfrotto BeFree Tripod, Aluminum Model

These models both are versions of the BeFree tripod by Manfrotto. The version shown in Figure A-15, model number MKBFRC4-BH, is especially light in weight because of its carbon fiber construction. Model number MKBFRA4-BH, shown in Figure A-16, is somewhat heavier because of its aluminum construction, but is considerable less expensive. Either one works very well with the ZS100 camera.

# APPENDIX B: QUICK TIPS

This appendix includes tips and hints for using the ZS100 that might be useful as reminders. These are small bits of information that might help you in certain situations, or that might not be obvious to everyone.

**Use the movable autofocus area in conjunction with Spot metering.** When you do this, using an AF Mode setting such as 1-Area or Pinpoint, you can move the focus and metering area together around the screen with the direction buttons or the touch screen, so you can focus and meter a small, specific area of your scene. This procedure can add precision to your metering and focusing, and give you more control over your results.

**Use Manual exposure mode with Auto ISO.** Not all cameras let you use Auto ISO with Manual mode. This feature lets you keep aperture and shutter speed at fixed values, while the camera adjusts ISO to obtain a normal exposure if possible. This is useful, for example, when you need to stop action with a fast shutter speed and also control depth of field with a narrow aperture. (This feature does not work when recording videos with the Creative Video version of Manual Exposure mode.)

**Diffuse your flash.** If you find the built-in flash produces light that's too harsh for macro or other shots, try using a piece of translucent plastic as a flash diffuser. Hold the plastic up between the flash and the subject. An approach you can try when using fill-flash outdoors is to use the Flash Adjustment menu setting to reduce the intensity of the flash by -2/3 EV. Also, you can bounce the flash off of the ceiling if you pull the flash unit gently back with your finger.

**Use the self-timer to avoid camera shake.** Press the Down button, scroll to the self-timer item, and press the Up button to choose your setting. This feature is not just for group portraits; you can use it whenever you'll be using a slow shutter speed and you need to avoid camera shake. It can be useful when you're doing macro photography, also.

**Use the 4K Photo option for burst shooting.** With this option, on screen 3 of the Recording menu (or assigned to a function button), you can set the camera to capture 4K-quality video that can generate a high-quality still image from each frame. This option gives you a burst shooting mode with Large-sized images and continuous focusing, at a rate of 30 frames per second (in the United States and other areas that use the NTSC video standard; 25 fps elsewhere). You have to use an SD card with a speed in UHS Class 3, but this is an excellent capability for action shots, shots of wildlife, and street photography.

**Create a custom autofocus zone that uses the entire focusing area.** Although the ZS100 has an AF Mode setting called 49-Area, that setting actually uses no more than nine of the 49 possible focus zones. If you want to have a setting that uses the full extent of the display area, you have to create it yourself. To do that, use the Custom Multi option of AF Mode to create a focus setting with all 49 zones. Chapter 5 explains how to do this.

**Use the zoom lever and the Display button to speed through menu screens.** These options can save time when you need to scroll through menus with as many as eight screens. When a menu screen is displayed, press the zoom lever in either direction to move forward or backward a full screen at a time. You also can press the Display button to move a screen at a time, in the forward direction only.

**Be careful of using Raw for Quality when shooting with filter effects using the Filter Settings option or Creative Control mode.** The ZS100 will let you set Quality to Raw when shooting with picture effects that are accessed through the Filter Settings menu option or Creative Control mode, such as Silky Monochrome, Impressive Art, Star Filter, and others. The recorded images will appear to have the effects added when viewed in the camera, but that is only because a small JPEG file is embedded in the Raw file. When you open the Raw file on a computer, the picture effect will not be there. You can try to recreate it using software settings, but I have not found any way to recover the full effect as recorded by the camera. So, you might think you have taken some great shots using creative effects, but when you view them on your computer the effects will have disappeared. To avoid this problem, shoot using Fine, or, probably the best option, Raw & Fine for Quality.

Use the in-camera processing features before uploading images. The ZS100 has a good set of options for transferring images using Wi-Fi to a smartphone, tablet, or computer, and for uploading directly to social networks. Before you do that, you may want to use options on the Playback menu such as Raw Processing, Cropping, and Resize in order to send images at the optimal size and with the appearance you want. You also can use the remarkably effective Clear Retouch menu option to remove an unwanted person or object from an image.

Use the remote control capability of the Panasonic Image App. With this app, you can take self-portraits and capture images and videos of birds and other subjects while controlling the camera from a distance through a wireless network. Set the camera on a good tripod near a bird feeder to catch shots of birds, or set the camera in a good location to record video of a school play while you sit nearby and control the camera from your smartphone. You can change settings on the camera while it is under remote control, and use functions such as burst shooting and stop motion animation.

Take advantage of the many shortcuts available with use of the touch screen. For example, when the camera is in Intelligent Auto mode, touch the iA icon in the upper left corner of the display to switch between Intelligent Auto and Intelligent Auto Plus modes. Or, in Scene Mode, touch the scene type icon in the upper left corner to select a different scene type.

Reassign a function button quickly. You can change the assignment of a function button to a menu option or other operation using the Function Button Set option on screen 7 of the Custom menu. To make that setting much more rapidly, press and hold a function button for several seconds, and the camera will display a menu that lets you change the button's assignment.

Use the Post Focus feature in tricky focusing situations. When you are shooting extreme closeups or other shots where focus is critical, take advantage of the Post Focus capability, as discussed in Chapter 4. The camera will shoot a 4K video sequence using multiple focus points, and you can choose the most sharply focused shot after the fact.

Set up the touch screen so it doesn't interfere with your shooting. When I use the viewfinder, I sometimes find that a movable focus frame or focus area appears unexpectedly in the viewfinder's display, interfering with my composition. This happens because my nose hits the LCD screen when the AF Mode option is set to 1-Area, 49-Area, or another setting that places a movable focus area on the display, with the Touch AF options turned on. To avoid this problem, go to Touch Settings on screen 8 of the Custom menu and set Touch AF and Touch Pad AF to Off.

# Appendix C: Resources for Further Information

## Photography Books

A visit to any large general bookstore or library, or a search on Amazon.com or other sites, will reveal the vast assortment of currently available books about digital photography. Rather than trying to compile a long bibliography, I will list a few books I have found especially helpful.

C. George, *Mastering Digital Flash Photography* (Lark Books, 2008)

C. Harnischmacher, *Closeup Shooting* (Rocky Nook, 2007)

H. Horenstein, *Digital Photography: A Basic Manual* (Little, Brown, 2011)

## Websites

Following are several sites that are useful for finding further information about the ZS100 or about digital photography in general:

Digital Photography Review

http://forums.dpreview.com/forums/forum.asp?forum=1033

This is the current web address for the "Panasonic Compact Camera Talk" forum within the dpreview.com site. Dpreview.com is one of the most established and authoritative sites for reviews, discussion forums, technical information, and other resources concerning digital cameras. If you have a question about a feature of the ZS100, there is a good chance you can find an answer through this forum.

Official Panasonic and Related Sites

http://shop.panasonic.com/shop/model/DMC-ZS100K?support

The Panasonic company provides resources for the ZS100 at this web address, including the downloadable version of the user's manual for the ZS100 and other technical information.

http://panasonic.jp/support/global/cs/dsc/

This is another address where Panasonic provides support information for the ZS100, the Panasonic Image App, and other devices and software.

http://lumixclub.panasonic.net/eng/c/

At this address, you can get information about the Lumix Club, which you need to join in order to upload images from the ZS100 to social network sites.

http://panasonic.net/avc/sdcard/information/sdxc.html

This site provides information about the compatibility of SDXC cards with the ZS100.

http://www.isl.co.jp/SILKYPIX/english/p/support/

At this site, you can download the manual for the Silkypix software included with the ZS100.

http://loilo.tv/product/20

This site is where you can download the manual for the LoiLoScope software for editing videos, a trial version of which is provided with the ZS100 camera.

http://panasonic.jp/dc/dpof_110/white_e.htm

This site provides information about the Print Set option for printing images directly from an SD card used in the ZS100.

http://www.cambridgeincolour.com

This site is an excellent resource for general information about a wide range of photographic topics.

# Videos

https://youtu.be/-Cjk9x5zsuE

This video gives a good hands-on review of the ZS100 camera.

https://youtu.be/lmV715l8-b4

The link above also leads to a detailed review of the ZS100.

https://youtu.be/VFQS3BQPihY

The link above is an update of the previous review of the camera.

https://youtu.be/WGPyFrkZkL0

The link above is to another detailed review of the camera.

https://youtu.be/g2JgpYX0bZg

This link is to a video that compares the ZS100 to the Sony DSC-RX100 IV, another high-quality compact camera.

https://youtu.be/yDWr4iWwD48

The link above is to a video that gives detailed instructions for making a filter adapter for a compact Panasonic camera.

Reviews of the ZS100

Following are links to written reviews of the ZS100:

http://www.dpreview.com/reviews/power-zoom-panasonic-lumix-dmc-zs100-tz100-review

http://www.cameralabs.com/reviews/Panasonic_Lumix_TZ100_ZS100/

http://www.cnet.com/products/panasonic-lumix-zs100/

http://www.imaging-resource.com/PRODS/panasonic-zs100/panasonic-zs100A.HTM

http://www.techradar.com/us/reviews/cameras-and-camcorders/cameras/compact-cameras/panasonic-tz100-zs100-1312056/review

http://cameradecision.com/review/Panasonic-Lumix-DMC-ZS100

http://www.pocket-lint.com/review/136159-panasonic-lumix-tz100-review-imaging-liberation-meet-lens-limitation

# Index

CPSIA information can be obtained
at www.ICGtesting.com
Printed in the USA
BVHW02s1202260218
508734BV00009B/65/P

9 781937 986520